Timeless Treasures

Landmarks of Southern Cuisine

Valdosta Junior Service League

Valdosta, Georgia

www.vjsl.org

The purpose of the Valdosta Junior Service League is to improve cultural, welfare, recreational, civic and educational conditions in the community, to promote volunteerism, and to cooperate with other organizations performing similar services.

First Printing   May, 1993
Second Printing   February, 2006

Copies of *Timeless Treasures* may be obtained by contacting the Valdosta Junior Service League at valdostajsl@yahoo.com, by using the order forms provided in the back of this edition, or at the address provided below.

Valdosta Junior Service League
P. O. Box 2043
Valdosta, GA 31603-2043

Other cookbooks published by the Valdosta Junior Service League include *Who's Cooking in Valdosta, Valdosta Recipes, the hors d'oeuvre tray, Taster's Luncheon, The Holiday Hostess,* and *Southern Treasures.*

Library of Congress Catalog Card Number 92-85153
ISBN 0-9635249-0-9

WIMMER
COOKBOOKS

A CONSOLIDATED GRAPHICS COMPANY

800.548.2537   wimmerco.com

Introduction

The Valdosta Junior Service League was founded in 1936 by a group of young Valdosta women who wanted to work for the betterment of their community. Many important projects have been started by the League and either continue to be serviced by its members or, once organized and in successful operation, have been absorbed by other agencies. Some of those projects include:

Converse-Dalton-Ferrell House — restore and preserve this nationally registered historic landmark to serve as the League's home, share with the public, and rent for special occasions.

Educational Scholarships — fund the Speech and Hearing Scholarship awarded to a speech and hearing major at Valdosta State University.

Habitat for Humanity — assist in the building of new Habitat homes, including the solely League funded and constructed Valdosta Women's Build in 2003.

Koats for Kids — collect and distribute winter coats for area children in need.

Learning Enhancement Grants — award grants to area teachers for special classroom projects.

Lowndes-Valdosta Arts Commission — support and provide staff for art shows and Presenters Series.

School Hearing and Vision Screening — conduct hearing and vision tests for all city, county, and private school third and sixth graders.

Other League sponsored projects: Arts & Crafts Show Christmas Spectacular, CPIE, Foster Parents Banquet, Jacob's Ladder Horse Camp, Jingle Bell Run, Kids Café, the Salvation Army, South Georgia Medical Center Spice of Life, the United Way's Day of Caring, and Valdosta Technical College's HarvestEd.

Our civic-minded members are dedicated to identifying and meeting our community's future needs. Your purchase of *Timeless Treasures* will allow us to continue to serve our community and surrounding areas.

We appreciate your support of our organization.

Cookbook Committee

Co-Chairmen
Janice Worn   Patti Wright

Design and Format
Janet Nichols — Chairman
Mary Perry
Jana Yates

Marketing
Debbie Hobdy — Chairman

Elizabeth Butler	JaBra Harden
Carol Cowart	Zan Martin
Brenda Davis	Monique Sineath
Jan Girardin	Diane Stewart

Committee

Susan Allison	Carol Giles	Margaret Perryman
Jan Anderson	Lisa Harris	Jadan Pitcock
Cheryl Arnold	Lisa Henry	Mary Powell
Janet Blalock	Judith Joseph	Denise Retterbush
Jan Blanton	Honey Kendrick	Chris Roan
Vallye Blanton	Renee Land	Cathy Sheats
Claire Buescher	Lee Limbocker	Debbie Smith
Sandi Chambless	Kathy Lincoln	Becky Stewart
Ellen Clary	Floye Luke	Kim Strickland
Sue Clary	Pam Mackey	Beth Sullivan
Scarlett Cooper	Linda McCrary	Julie Taylor
Mary Corbett	Debi McNeal	Charlotte Thomas
Jeanne Cowart	Marcia McRae	Cheri Tillman
Debbie Davis	Donna Miller	Marcia Tillman
Jan Fackler	Lynn Minor	Kathy Turner
Marcia Felts	Beverly Moye	Vickie Wilkinson
Libby George	Mary Beth Meyers	Pam Woodward

Special Thanks

Alday, Tillman, Wright & Giles, P.C.	Lori Cannon
	Dot Gibson
Goddard, Henderson, Godbee & Nichols	Sally Kurrie
	Sharon Stalvey
Sheri Batten	Beth Sullivan

Suzanne Sullivan

Valdosta Junior Service League

Active Members

Susan Allison	Dale Crane	Pam Mackey	Monique Sineath
Jan Anderson	Becky Crosby	Zan Martin	Janice Smith
Cheryl Arnold	Nan Dame	Jani Martin	Debbie Smith
Barbara Bankston	Brenda Davis	Debi McNeal	Susan Smith
Jamie Bird	Pam Davis	Marcia McRae	Tonya Smith
Karen Bishop	Ann Edwards	Kellie McTier	Sharon Stalvey
Jan Blanton	Pam Edwards	June Mercer	Susan Steel
Vallye Blanton	Sharon Everson	Claire Miller	Becky Stewart
Mary Young	Jan Fackler	Donna Miller	Diane Stewart
Boatenreiter	Marcia Felts	Jessie Miller	Kim Strickland
Elaine Bridges	Sally Gaskins	Lynn Minor	Leslie Strickland
Judy Bridges	Cheryl Gaston	Stephanie Mize	Beth Sullivan
Claire Buescher	Libby George	Mary Beth Meyers	Amy Swindle
Jane Burgsteiner	Carol Giles	Janet Nichols	Sharon Swindle
Elizabeth Butler	Jan Girardin	Debbie Parker	Barbara Tampas
Stacey Bynum	Carolyn Gish	Mary Perry	Julie Taylor
Melissa Carter	Susan Golden	Margaret Perryman	Charlotte Thomas
Sandi Chambless	Barbara Hacker	Jadan Pitcock	Terry Thomson
Pam Chapman	Laura Hansen	Jamie Pitts	Cheri Tillman
Pat Chitty	JaBra Harden	Mary Powell	Marcia Tillman
Donna Clary	Lisa Harris	Peggi Pulido	Nan Troutman
Ellen Clary	Lisa Henry	Denise Retterbush	Kathy Turner
Sue Clary	Debbie Hobdy	Chris Roan	Merry Jo Whidby
Robin Coleman	Judith Joseph	Denise Rountree	Vickie Wilkinson
Scarlett Cooper	Honey Kendrick	Lorraine Scott	Pam Woodward
Vickie Copeland	Renee Land	Cathy Sheats	Janice Worn
Mary Corbett	Sybil Langdale	Cay Simmons	Patti Wright
Carol Cowart	Lee Limbocker	StuartLynn Simpson	Jana Yates

Non-Resident Members

Frances Campbell	Mary Smith
Claire Hiers	Nancy Warren
Emily Reilly	Denise Watt

Associate Members

Sue Addington	Janet Blalock	Jean Bynum	Jeanne Cowart
Cathy Alday	Becky Bowling	Ingrid Carroll	Sue Cox
Sandra Allen	Rosemary Brannen	Shirlee Carroll	Susan Crago
Gloria Anderson	Dee Broadfoot	Patty Castleberry	Jane Crick
Sandra Anderson	Dean Brooks	Dorothy Chandler	Ann Dasher
Janice Baker	Brenda Brown	Laverne Coleman	Debbie Davis
Carol Barker	Julie Budd	Kay Coleman	Judy DeMott
Sue Bentley	Ann Burnette	Sharon Coleman	Sue Dennard

Nancy Dewar
Lyn Dickey
Martha Dover
Phyllis Drury
Carolyn Eager
Karen Eager
Beverly Edwards
Cindy Fann
Jean Fowler
Peggy Gayle
Ann Godbee
Careen Golivesky
Frances Golivesky
Mary Gray
Barbara Griffin
Jeneane Grimsley
Martha Grow

Caroline Harris
Marilyn Henderson
Barbara Hendrix
Clod Holt
Susie Kaiser
Marilyn Kemper
Christy Kirbo
Sally Kurrie
Russell Lawrence
Kathy Lincoln
Floye Luke
Susan Mackey
Kay McBride
Laurie McCall
Shirley Miller
Linda Miller
Teresa Minchew

Sharon Mink
Sally Moritz
Jan Moseley
Beverly Moye
Sheila Myddleton
Ann Norris
Catherine Parramore
Nancy Parris
Sarah Parrish
Sue Ellen Patterson
Ginger Paulk
Ann Plageman
Jerry Powers
June Purvis
Jane Rainey
Anita Reames

Jeannie Respess
Dawn Rodgers
Marsha Rudolph
Jane Sherwood
Leigh Smith
Kaye Smith
Jane Stanaland
Teresa Steinberg
Julie Street
Polly Talley
Betty Dow
　Templeton
Donna Thornton
Mala Vallotton
Rose Ware
Carol Woodall

Lifetime Members

Emily Anderson
Tootsie Anderson
Jane Anthony
Martha Barham
JoAnn Bassford
Virginia Beckmann
Myra Jane Bird
Patsy Brogdon
Jan Carter
Marion Anice Cross
Margaret Dasher

Mary Dasher
Mary Dickey
Peggy Durden
Billie Ruth Fender
Margaret Ann
　Griffin
Lilla Kate Hart
Mary Ann Heard
Barbara Hornbuckle
Lamar Jackson
Dottie Keller

Susan Klanicki
Lamb Lastinger
Barbara Lester
Jane McLane
Liz Mixson
Emma Murrah
Mary Young Oliver
Joyce Paine
Barbara Parks
Mary Remer
　Parramore

Sue Nell Scruggs
Sadie Shelton
Janet Smith
Harriet Smith
Suzanne Sullivan
Cissy Taylor
Georgia Thomson
Tootsie Tillman
Emma Wainer
Henrietta Walker
Joanne Youles

During the three years of compiling and testing recipes, words cannot begin to express the enthusiasm and commitment shared among our active, associate and lifetime members.

Our efforts in providing you with these "Timeless Treasures" couldn't have been possible without the help of our family and friends, who so graciously tested these recipes and who so honestly selected the best.

After being shared over many a dinner table, we are proud to present these treasures that have been passed down through generations and enjoyed at our own family table.

Co-Chairmen,
Janice Worn
Patti Wright

Table of Contents

The laurel wreath is a symbol of distinction, honor, and achievement. Intricate wood carvings of the laurel wreath are seen throughout the interior and exterior of the Converse-Dalton-Ferrell House, home of the Valdosta Junior Service League. Originally built in 1902 for the Thomas Briggs Converse, Sr. family, the house was restored to its original splendor in 1983. It was also placed on the National Historical Register in 1983. We are proud to honor this great landmark and to call it our home.

The cover is an original watercolor of the Converse-Dalton-Ferrell House, painted by Lynwood Hall. Mr. Hall was the 1992 Georgia Artist of the Year. He is a graduate of the University of Georgia with a degree in art. He lived in Washington, D.C. for five years and worked with the U.S. Senate. In January, 1979, Hall was commissioned by the Senate to paint a watercolor of the Capitol that was presented to Vice Premier Deng Xiao Ping from China. In April of that year, The Hearst Corporation commissioned Hall to paint a watercolor of the White House that was presented to President Anwar Sadat of Egypt. Hall has exhibited in ten Georgia cities as well as Washington, D.C. and New York. He is a native of Moultrie, Georgia, and currently resides on a farm outside Moultrie, where his studio is located.

The divider page artwork features other Valdosta landmarks listed on the National Historical Register. This artwork was accomplished entirely in pen and ink medium by Ralph Avila of Valdosta, Georgia. Mr. Avila has been active as an artist for twenty years. He works in a number of medias, including color renderings of all types. His pen and ink renderings, particularly in this exclusive artist cookbook, is a testimony to his skill as an artist. Mr. Avila is currently working on other pen and ink commissions involving local scenes in various Georgia cities and counties. Some artwork used on the divider pages is being used with the permission of Mr. Avila.

Beautiful pink azaleas are in bloom each spring in Valdosta, Georgia making our city proud to be known as the "Azalea City." We have used azaleas throughout the cookbook to designate favorite recipes originally included in the no longer in print, *Valdosta Recipes*, which was compiled and published by our League's associate members in the late 60's.

Treasured Menus

Chamber of Commerce
Ola Barber/Pittman Home
Built 1915

Bridge Brunch Buffet

Bloody Mary Mix

Olive Surprises   Almond Asparagus Casserole

Grand Marnier Grapes

Party Ham Rolls   Sausage Pinwheels

Breakfast/Brunch Casserole

Caramel Nut Ring   Covington's Cinnamon Rolls

King and Prince Oatmeal Raisin Muffins

South of the Border

Margaritas

Mexican Delights   Tex-Mex Dip

Chicken Fajitas Valdosta Style

Fiesta Coleslaw

Corn Bake   Baked Cheese Stuffed Tomatoes

Buttered Rum Pound Cake

Summer Sizzling Cookout

Spinach Dip served with raw vegetables

Layered Cabbage Salad

Grilled Sirloin

Sautéed Mushrooms   Baked Potato with Potato Topper

Cheese Bread

Mint Ice Cream Pie

Tailgate for Touchdowns

Flaming Cabbage

Asparagus Filling or Spread

Chicken Bacon Sandwich Filling

Marinated Chicken Wings

24 Hour Layered Vegetable Salad

Peanut Blossoms $250 Cookie Recipe

Azalea City Southern Style Supper

(From Local Chef's Treasures)

Chicken and Dumplings

Everyone's Favorite Fried Eggplant

Sweet Potato Apple Casserole

Bourbon Pecan Pie

Refreshing Mid-Summer Iced Tea

Treasures from the Sea

Oysters Pierre

Herbed Tomato Platter

Grilled Fresh Tuna

Baked Broccoli Continental   Garlic Grits

Hush Puppies #1

Peach Melba Trifle

Wild Game Dinner

Duck Dip   Swamp Salad

Venison Stew

Bacon Dove Bake

Marinated Carrots   Broccoli and Wild Rice Bake

Beer Bread

Everyone's Favorite Chocolate Cheesecake

Holiday Hostess

(By Candlelight)

Mrs. Register's Cheese Spread

Chilled Minted Canteloupe Soup

Fresh Spinach with Spinach Salad Dressing

Porc à l'Orange

Epicurean Peas   Sweet Potato Soufflé

Tarragon and Oregano Butter

served with Dinner Rolls

Glazed Almond Amaretto Cheesecake

Appetizers

First Presbyterian Church
Built 1909

 ## Bacon Crisps

1   (16 ounce) box club
    crackers

1   (2 pound) package thinly
    sliced breakfast bacon
    paprika

Break crackers along perforation. Wrap ½ piece bacon around cracker, may need to secure with toothpick. Sprinkle heavily with paprika. Bake at 200 degrees for 45 minutes to 1 hour. Let set a few minutes so bacon can crisp. Serve warm.

Yield: 48 servings   Suzanne Sullivan

Hot Bacon-Cheese Roll-Ups

1   loaf thinly sliced bread
1   (6 ounce) jar cheese spread

15   slices bacon

Trim crusts from thin sliced bread. Cut each slice in half. Spread lightly with cheese spread. Roll up, wrap with a half slice of bacon, and secure with wooden toothpick. Bake on a rack at 400 degrees until bacon is crisp. These may be cooked halfway, cooled, and frozen until needed. When ready to use, put frozen roll-ups on cookie sheet and bake.

Yield: 30 servings   Myra Jane Bird

Broccoli In A Biscuit

1   (10 ounce) package frozen
    broccoli
2   (8 ounce) cans biscuits, 20
    biscuits

1   (10¾ ounce) can cream of
    chicken soup
2   cups cooked chicken
    shredded cheese

Cook broccoli according to package directions. Flatten each biscuit and place in greased muffin pans. Smooth biscuit dough up the sides. In a separate bowl, combine soup, cooked broccoli and chopped chicken. Spoon mixture into muffin pans on top of the flattened biscuits. Sprinkle with cheese. Bake 30 minutes at 350 degrees.

Yield: 20 servings   Floye Luke

Herb Bacon Cheese Ball

2 (8 ounce) packages cream cheese, softened

1 (.04 ounce) envelope ranch dressing
1 (3 ounce) jar bacon bits

Combine cream cheese and envelope of ranch dressing and mix well. Shape into ball and roll in bacon bits. Chill 3 to 4 hours or overnight. Serve with crackers.

Yield: 4-inch cheese ball

Jan Fackler

Bourson Cheese Ball

3 (8 ounce) packages cream cheese, softened
¾ cup butter, not margarine, softened

1 (8 ounce) bottle ranch or green goddess dressing
2 teaspoons garlic salt or powder
coarse ground black pepper

Beat softened cream cheese, butter, salad dressing and garlic well with mixer. Refrigerate mixture until firm. Shape into two balls and roll each in ground pepper.

Yield: two 3-inch cheese balls

Vickie Wilkinson

These may be frozen by wrapping in a moist paper towel, then in plastic wrap.

Pineapple Cheese Ball

2 (8 ounce) packages cream cheese, softened
1 (7¾ ounce) can crushed pineapple, well-drained
2 tablespoons finely chopped onion

¼ cup chopped green pepper
¼ cup chopped celery
1 tablespoon seasoned salt
2 cups chopped pecans

Mix cream cheese, crushed pineapple, onion, green pepper, celery, seasoned salt and 1 cup chopped pecans. Refrigerate in covered bowl for 24 hours to blend flavors. Before serving, form into ball (will be flattened ball due to softness of ingredients) and roll in remaining cup chopped pecans. Serve with crackers.

Yield: 4-inch cheese ball

Carol Giles

Cheese Appetizers

1 cup chopped ripe olives	½ cup mayonnaise
½ cup chopped green onions	6 English muffins
1½ cups shredded Parmesan cheese	

Mix olives, onions, and cheese with mayonnaise. Open muffins. Spread mixture on English muffins. Cut split muffins in fourths. Place on cookie sheet. Bake at 350 degrees for 15 minutes.

Yield: 24 servings   Vallye Blanton

Confetti Cheese Dip

6 slices bacon, cooked and
    crumbled
	1 bunch green onions,
	    chopped

1 (8 ounce) block Cheddar cheese, shredded	3 tablespoons mayonnaise

½ cup almonds, chopped	1 (8 ounce) carton sour
	    cream
	    dash of garlic powder

Mix bacon, cheese, almonds, onions, mayonnaise and sour cream. Add garlic powder. Mix well. Chill. Serve with crackers.

Yield: 24 servings   Vallye Blanton

Layered Nacho Dip

1 (16 ounce) can refried
    beans
	1 (4½ ounce) can chopped
	    ripe olives

½ (1¼ ounce) package taco seasoning mix	2 large tomatoes, diced
1 (6 ounce) carton avocado dip	1 small onion, finely chopped

1 (8 ounce) carton sour
    cream
	1 (8 ounce) block Monterey
	    Jack cheese, shredded

Combine the refried beans and taco seasoning mix. Spread evenly in a 13x9x2-inch dish. Layer the following ingredients in order: avocado dip, sour cream, ripe olives, tomatoes, onion and top with Monterey Jack cheese. Place in refrigerator for 1 hour before serving. Serve with large chips.

Yield: 24 servings   Barbara Bankston

 ## Cream Cheese Pickapeppa

1	(8 ounce) package cream cheese	1	(8 ounce) jar Pickapeppa sauce

Cover 1 block of cream cheese with Pickapeppa sauce. Serve with crackers.

Yield: 48 servings — Ginna Drumheller

Hot—but good!

Taco Dip

1	(8 ounce) package cream cheese, softened	1	(4½ ounce) can sliced ripe olives, drained
1	(16 ounce) can chili with beans	1	small onion, finely chopped
1	(8 ounce) package grated Monterey Jack cheese	1	(8 ounce) package grated Cheddar cheese

Layer the above ingredients in order in a 13x9x2-inch baking dish. Bake at 350 degrees for 15 minutes. Serve with dip size corn chips or tortilla chips.

Yield: 10 to 12 servings — Barbara Bankston

This dip can be made ahead of time and placed in the freezer. Then cook when you need it.

Mexican Cheese Squares

½	cup margarine	1	(4 ounce) can chopped green chilies
10	eggs	1	pint cottage cheese
½	cup all-purpose flour	1	(16 ounce) block Monterey Jack cheese, grated
1	teaspoon baking powder dash of salt		
1	tablespoon chopped jalapeño peppers		

Melt margarine; set aside. Beat eggs slightly, add flour, baking powder and salt. Mix together. Add melted margarine, peppers, chilies, cottage cheese and Monterey Jack cheese. Mix well but don't beat. Pour into lightly greased 13x9x2-inch dish. Bake at 350 degrees for 35 to 40 minutes.

Yield: 2 dozen — Barbara Hendrix

Mexican Dip

1 (12 ounce) package
mushrooms and onions rice
pilaf

1 (10¾ ounce) can condensed
Cheddar cheese soup
4 teaspoons taco sauce
1 to 4 drops hot pepper sauce

In medium saucepan, cook rice according to package directions. Combine rice, Cheddar soup, taco sauce and hot pepper sauce until heated thoroughly. Serve warm with corn chips for dipping.

Yield: 3 cups   Marcia McRae

Tex-Mex Dip

2 (10½ ounce) cans bean dip
3 avocados, mashed with salt
and pepper
2 tablespoons lemon juice
1 (8 ounce) carton sour
cream
1 (1¼ ounce) package taco
seasoning mix

1 bunch green onions,
chopped
3 large tomatoes, chopped
1 (6 ounce) can sliced ripe
olives
1 (12 ounce) block Cheddar
cheese, shredded

In 12x8x2-inch glass casserole dish, layer the following: bean dip, avocados mixed with lemon juice, sour cream mixed with taco seasoning, green onions, tomatoes, olives and cheese. Serve with corn chips.

Yield: 5½ cups   Beth Sullivan

Mexican Delights

2 (8 ounce) packages cream
cheese
1 (4 ounce) can chopped
green chilies, drained

1 (4½ ounce) can chopped
ripe olives, drained
4 to 5 green onions, chopped
3 to 5 flour tortillas
1 (8 ounce) jar picante sauce

Combine cream cheese, chilies, olives and green onions. Spread thin layer evenly on tortilla. Repeat layers. Cut into approximately 1x2¼-inch rectangles. Serve with picante sauce.

Yield: 20 servings   Jan Anderson

21

Mexican Roll-Ups

1 cup sour cream	1 bunch green onions
1 (8 ounce) package cream cheese, softened	1½ cups grated Cheddar cheese garlic powder to taste
1 (4 ounce) can green chilies, drained	1 package of 10 flour tortillas
	1 (8 ounce) jar salsa

Mix sour cream and cream cheese together. Chop green chilies and add to sour cream mixture. Chop onions and add to mixture. Add grated cheese and garlic powder. Spread mixture on flour tortilla and roll up in jellyroll fashion. Cover with plastic wrap and chill. When chilled, remove wrap and cut tortillas ¼-inch thick. Secure with toothpick. Serve with salsa.

Yield: 40 to 50 servings   Vallye Blanton

Party Ham Rolls

1 small onion, finely chopped	3 packages party rolls, 20 to 24 per package
3 tablespoons mustard	
3 tablespoons poppy seeds	1½ pounds deli ham, thinly sliced
½ pound butter or margarine, softened	
1 teaspoon Worcestershire sauce	1 pound Swiss cheese, thinly sliced

Place chopped onion in microwave and cook for one minute and set aside. Mix together mustard, poppy seeds, butter or margarine, Worcestershire sauce and onion. Split package of rolls in half. Spread mixture on both sides of rolls. Spread thinly but cover rolls completely. Place ham on bottom of rolls and place cheese on top and replace top half of rolls. Bake, in aluminum package, at 350 degrees for 15 minutes or until cheese has melted.

Yield: 10 to 12 servings   Janice Worn

These can be made in advance and refrigerated or frozen. If refrigerated, they will take longer than 15 minutes in regular oven. If frozen, take out of freezer and remove from aluminum pan and heat in microwave for 2 to 3 minutes on full power, 1 package at a time. Separate each roll and keep hot.

Fox's Georgia-Florida Party Spread

1	(16 ounce) can refried beans	1	tomato, chopped
1	(8 ounce) carton sour cream	½	head of lettuce, shredded
2	(8 ounce) packages cream cheese, softened	½	cup chopped onion
		1	cup shredded Cheddar cheese
1	(1¼ ounce) package taco seasoning mix	1	cup shredded mozzarella cheese
2	jalapeño peppers, chopped	2	(12 ounce) bags tortilla chips

Mix beans, sour cream, cream cheese and taco seasoning mix together. Spread mixture, approximately 1-inch thick, onto large serving platter. Top with peppers. Mix tomatoes, lettuce and onions together and pour over peppers. Mix Cheddar and mozzarella cheese together and sprinkle over all. Serve with tortilla chips.

Yield: 48 servings   Margaret Perryman

Mrs. Register's Cheese Spread

10	ounces sharp Cheddar cheese, grated	1	teaspoon garlic powder
		1	teaspoon paprika
1	(8 ounce) package cream cheese, softened	4	to 6 drops hot pepper sauce
⅓	cup mayonnaise	½	cup chopped or ground pecans, optional
1	heaping tablespoon onion flakes or grated onion	1	(10 ounce) jar strawberry preserves

Cream grated cheese, cream cheese and mayonnaise to smooth consistency. Add onion flakes, garlic powder, paprika, hot pepper sauce and pecans, if desired. Mix together until well blended. Place in ring mold or shape into ball and roll in chopped pecans. Serve with crackers and strawberry preserves. If made in ring mold, unmold and place preserves in center.

Yield: 24 servings   Vickie Wilkinson

This recipe can be easily doubled and freezes without separating.

Norma Gail's Hawaii Five-O Delight

1   (18 ounce) jar pineapple or
    apricot preserves
1   (18 ounce) jar apple jelly
1   ounce dry mustard

dash of pepper
1   (4 ounce) jar horseradish
1   (8 ounce) package cream
    cheese, softened

Mix preserves, jelly, mustard, pepper, horseradish and cream cheese. Serve with crackers. Store in refrigerator until ready to serve.

Yield: 5 cups   Floye Luke

Beef And Mushrooms

1   (5 pound) whole beef
    tenderloin
½   cup butter
    juice of 1 lemon
1   (5 ounce) bottle steak sauce

2   tablespoons ketchup
    salt and pepper to taste
3   (4 ounce) jars mushroom
    caps

Strip membrane from tenderloin. Bake, uncovered, at 400 degrees for 20 minutes in a roasting pan. Baste, while baking, with melted butter and lemon juice. Remove meat to platter to cool, saving drippings. Add steak sauce, ketchup, salt and pepper to taste to drippings. Heat to boiling. Cut beef into 1-inch cubes. Add beef and mushrooms to sauce. Let cool. Refrigerate for 24 hours. Heat to boiling and serve in chafing dish with toothpicks.

Yield: 20 servings   Jan Carter

Cheese Corned Beef Dip

1½ cups mayonnaise
1   (12 ounce) package cream
    cheese, softened
1   (8 ounce) carton sour
    cream
2   (2½ ounce) bags corned
    beef, chopped

dash of garlic salt
1   (8 ounce) package shredded
    mozzarella cheese
1   (4 ounce) package grated
    Swiss cheese
    round rye bread

Blend mayonnaise, cream cheese and sour cream. Mix corned beef, garlic salt, and cheeses. Combine mayonnaise and corned beef mixtures together. Hollow out round rye bread. Pour in mixture. Wrap in tin foil. Bake at 325 degrees for 1½ hours.

Yield: 5 cups   Lynn Minor

Chili Con Queso Dip

1½ pounds ground chuck	1 bunch green onions, chopped
1 (8 ounce) jar taco sauce	½ teaspoon salt
2 (4 ounce) cans chopped chilies	¼ teaspoon pepper
1 tablespoon sugar	3 cloves garlic, minced
1 teaspoon vinegar	2 teaspoons paprika
⅓ (5 ounce) bottle hot pepper sauce to taste	2 pounds pasteurized process cheese spread

Brown ground chuck, drain and set aside. Combine taco sauce, chilies, sugar, vinegar, hot pepper sauce, onions, salt, pepper, garlic and paprika. Simmer 1 to 1½ hours. Add cheese, simmer an additional 30 minutes. Add browned meat to mixture. Serve in warming dish with tortilla chips.

Yield: 2 quarts   Beth Sullivan

This dip may be frozen.

Chinese Chicken Wings

1 garlic clove, minced	¼ cup honey
2 green onions, chopped	1 tablespoon sugar
¼ cup soy sauce	3 tablespoons oyster sauce, optional
1 tablespoon sherry wine	12 chicken wings
½ cup water	

Combine garlic, onions, soy sauce, wine, water, honey, sugar, and oyster sauce, if desired, in a Dutch oven. Stir well. Add wings. Bring to boil then simmer, covered, for 30 to 40 minutes, shake occasionally. Uncover and simmer an additional 15 minutes stirring and basting frequently. Remove wings and reserve liquid. When ready to serve, broil and sprinkle with reserved liquid. Broil until brown and crisp, turning once.

Yield: 6 servings   Kellie McTier

These make great appetizers that men love.

Texas Marinated Chicken Wings

2	cups red wine or apple cider vinegar	2	tablespoons garlic powder
1	cup water	½	cup margarine, melted
½	cup salt	2	ounces hickory liquid smoke
1	tablespoon cayenne pepper	4	pounds chicken wings
1	tablespoon black pepper		

Combine all ingredients and pour over wings. Marinate in refrigerator one day for average and two days for a really hot taste. Cook chicken on grill until done.

Yield: 8 to 10 servings   Sharon Coleman

Marinated Chicken Wings

6	pounds chicken wings	⅓	cup sugar
1	teaspoon ground ginger	⅓	cup cider vinegar
⅔	cup soy sauce	2	teaspoons garlic powder

Cut chicken wings in two pieces and discard end piece. Mix ginger, soy sauce, sugar, vinegar and garlic powder. Pour over chicken and marinate overnight. Then place chicken in large metal pan(s) in single layer and baste with leftover marinade. Bake, uncovered, at 375 degrees for 45 minutes. Baste every 15 minutes until done.

Yield: 25 to 30 servings   Carol Giles

 # Chicken Liver Wrap-Ups

½	pound chicken livers, cut into thirds	1	(5 ounce) can whole water chestnuts, cut into thirds
¼	cup soy sauce	15	slices thin sliced breakfast bacon, cut in halves
1	clove garlic, minced		

Marinate livers in soy sauce and garlic 3 hours at room temperature or overnight in refrigerator. Wrap livers and water chestnuts in bacon and secure with toothpick. Place on wire rack over shallow pan. Bake at 425 degrees for 25 minutes. Cook until bacon is crisp, turning occasionally. Keep some water in shallow pan to keep drippings from burning. May also be charcoaled.

Yield: 15 appetizer servings   Mary Dodson

Chicken Roll-Ups

2 cups cooked, chopped chicken	2 tablespoons milk
2 (3 ounce) packages cream cheese, softened	3 tablespoons pimentos
	salt and pepper to taste
2 tablespoons butter, melted	1 (8 ounce) package crescent rolls

Mix chicken, cream cheese, butter, milk, pimentos, salt and pepper together. Spread crescent roll dough out and press seams together. Spoon chicken mixture onto dough. Roll dough in jellyroll fashion. Cut into ½-inch pieces. Bake according to directions on crescent roll package. Serve hot.

Yield: 24 servings   Barbara Hendrix

Duck Dip

12 duck breasts	1 teaspoon chili powder
⅛ teaspoon black pepper	1 stalk celery, chopped
¼ teaspoon salt	2 onions, chopped
2 bay leaves	2 hard boiled eggs, chopped
⅛ teaspoon red pepper	2 cups mayonnaise

Wash duck and place in Dutch oven. Cook with pepper, salt and bay leaves until tender. Remove meat from bone. Process in food processor until chopped. Combine with red pepper, chili powder, celery, onions, eggs and mayonnaise and mix well. Cover and refrigerate overnight. Ducks may be smoked instead of boiled. Serve with crackers.

Yield: 6 servings   Sue Clary

Sausage Stuffed Mushrooms

30 large fresh mushrooms	½ cup pizza sauce
3 tablespoons butter, melted	1 egg
1 (16 ounce) package bulk sausage	1 (6 ounce) package mozzarella cheese
½ cup breadcrumbs	

Remove stems from mushrooms. Dip mushroom caps in butter and arrange on cookie sheet. Brown and drain sausage. Mix sausage, bread crumbs, pizza sauce and egg. Stuff mushrooms. Top with 1-inch square of cheese. Bake at 425 degrees for 10 to 15 minutes.

Yield: 15 servings   Vallye Blanton

Sausage Pinwheels

1 (16 ounce) package bulk
  sausage
1 (8 ounce) package cream
  cheese, softened

2 (8 ounce) cans crescent rolls
1 egg, beaten
  poppy seeds

Brown sausage and drain. While warm, mix with cream cheese. Cool completely in refrigerator. Then spread the mixture on the crescent rolls put together to make a square. The sausage/cream cheese mixture should be spread evenly and to all edges. Roll and place on wax paper. Freeze or refrigerate until firm. When ready to bake, slice the roll into small individual pieces. Spread a small drop of the beaten egg on each piece and sprinkle poppy seed on each. Bake at 350 degrees for 20 to 30 minutes until brown.

Yield: 48 servings

Mary Young Boatenreiter

Crabmeat Spread

3 (8 ounce) packages cream
  cheese, softened
3 to 5 tablespoons milk
1 or 2 tablespoons minced
  onion

3 tablespoons horseradish
  salt and pepper to taste
2 (6 ounce) cans crabmeat,
  drained
  paprika

Blend cream cheese, milk and onion. Mix in horseradish. Salt and pepper to taste. Add crabmeat. Place in 13x9x2-inch baking dish. Top with paprika. Bake, uncovered, at 325 degrees for 30 minutes. Serve hot on crackers or cocktail bread.

Yield: 30 servings

Floye Luke

Caviar Dip

2 (8 ounce) packages cream
  cheese, softened
2 bunches green onions

3 eggs, boiled
1 (2 ounce) can black caviar

Shape cream cheese into a mound. Chop onions, including tops. Sprinkle onions over cream cheese. Grate eggs over onions. Place caviar on top in the middle. Serve with crackers.

Yield: 4-inch ball

Patti Wright

 *Hot Clam Dip*

3 tablespoons butter	½ green pepper, finely
1 small onion, finely chopped	chopped

In the top of a double boiler, melt butter. Sauté onion and green pepper over direct heat for 3 minutes. Add:

1 (10½ ounce) can clams, drained	4 tablespoons ketchup
½ pound or more pasteurized process cheese spread	1 tablespoon Worcestershire sauce
1 tablespoon sherry	¼ teaspoon cayenne pepper

Cook in double boiler until cheese has melted, stirring often. Transfer to chafing dish. Serve with melba toast.

Yield: 18 to 24 servings   Myra Jane Bird

Shrimp Dip

dash hot pepper sauce	4 ounces sour cream
1 (3 ounce) package cream cheese, softened	3 tablespoons chili sauce
½ small onion, grated	1 (6 ounce) can deveined shrimp, drained
2 teaspoons lemon juice	1 tablespoon Worcestershire sauce
¼ cup thousand island dressing	

Mix hot pepper sauce, cream cheese, grated onion, lemon juice, thousand island dressing, sour cream, chili sauce, shrimp and Worcestershire sauce together. Serve with chips.

Yield: 2 cups   Kathy Turner

Spicy Seafood Dip

1   large green pepper,
    chopped
1   tablespoon olive oil
1   pound small shrimp,
    shelled and deveined
2   tablespoons butter
2   (14 ounce) cans artichoke
    hearts, drained and finely
    chopped
2   cups mayonnaise
½   cup thinly sliced green
    onions
½   cup drained and chopped
    hot red peppers

1   cup freshly grated
    Parmesan cheese
2   tablespoons lemon juice
4   teaspoons Worcestershire
    sauce
3   pickled jalapeño peppers,
    seeded and minced; may
    use only 1½ or 2, if desired
    dash of hot pepper sauce
½   teaspoon salt
1   pound crabmeat
⅓   cup sliced almonds, lightly
    toasted

Preheat oven to 375 degrees. In heavy frying pan, sauté green pepper in olive oil over medium heat until soft. Cool. Sauté shrimp in butter for 1½ minutes. In large bowl, mix green pepper, artichokes, mayonnaise, green onion and red peppers. Add Parmesan cheese, lemon juice, Worcestershire sauce, jalapeño peppers, hot pepper sauce and salt. Gently stir in shrimp and crabmeat. Place in greased 11x7x2-inch baking dish and sprinkle with almonds. Bake, uncovered, at 375 degrees for 25 to 30 minutes until golden brown and bubbly. Serve in a chafing dish with your favorite crackers.

Yield: 1½ quarts   Tonya Smith

This hors d'oeuvre may be prepared a day in advance and baked just before serving.

Hot Artichoke Dip

½   cup mayonnaise
1   cup grated Parmesan and
    Romano cheese

1   (14 ounce) can artichoke
    hearts, drained and
    chopped

Mix mayonnaise and grated cheese in 8 or 9-inch pie plate. Stir in artichoke hearts. Bake at 350 degrees for 20 to 30 minutes or until bubbly and light brown. Serve warm with crackers.

Yield: 3 cups   Carol Giles

Oysters Pierre

1	cup cracker meal	1	teaspoon garlic powder
½	cup grated Parmesan cheese	1	pint fresh shucked oysters, drained
1	teaspoon oregano leaves, crushed	1	pound bacon

In pie pan, or similar container, combine cracker meal, cheese, oregano and garlic powder. Mix well. Coat oysters in meal mixture and wrap in ⅓ strip of bacon. Secure with toothpick. Place on broiler pan and broil, turning once, until bacon is crisp. Serve at once.

Yield: 40 to 50 oysters   Cheryl Arnold

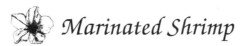 *Marinated Shrimp*

2	pounds shrimp, boiled and peeled	2	lemons, sliced thin
2	large onions, sliced into rings	1½	cups salad oil

Bring to boil:

1	pint apple cider vinegar	1	blade mace
1	teaspoon salt	1	teaspoon sugar
¼	teaspoon dry mustard	½	teaspoon black peppercorns
4	medium bay leaves	⅓	cup mixed pickling spices
1	small ginger root		

Cool and strain and pour over shrimp. Marinate overnight. Will keep for days in refrigerator.

Yield: 8 to 10 servings   Mary Dodson

Salmon Mousse

1	tablespoon unflavored gelatin	½	teaspoon hot pepper sauce
¼	cup cold water	4	teaspoons grated onion
½	cup boiling water	1	teaspoon salt
½	cup mayonnaise	2	tablespoons capers
1	tablespoon fresh lemon juice	2	cups salmon; strained, cleaned and washed
½	teaspoon paprika	½	cup heavy cream, whipped stiff, but not dry

Dissolve gelatin in cold water; melt in boiling water. Cool and add mayonnaise, lemon juice, paprika, hot pepper sauce, onion and salt until blended. Add capers and salmon to mixture. Fold in whipped cream. Pour into mold and refrigerate until congealed.

Optional Dill Sauce:

1	teaspoon salt	¼	teaspoon lemon juice
1	cup sour cream	3	tablespoons chopped dill
¼	teaspoon white pepper		

Mix ingredients together and serve with mousse.

Yield: 10 to 12 servings   Vickie Wilkinson

This looks good prepared in a fish mold and when removed, garnish with almond slices for scales, an olive for the eye and green onion strips for the gills.

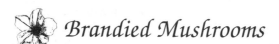 Brandied Mushrooms

1	pound mushrooms, sliced	salt, pepper and chopped
2	tablespoons butter	parsley to taste
¼	cup brandy	

Sauté mushrooms in butter over high heat. When mushrooms are browned, add brandy. Set a match to it for flaming. Shake the skillet as the flame catches and gradually goes out. Season with salt, pepper and chopped parsley.

Yield: 12 servings   Margaret Ann Griffin

Asparagus Filling Or Spread

3 tablespoons mayonnaise
2 tablespoons dried onion
   flakes
1 (8 ounce) package cream
   cheese, softened

1 (15 to 16 ounce) can
   asparagus, drained
1 (2 ounce) package blanched
   slivered almonds, toasted

Cream mayonnaise, onion flakes, and cream cheese together. Chop asparagus. Stir asparagus and almonds together with fork. Combine both mixtures and blend well. Refrigerate overnight. As a spread, serve with favorite party bread. As a dip, place into carved out round loaf of Hawaiian bread. Serve with pieces of remaining bread.

Yield: 4 cups   Floye Luke

Flaming Cabbage

1 large purple cabbage
1 (8 ounce) jar stuffed olives

1 (16 ounce) package cocktail
   sausages

Wash cabbage and curl outer leaves out from top. Hollow out center about 6-inches deep. Place a small can of sterno in cavity. Place a stuffed olive and a cocktail sausage on each wooden toothpick and stick into sides of cabbage. Light sterno and let guests roast their own sausages. Barbecue sauce or a sharp mustard is nice to use as a dip.

Yield: 8 to 10 servings   Myra Jane Bird

This is good for an "after the game" party or at Halloween.

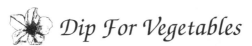

Dip For Vegetables

1 package blue cheese salad
   dressing mix

1 (8 ounce) carton sour
   cream
½ cup mayonnaise

Mix and refrigerate several hours. Serve with carrots, cauliflower, and celery cut into bite-size pieces.

Yield: 1½ cups   Suzanne Sullivan

33

Spinach Dip

1 (10 ounce) package frozen chopped spinach	1 medium onion, chopped
1 cup mayonnaise	1 (8 ounce) can water chestnuts, chopped
1 cup sour cream	dash of lemon pepper
1 packet dry vegetable soup mix	1 loaf Hawaiian bread

Thaw spinach. Place into colander and press out all moisture using back of spoon. Mix mayonnaise, sour cream, soup mix, onion, water chestnuts, and lemon pepper seasoning. Prepare ahead of time so dried particles in soup mix will soften. Then add spinach. Mix together. Place into carved out round loaf of Hawaiian bread. Serve with pieces of remaining bread.

Yield: 4 cups   Marcia Tillman

Swamp Salad

5 pounds tomatoes, sliced	1 quart cider vinegar
2½ pounds sweet white onions, sliced	½ pound light brown sugar
	salt and pepper to taste
1 quart dill pickle slices, drained	

Layer tomatoes, onions, and pickles. Mix vinegar, sugar, salt and pepper. Pour over and toss with vegetables. Marinate in refrigerator at least one hour. Serve with saltine crackers. Guests should layer vegetables on crackers to eat.

Yield: 20 to 30 servings   Melissa Carter

No Valdosta oyster roast, fish fry or large outdoor party is complete without this unique appetizer.

Olive Surprises

½ cup butter or margarine, softened
1 cup grated sharp Cheddar cheese
½ cup sifted all-purpose flour
¼ teaspoon salt
¼ teaspoon pepper
36 stuffed olives, drained

Cream butter or margarine and cheese until blended. Add flour, salt and pepper. Mix well. Chill 15 to 20 minutes. Shape a small portion of dough around each olive. Bake on cookie sheet at 400 degrees for 15 minutes.

Yield: 8 to 10 servings   Jeanette Oliver

If desired, these may be frozen on a cookie sheet, put in plastic bags, and stored in freezer until needed. Best when served hot.

 Marinated Mushrooms

½ pound fresh mushrooms, thinly sliced
½ cup salad oil
½ cup lemon juice
2 teaspoons seasoned salt
½ teaspoon sugar
½ teaspoon cracked black pepper
¼ teaspoon basil
¼ teaspoon marjoram
¼ teaspoon oregano
¼ teaspoon salt
¼ teaspoon garlic powder

Wash mushrooms and set aside to dry. Combine oil, lemon juice, seasoned salt, sugar, pepper, basil, marjoram, oregano, salt, and garlic powder. Shake well in a jar. Pour over mushrooms. Place in marinating container in refrigerator for 6 to 8 hours.

Yield: 6 to 8 servings   Suzanne Sullivan

Zesty Party Mix

1 (6 ounce) package Cheddar goldfish
1 (6 ounce) package Parmesan goldfish
1 (6 ounce) package plain goldfish
1 (6 ounce) package pretzel goldfish
3 cups Wheat Chex cereal
3 cups Corn Chex cereal
3 cups Crispix cereal
2 cups regular Cheerios

8 to 10 cups peanuts or pecans, unsalted
2 tablespoons onion powder
2 tablespoons celery salt
1 tablespoon garlic powder
1 tablespoon black pepper
½ cup butter
½ cup bacon drippings
2 tablespoons Worcestershire sauce
1 tablespoon hot pepper sauce

Combine goldfish, cereal and nuts. Mix together onion powder, celery salt, garlic powder and pepper, then shake over cereal mixture. Let sit eight hours or overnight, shaking occasionally. Melt butter and stir in bacon drippings, Worcestershire sauce and hot pepper sauce. Pour over seasoned cereal mixture, toss to coat evenly. Bake at 200 degrees for 1 hour, stirring every 15 minutes.

Yield: 8 quarts

Cay Simmons

Beverages

Lowndes County Courthouse
Built 1905

Banana Smasher

1	(6 ounce) can frozen orange juice, undiluted	1	banana, sliced approximately 3 cups crushed ice
¼	cup light rum		
⅓	cup powdered sugar		

Combine first 4 ingredients in electric blender, add ice and blend until smooth.

Yield: 4 servings   Pat Chitty

The rum can be substituted with apple juice for a great breakfast drink for children and adults.

Bloody Mary Mix

1	(58 ounce) can cocktail vegetable juice		salt to taste juice of 4 lemons
1	(46 ounce) can tomato juice	1	teaspoon hot pepper sauce
2	(10½ ounce) cans beef consommé soup	2	tablespoons Worcestershire sauce

Mix all ingredients in a 1 gallon container.

Yield: 18 to 20 servings   Sybil Langdale

Spiced Hot Chocolate

8	(1 quart) packages powdered milk	12	ounces dry coffee creamer
2	pounds instant chocolate flavored drink mix	1½	cups powdered sugar
		1	tablespoon cinnamon

Mix all ingredients together. Store in large container. To make 1 serving, add 3 to 4 teaspoons in 1 cup boiling water. Stir and enjoy.

Yield: 10 cups mix   Pat Chitty

Makes a great Christmas gift to give to friends when packed in clear jars with bright ribbons or in a colorful tin.

Hot Mocha Mix

2½	cups sugar	2	cups non-fat powdered milk
1	cup unsweetened cocoa	½	cup instant coffee
2	cups dry coffee creamer	1	vanilla bean, quartered

Combine ingredients in large bowl, stir until well-blended. Place 2 cups mixture with one vanilla bean section in each jar. Seal and label. Store in refrigerator at least 1 week to absorb vanilla.

Yield: 8 cups mix

Kathy Turner

Rich and Creamy Coffee Punch

5	tablespoons instant coffee	1	gallon vanilla ice cream, softened
3	cups sugar		
1	gallon cool water	1	(12 ounce) container frozen whipped topping

Dissolve coffee and sugar in enough hot water to cover. Pour coffee/sugar mixture and 1 gallon cool water in large bowl. Place in refrigerator to chill. When ready to serve punch, pour coffee and water mixture in punch bowl, add ice cream. Fold in whipped topping.

Yield: 15 servings

Julie Taylor

Hot Mulled Punch

1	(1½ quart) bottle cranberry juice	½	teaspoon salt
2	(1 quart) bottles apple juice	4	cinnamon sticks
½	cup brown sugar	1½	teaspoons whole cloves

Pour juices into a 24 to 30 cup coffee maker. Place sugar, salt, cinnamon sticks and cloves in coffee basket. Let perk until cycle is complete. Remove basket. Serve hot in mugs or cups.

Yield: 24 to 30 cups

Karen Bishop

A quick holiday crowd pleaser.

Party Punch Pizzazz

2	(3 ounce) packages lemon flavored gelatin mix		juice of 8 lemons
1	cup hot water	2	(46 ounce) cans natural pineapple juice
4	cups sugar	2	quarts ginger ale, chilled

Dissolve gelatin in hot water. Combine with sugar, lemon juice and pineapple juice. Mix together well. Pour into 2 one-gallon containers. Add water until each container is full. Shake and freeze. Remove from freezer approximately 2 to 3 hours before serving. Pour into punch bowl and add 2 quarts of cold ginger ale.

Yield: 2½ gallons   Pat Chitty

Light rum can also be added for more festive taste.

Party Fruit Punch

3	cups sugar		juice of 6 oranges
6	cups water	1	(46 ounce) can pineapple or raspberry juice
5	large bananas, pureed	3	quarts ginger ale
	juice of 3 lemons		

Boil sugar and water for 3 minutes and cool. Combine bananas, lemon juice, orange juice, and pineapple juice with sugar/water mixture and freeze in mold. Add ginger ale approximately 3 to 5 minutes before serving.

Yield: 2 gallons   Sharon Swindle

Citrus Punch

2	(3 ounce) packages citrus flavored gelatin	1	(6 ounce) can frozen lemonade, thawed
2	cups boiling water	½	cup sugar
1	(46 ounce) can pineapple juice	6	cups water
1	(6 ounce) can frozen orange juice, thawed	1	(33.8 ounce) bottle ginger ale

Dissolve gelatin in boiling water. Add ginger ale, juices, lemonade, sugar and 6 cups water and freeze in 1 gallon container. Thaw 2 to 3 hours before serving. Pour in bowl and add ginger ale. Stir to "slush".

Yield: 1 gallon   Melissa Carter

Symphony Punch

1   (46 ounce) can orange juice
1   (46 ounce) can pineapple
    juice
1   (.31 ounce) package lemon-
    lime powdered drink mix

6   cups water
2   cups sugar
1   (16 ounce) bottle lemon
    juice

Mix all ingredients well. Pour into freezer container to freeze. Stir frequently as it begins to freeze. Serve directly from freezer, to avoid thawing. It will be slushy and does not require ice.

Yield: 1½ gallons   Barbara Bankston

Punch With a "Kick"

2   cups pineapple juice
1   cup sugar
1   cup lemon juice
1½ cups brandy

1½ cups white wine
2½ teaspoons bitters
1   (750 ml) bottle chilled
    champagne, white or pink

Mix together all ingredients, except champagne, and let stand for 24 hours in refrigerator. Add champagne before serving.

Yield: 2½ quarts   Pat Chitty

Kentucky Fruited Mint Tea

3   cups boiling water
4   regular-size tea bags
12 fresh mint sprigs
1   cup sugar
¼   cup lemon juice

1   cup frozen orange juice,
    undiluted
5   cups water
    fresh mint sprigs and
    orange slices for garnish

Pour boiling water over tea bags and mint; cover and steep 5 minutes. Remove tea bags and mint, squeezing gently. Stir in sugar, lemon juice, orange juice and water. Serve over ice. Garnish with mint sprigs and orange slices.

Yield: 2½ quarts   Pat Chitty

Frozen Lime Daiquiris

1 quart dry ginger ale	12 ounces white rum
1 (12 ounce) can frozen lemonade concentrate	2 tablespoons grenadine syrup
1 (6 ounce) can frozen limeade concentrate	

Place all ingredients in freezer container. Stir well and freeze overnight. Daiquiris will be "slushy", not frozen solid, and can be kept in freezer indefinitely. No need to thaw before serving.

Yield: 2 quarts   Patti Wright

Margaritas

1 lime	6 to 8 ounces tequila
salt	1½ to 2 cups crushed ice
16 ounces (liquid) margarita mix	1 (10 ounce) package sliced strawberries, optional

Cut lime into four thin slices. Set aside. Reserve end pieces of lime. Moisten rim of 4 (6 ounce) glasses with end pieces. Pour salt into a saucer and dip each glass in salt to coat rim. In blender, combine margarita mix, tequila and ice. Whip in blender to get a slushy, frothy consistency. Pour liquid into glasses. Garnish each glass with a lime slice.

Yield: 4 servings   Jana Yates

To make strawberry margaritas, only use 1 cup crushed ice.

Soups & Sauces

J.T. Roberts Home
Built 1840

New England Clam Chowder

¼	pound salt pork, diced	4	(6½ ounce) cans minced
1	medium onion, chopped		clams, drained, reserve
2	tablespoons all-purpose		juice
	flour	3	cups milk
3	medium potatoes, peeled	3	tablespoons butter
	and diced		salt and freshly ground
			pepper to taste

Cook salt pork over low heat in Dutch oven until browned and the fat is cooked out of diced pork. Remove pork with slotted spoon and pour off all fat except 2 tablespoons. Add onion to fat in pot and cook slowly until golden. Sprinkle flour over onions and cook, stirring, 2 to 3 minutes. Add potatoes and reserved clam juice; add water to reserved juice if needed to make 2½ cups liquid. Cover and simmer 10 minutes. Add clams and cook an additional 10 minutes until clams and potatoes are soft. Add milk, butter, salt, pepper and pork. Heat slowly. Do not boil.

Yield: 6 to 8 servings   Suzanne Sullivan

Clam Chowder

1	onion, finely chopped	1	(16 ounce) can tomatoes
3	strips bacon, finely chopped	2	cups milk
2	cups water	1	tablespoon Worcestershire
1	or 2 (6½ ounce) cans		sauce
	minced clams, undrained	⅛	teaspoon pepper
4	medium potatoes, grated		salt to taste
1	green pepper, finely	1	lemon
	chopped		

Brown onion and bacon slowly in Dutch oven. Add water, undrained clams, potatoes, green pepper and tomatoes. Cook until potatoes are just done. Just before serving, add milk, Worcestershire sauce, pepper and salt. Do not let boil after milk has been added. Serve with a thin slice of lemon in each bowl.

Yield: 6 servings   Jan Carter

Sausage Chowder

1	pound bulk sausage	1	large onion, chopped
2	(14½ ounce) cans stewed tomatoes, undrained	1	green pepper, chopped
		1	rib celery, sliced
2	cups tomato juice	½	teaspoon thyme
4	bay leaves	½	teaspoon garlic salt
1	(16 ounce) can whole kernel corn	1½	teaspoons seasoned salt
		1	teaspoon chili powder
2	(16 ounce) cans kidney beans	¼	teaspoon pepper

Brown sausage and drain. Combine remaining ingredients. Simmer 1 hour. Serve with garlic bread and salad.

Yield: 10 to 12 servings   Patti Wright

Shrimp Chowder

8	slices bacon	1	(10¾ ounce) can cream of celery soup
1	onion, chopped		
1	rib celery, chopped	2	(4¼ ounce) cans small shrimp, drained and rinsed
1	green pepper, chopped		
2	(10¾ ounce) cans cream of potato soup	4	cups milk
		¼	teaspoon pepper

Cook bacon in a large Dutch oven until crisp. Remove bacon, reserving 1 tablespoon drippings in Dutch oven. Crumble bacon and set aside. Sauté onion, celery and green pepper in bacon drippings until tender. Add potato and celery soup, shrimp, milk and pepper, stirring well. Cook over medium heat until thoroughly heated. Sprinkle each serving with bacon.

Yield: 2½ quarts   Susan Smith

Ione's Fish Chowder

1	pound mild fish fillets; flounder, orange roughy, etc.	2	carrots, grated
		4	sprigs fresh parsley leaves, chopped
3	cups water		salt to taste
4	chicken bouillon cubes	2	tablespoons butter or margarine
5	to 6 green onions, chopped		
3	potatoes, cubed	2	cups milk

In Dutch oven on stove top, cook fillets in water until tender. Add bouillon cubes, onions, potatoes, carrots, parsley and salt. When vegetables are tender, add butter and milk. Heat thoroughly.

Yield: 4 servings   Carol Giles

Seafood Chowder

1	(10¾ ounce) can cream of celery soup	1	pound shrimp, peeled
		1	pound crabmeat
2	(10¾ ounce) cans cream of potato soup	1	tablespoon butter
		¼	cup sherry or white wine
3	soup cans of milk		

Mix all ingredients, stirring until shrimp are done. Do not boil.

Yield: 8 to 10 servings   Zan Martin

The 2 pounds of seafood can be shrimp, crabmeat, clams, oysters or any combination.

Chilled Minted Cantaloupe Soup

2½	cups cubed cantaloupe	¼	cup Chablis
1½	tablespoons sugar	3	tablespoons plain yogurt
1½	teaspoons chopped fresh mint		fresh mint sprigs

Combine cantaloupe, sugar and chopped mint in blender or food processor. Process until mixture is smooth. Transfer mixture to medium bowl. Add Chablis and yogurt, stirring with a wire whisk until smooth. Cover and chill at least 2 hours. Serve in individual bowls. Garnish with fresh mint sprigs.

Yield: 2 cups   Honey Kendrick

Wild Duck Gumbo

8	ducks, preferably Mallards	2	(6 ounce) cans tomato paste
1	(8 ounce) bottle Italian dressing	1	(16 ounce) can tomatoes, undrained
3	to 5 pounds shrimp	2	teaspoons thyme
½	cup butter	2	teaspoons basil
½	cup bacon drippings	2	teaspoons oregano
½	cup all-purpose flour	½	teaspoon cayenne pepper
3	cloves garlic, chopped	1	tablespoon seasoned salt, optional
3	large green peppers, chopped	1	tablespoon pepper
2	cups chopped celery	2	tablespoons parsley flakes
2	large yellow onions, chopped	1	tablespoon Filé, optional
2	large bunches green onions, chopped	4	cups cut okra, optional

Rinse and wash ducks. Soak 7 ducks in Italian dressing overnight. Reserve 1 duck. Smoke or grill marinated ducks until meat is very tender. Take meat off and cut into bite-size pieces. Cook the 1 reserved duck in water in large saucepan until tender. Cool and cut up. Strain and reserve broth. Peel and clean shrimp. Cook butter, bacon drippings and flour in skillet until a copper color, stirring constantly. Add garlic, green pepper, celery, yellow and green onions. Cook until vegetables are light brown, stirring constantly. Add tomato paste and undrained tomatoes. Mix well, breaking tomatoes. Add all seasonings, except Filé. Add enough duck broth to make desired consistency. Add okra, if desired, and simmer, covered, 1 hour or longer. Add duck and shrimp and cook 30 to 45 minutes. Add additional broth to make desired consistency. Optional: bring to boil and add Filé. Cook 3 minutes. Serve over hot cooked rice.

Yield: 15 servings   Sue Clary

All ducks can be boiled, but grilling or smoking gives a better taste. Do not use Italian dressing if boiling all ducks.

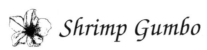 *Shrimp Gumbo*

6	tablespoons all-purpose flour	3	teaspoons salt
5	tablespoons bacon drippings	1	teaspoon pepper
2	medium onions, chopped	1	(10 ounce) package frozen okra, thawed
1½	cups chopped celery	2	pounds shrimp
1	clove garlic, minced	1	pint small oysters, optional
2	(15 ounce) cans tomatoes, undrained	1	(6 ounce) can crabmeat, optional
1	(15 ounce) can tomato sauce	3	tablespoons Worcestershire sauce
2	to 3 cups water (add more depending on thickness)		hot pepper sauce and ground red pepper to taste

In a heavy skillet, make a golden roux with flour and drippings. Add onions, celery and garlic and brown. Add tomatoes, tomato sauce, water, salt and black pepper. Simmer for 1 hour. Add okra and seafood. Cook 20 minutes longer. Add Worcestershire sauce, hot pepper sauce and ground red pepper. Serve over hot rice, or as a heavy soup with hard bread.

Yield: 8 servings

Joanne Youles

 *Crab Soup*

⅓	cup chopped onion		salt and pepper to taste
⅓	cup chopped green pepper		Worcestershire sauce to taste
⅓	cup chopped celery		hot pepper sauce to taste
½	cup butter	½	cup sherry
1	quart milk		nutmeg, optional
2	tablespoons cornstarch		
1	pound crabmeat		

Sauté onion, green pepper and celery in butter. In separate saucepan, thicken 1 cup of milk with cornstarch. Add to sautéed vegetables. Add remainder of milk. When milk is warm add crabmeat, salt, pepper, Worcestershire sauce, hot pepper sauce and sherry. Heat, but do not boil. Sprinkle nutmeg on top, if desired.

Yield: 8 to 12 servings

Betty Oliver

French Onion Soup

½	cup butter or margarine	¼	cup dry white wine
4	large onions, thinly sliced and separated into rings	¾	teaspoon salt
		¼	teaspoon pepper
1	tablespoon all-purpose flour	1	(6 ounce) box croutons
2	cups chicken broth	6	to 8 slices cheese; Swiss, Gruyère or mozzarella Parmesan cheese to taste
1	(10½ ounce) can beef broth		
1	cup water		

Melt butter in large Dutch oven. Add onion and cook over medium heat until tender, stirring frequently. Blend in flour, stirring until smooth. Stir chicken broth, beef broth, water and wine into onion mixture. Bring to a boil. Reduce heat, cover and simmer 20 to 30 minutes. Add salt and pepper. Ladle soup into individual ovenproof bowls. Top each bowl with 6 to 8 croutons, slice of cheese and sprinkle with Parmesan cheese. Place bowls in oven and bake at 350 degrees approximately 10 minutes until cheese is melted and soup is hot.

Yield: 6 to 8 servings   Suzanne Sullivan

Cream of Broccoli Soup

1	bunch fresh broccoli or 2 (10 ounce) packages frozen broccoli	5	tablespoons all-purpose flour
3	cups chicken stock or chicken bouillon		half-and-half or milk as needed
1	medium onion, chopped		salt and white pepper to taste
4	tablespoons butter or margarine		

Cook broccoli in stock or bouillon with onion until soft. Place in blender and blend quickly. Leave small pieces of broccoli. Make a roux using butter or margarine and flour. Cook 3 minutes, stirring constantly. Add small amount of broccoli liquid to roux. Stir until smooth. Add mixture to rest of soup stirring constantly to avoid lumps as it thickens the liquid. Thin to preferred consistency with half-and-half or milk. Add salt and white pepper to taste.

Yield: 6 servings   Vickie Wilkinson

Très Bon French Onion Soup

¼	cup butter	1	(1½ ounce) package dry
¼	cup oil		onion soup mix
8	cups sliced onions		salt and pepper to taste
2	garlic cloves, pressed		dash of Accent
1	bay leaf, optional	2	tablespoons Worcestershire
8	cups stock; 4 beef and 4		sauce
	chicken bouillon cubes in 8	½	cup sauterne
	cups water	1	loaf French bread, sliced
1	(10½ ounce) can beef	1	(16 ounce) package Swiss
	consommé		cheese

In Dutch oven melt butter and oil. Add onions and garlic. Brown lightly. Add remaining ingredients except bread and cheese. Simmer 2 hours. Toast slices of French bread and place one slice on bottom of each bowl. Fill bowl almost full with soup and place 2 slices of cheese on top. Place under broiler until bubbly.

Yield: 8 servings   Diane Stewart

Taco Soup

2	pounds ground beef	1	(16 ounce) can red beans
1	large onion, chopped	1	(1 ounce) package ranch
1	(16 ounce) can whole kernel		dressing mix
	corn, drained	1	(1¼ ounce) package taco
1	(4 ounce) can green chilies,		seasoning mix
	chopped and drained	1	(8 ounce) carton sour
4	(16 ounce) cans tomatoes		cream
1	(16 ounce) can pinto beans	1	cup grated Cheddar cheese

Brown ground beef and onion together and drain. Add corn, chilies, tomatoes, pinto beans, red beans, dressing mix and taco mix to beef mixture. Simmer one hour. Serve in soup bowls with a dollop of sour cream and grated cheese in the middle. Serve with nacho chips on the side.

Yield: 10 to 12 servings   Brenda Davis

Oyster Stew

2	tablespoons butter	1	quart milk
½	cup chopped celery	½	teaspoon salt
1	small onion, chopped	1	pint oysters, undrained

Melt butter. Cook celery and onion in butter until transparent. Add milk and salt. Let milk get hot, but do not boil. Add undrained oysters. Cook until the edges of the oysters curl.

Yield: 10 to 12 servings   Vallye Blanton

Shrimp Stew

2	cups margarine	6	(10½ ounce) cans shrimp stock; may substitute 6 (10¼ ounce) cans chicken stock
2	cups all-purpose flour		
2	cups chopped green pepper		
6	cups chopped yellow onion		
2	cups chopped celery	3	tablespoons black pepper
¼	cup minced garlic	1	teaspoon red pepper; less, if preferred less spicy
3	cups whole, peeled tomatoes, drained and diced		
		1½	tablespoons Worcestershire sauce
3	cups tomato sauce	1	tablespoon sugar
2	pounds shrimp	½	cup parsley, chopped

Make a roux by warming margarine and stirring in flour a little at a time until well browned. Do not burn. Sauté green pepper, onion, celery and garlic in hot roux. Stir 5 minutes, then stir in tomatoes and tomato sauce on low heat. Add shrimp and stock. Stir well over low heat. Add black pepper, red pepper, Worcestershire sauce and sugar. Cook over medium heat 15 minutes. Turn off heat and add parsley. Serve over fluffy rice. Very spicy.

Yield: 25 servings   Sharon Swindle

Cream of Mushroom Soup

2	cloves fresh garlic, minced	1	pound fresh mushrooms, sliced
½	cup chopped celery		
½	cup chopped onion	½	cup butter
½	pound fresh mushrooms, chopped	4	cups chicken stock
			salt to taste
¼	cup olive oil	1	teaspoon pepper
		2	cups half-and-half

Sauté garlic, celery, onions and chopped mushrooms in olive oil until tender. Puree in food processor. In large pot, sauté sliced mushrooms in butter until beginning to get tender, 5 to 6 minutes. Pour in chicken stock and add pureed mixture. Stir well, add salt and pepper. Simmer 1½ to 2 hours. Before serving, heat well and add half-and-half. Heat only. Serve with French bread.

Yield: 8 to 10 servings   Denise Retterbush

Easy And Delicious Vegetable Soup

1½	pounds ground beef	1	(6 ounce) can tomato paste
½	(20 ounce) package frozen vegetables for stew	⅓	cup barley
		½	tablespoon Worcestershire sauce
½	(20 ounce) package frozen vegetables for soup		
		3	beef bouillon cubes
1	(15 ounce) can tomatoes		salt and pepper to taste
1	(15 ounce) can tomato sauce	1	tablespoon parsley flakes

Brown ground beef in Dutch oven. Drain off fat. Add remaining ingredients to ground beef plus enough water to fill the Dutch oven ¾ full. Cook on low heat 6 to 8 hours, stirring frequently. Add water as necessary.

Yield: 6 to 8 servings   Julie Taylor

Potato Soup

1 medium onion, chopped	1 (10¾ ounce) can cream of
½ cup butter	chicken soup
7 large potatoes, cut into	1½ soup cans water
small cubes	garlic salt to taste
¾ pound pasteurized process	pepper to taste
cheese spread	

Sauté onion in butter. Set aside. Barely cover cubed potatoes with water and boil until soft. After potatoes have cooked, add cheese, soup, water, garlic salt, pepper and sautéed onion. Cook until heated thoroughly and serve.

Yield: 6 to 8 servings   Karen Bishop

 *Turkey Soup*

1 turkey carcass with some	1 tablespoon parsley flakes
meat	salt and pepper to taste
6 small ribs celery, diced	½ cup raw rice
1 large onion, chopped	1 cup uncooked, broken
½ cup barley	spaghetti
2 chicken bouillon cubes,	
dissolved in 1 cup boiling	
water	

Combine turkey carcass, celery, onion, barley, bouillon, parsley flakes, salt and pepper in large kettle with water to cover the carcass. Simmer 2 hours. Cool. Remove bones. A half hour before serving, bring to a boil and add rice and spaghetti. Cook until rice and spaghetti are done, approximately 20 minutes.

Yield: 10 servings   Jan Carter

Tessie's Brunswick Stew

1½	pounds ground beef	2	(15 ounce) cans stewed
1	pound lean ground pork		tomatoes
1	large onion, chopped	2	(15 ounce) cans cream corn
1	cup chicken stock	1	teaspoon pepper, red
1	cup water		pepper is best
1	fryer or hen, cooked, boned		salt to taste
	and chopped		hot pepper sauce, optional
1	(14 ounce) bottle ketchup		

Brown beef, pork and onion in Dutch oven. Drain well. Add chicken stock and water. Mix in all other ingredients. Bring to a boil then reduce heat and cook on low for 3 hours or longer, stirring occasionally. Be careful not to scorch.

Yield: 6 to 10 servings   Sue Clary

Venison Stew

3	pounds venison cut into	1	bay leaf
	2-inch cubes	½	teaspoon thyme
	salt and pepper	1	tablespoon all-purpose
2	tablespoons margarine or		flour
	butter	2	cups warm water
1	onion, chopped	4	cups consommé
1	1-inch cube of ham, minced	½	pound fresh mushrooms,
1	clove garlic, minced		chopped

Salt and pepper venison generously. Heat margarine or butter in skillet and brown venison slowly. When almost done, add onion. Brown slightly. Add ham, garlic, bay leaf and thyme. Stir and simmer 2 minutes. Add flour and cook an additional 2 minutes. Add warm water and consommé. Cook slowly for 1 hour. Add mushrooms and simmer an additional 30 minutes. Serve over rice or noodles.

Yield: 8 servings   Chris Roan

Barbecue Sauce

¾ cup chopped onions
½ cup vegetable oil
¾ cup ketchup
¾ cup water
⅓ cup lemon juice
3 tablespoons sugar

3 tablespoons Worcestershire sauce
2 tablespoons mustard
2 teaspoons salt
½ teaspoon pepper
¼ cup vinegar

Cook onions in oil until soft. Add ketchup, water, lemon juice, sugar, Worcestershire sauce, mustard, salt, pepper and vinegar. Simmer 20 minutes.

Yield: 1¾ cups   Pam Mackey

Great for ribs.

Mom's Barbecue Sauce

5   ounces vinegar
2½ ounces Worcestershire sauce
1   cup margarine
1   teaspoon lemon juice

1   teaspoon mustard
½   cup ketchup
½   cup water
⅛   teaspoon red pepper
1   onion, thinly sliced

Combine all ingredients in a saucepan and simmer 15 minutes over low heat.

Yield: 1½ cups   Lee Limbocker

Great on chicken, ribs, etc. Will keep for weeks in refrigerator.

Fresh Tartar Sauce

1   cup mayonnaise
2   teaspoons lemon juice
⅓   cup dill pickles, coarsely chopped

½   small onion, coarsely chopped
½   teaspoon dill weed, may add more
     pepper to taste

Combine all ingredients and chill several hours. Serve with your favorite fish or Beer Battered Fried Shrimp or Grouper. (See recipe under seafood.)

Yield: 1 cup   Pat Chitty

Blender Hollandaise Sauce

½	cup butter or margarine		dash of cayenne pepper
3	egg yolks	¼	to ½ teaspoon salt
2	tablespoons lemon juice		

Melt butter or margarine in saucepan until very hot but do not brown. Place egg yolks, lemon juice, cayenne pepper and ¼ teaspoon salt in blender. Cover and set blender on mix for 30 seconds. Remove cover. Continue blending on mix and pour hot butter or margarine into blender starting a drop at a time, then gradually adding remaining butter or margarine. When all the butter or margarine is added, turn blender off. Sauce should be creamy and lemony. Taste and add more salt, if desired.

Yield: ¾ cup   Jan Fackler

Sesame Sauce For Broccoli

2	tablespoons vegetable oil	1	tablespoon sugar
2	tablespoons vinegar	1	bunch fresh broccoli,
2	tablespoons soy sauce		cooked
2	tablespoons sesame seed, toasted		

Combine all ingredients in a saucepan. Bring to a boil. Pour over 1 bunch of cooked broccoli.

Yield: 6 servings   Elaine Bridges

 # Tangy Sauce For Vegetables

⅓	cup mayonnaise	1	teaspoon sugar
¼	cup milk	½	teaspoon prepared mustard
4	teaspoons vinegar		

Heat mayonnaise and milk in small saucepan and stir until smooth. Add vinegar, sugar and prepared mustard. Mix well and stir over low heat until hot. Pour over well-drained cooked vegetables.

Yield: ½ cup   Martha Barham

This sauce is good over cabbage or broccoli.

Horseradish Sauce

6	tablespoons butter	3	cups beef stock
6	tablespoons all-purpose flour	1	cup sour cream
		¼	cup prepared horseradish

Melt butter. Add flour and stir. Add beef stock and heat thoroughly. Remove from stove and add sour cream and horseradish.

Yield: 4 cups   Cindy Fann

Delicious with steak!

Fruit Sauce

1	cup mayonnaise	1	teaspoon paprika
½	cup sugar	1	teaspoon celery seed
¼	cup vinegar		

Mix all ingredients together. Will keep in refrigerator up to 2 weeks. Serve over fresh fruit salad.

Yield: 1 cup   Mary Perry

Chocolate Sauce

2	squares bitter chocolate	½	cup evaporated milk
2	tablespoons margarine	1	teaspoon vanilla
⅔	cup sugar	¼	cup sherry or brandy

Melt chocolate and margarine. Add sugar and evaporated milk. Simmer over low heat until sauce thickens. Remove from heat and add vanilla and sherry or brandy.

Yield: ½ cup   Susie Kaiser

Sanders' Hot Fudge Sundae Sauce

12	ounces milk chocolate	14	ounces light corn syrup
1	(14 ounce) can sweetened condensed milk	1	cup butter

Place all ingredients in double boiler over simmering water. Stir until melted. Cook for 30 minutes. Remove from heat and beat with electric mixer until smooth. Serve over ice cream. May be rewarmed over hot water to serve later.

Yield: 5 cups   Linda McCrary

60

Breads

First Baptist Church
Built 1899

New Bride's Banana Bread

1	egg	1	teaspoon salt
¾	cup buttermilk	⅓	cup margarine, melted
2	cups all-purpose flour	2	bananas, sliced
1	teaspoon double-acting	¾	cup sugar
	baking powder	1	teaspoon vanilla
½	teaspoon baking soda		

Take out eggs and buttermilk to let them warm while you get the other ingredients ready. Preheat oven to 350 degrees. Grease loaf pan and assemble other ingredients. Sift flour and measure. Resift with other dry ingredients (baking powder, soda and salt). Set aside. In mixing bowl, with mixer if you like, beat melted margarine, bananas and sugar. Add egg and beat until well blended. Alternate adding dry ingredients and the buttermilk and vanilla. Start and finish with the dry ingredients. Turn batter into 8x4x3-inch loaf pan and bake for 1 hour. Watch last ten minutes in case of fast-cooking oven. Test with a toothpick. Loaf is done when nicely browned on top and toothpick inserted in center comes out clean, i.e. with no batter stuck to it.

Yield: 1 loaf   Jan Fackler

This recipe freezes extremely well. It also doubles well. Doubled, it will make three generous 7x3½-inch loaves with approximately ¼ cup batter left over. Reduce the cooking time to approximately 50 minutes, and watch during last 10 minutes again.

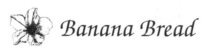

Banana Bread

½	cup butter	1	teaspoon soda
1	cup sugar	1	teaspoon salt
2	eggs	1	cup pecans, chopped
3	bananas, mashed	8	dates, cut in small pieces
2	cups all-purpose flour		

Cream butter and sugar. Fold in eggs. Add mashed bananas. Sift and beat in dry ingredients. Add nuts and dates. Turn into a greased 9x5x3-inch loaf pan and let stand 20 minutes. Bake in moderate oven at 350 degrees for 50 minutes.

Yield: 1 loaf   Suzanne Sullivan

Quick Banana Bran Bread

4	ripe bananas	½	cup chopped pecans,
2	eggs		optional
2	(7 ounce) packages bran muffin mix		

Mash bananas. Beat eggs and add to mashed bananas. Stir in bran mix until blended. Add pecans if used. Pour into a 9x5x3-inch greased and floured loaf pan. Bake at 350 degrees for 50 to 60 minutes.

Yield: 1 loaf   Vickie Wilkinson

Sour Cream Banana Nut Bread

¼	cup butter or margarine	2	cups all-purpose flour
1⅓	cups sugar	1	teaspoon baking powder
2	eggs	1	teaspoon baking soda
1	teaspoon vanilla	¾	teaspoon salt
1	cup sour cream	½	cup chopped nuts
1	cup mashed bananas		

Cream butter, sugar and eggs; add vanilla and sour cream. Add mashed bananas. Sift flour, baking powder, soda and salt. Add flour mixture to banana mixture. Fold in nuts. Pour into a greased 9x5x3-inch loaf pan coated with non-stick vegetable spray. Bake at 350 degrees for 40 to 45 minutes. Test for doneness in center.

Cream Cheese Icing:

1	(8 ounce) package cream cheese, softened	½	cup chopped nuts
¼	cup margarine, softened	1	(16 ounce) box 4X confectioners'sugar

Mix together and ice cake when cool.

Yield: 1 loaf   Sue Clary

Beer Bread

3	cups self-rising flour	1	(12 ounce) can beer
3	tablespoons sugar	½	cup melted butter

Stir flour, sugar and beer together. Pour into a 9x5x3-inch loaf pan. Pour melted butter over top. Bake at 350 degrees for 45 minutes.

Yield: 1 loaf

Cay Simmons

AubRay's Broccoli Cornbread

1 (10 ounce) package frozen chopped broccoli, cooked and drained
1 cup grated sharp Cheddar cheese
4 eggs, well-beaten
1 large onion, chopped
½ cup margarine, melted
1 teaspoon salt
1 (8½ ounce) box corn muffin mix
1 (6 ounce) carton cottage cheese, optional

Mix all ingredients. Pour into a greased 13x9x2-inch pan or 9-inch round or square cake pan. Bake at 400 degrees for 25 to 30 minutes.

Yield: 8 to 10 servings

Jane Stanaland

 # Owendaw Cornbread

2	cups cooked hominy grits	2	cups milk
4	tablespoons butter	1	cup cornmeal
4	eggs	1	teaspoon salt

Stir butter into hot hominy. Beat eggs until light and add to the hominy, then add milk and then cornmeal. Add salt last. Pour this thin batter into a well-greased 11x7x2-inch casserole dish. Bake at 375 degrees for 1½ hours or until center is firm. Spoon bread that will not fall!

Yield: 6 to 8 servings

Liz Mixson

Excellent with game, ham or roast.

Cheese Bread

¾ cup butter
1 teaspoon lemon juice
1 teaspoon poppy seeds
½ teaspoon Dijon mustard
½ cup minced onion

1 loaf of French, Vienna or
   Italian bread
1 (8 ounce) package Swiss
   cheese slices

Heat butter until melted. Add lemon juice, poppy seeds, mustard and onion to melted butter. Slice bread and spread butter mixture between slices and pour on top of bread. Cut sliced Swiss cheese into fourths and place a piece between each slice of bread. Wrap bread securely in foil. Bake at 350 degrees approximately 15 to 20 minutes. Open foil and bake an additional 5 minutes for crisp crust.

Yield: 6 to 8 servings

Jana Yates

Strawberry Bread

3 cups all-purpose flour
1 teaspoon soda
½ teaspoon salt
1 tablespoon cinnamon
2 cups sugar
3 eggs, beaten

1 cup vegetable oil
2 (10 ounce) packages frozen
   sliced strawberries, thawed
   and mashed
1 cup chopped pecans

Sift together flour, soda, salt, cinnamon and sugar. Add eggs, oil and strawberries. Stir well. Add pecans and combine gently. Pour into 2 greased and floured 8½x4½x2½-inch loaf pans. Bake at 350 degrees for 1 hour. Cool before slicing.

Yield: 2 loaves

Tonya Smith

Bread is good spread with softened cream cheese.

Zucchini Bread

3	eggs	2	teaspoons ground
2	cups sugar		cinnamon
1	cup vegetable oil	¼	teaspoon baking powder
3	cups self-rising flour	2	cups grated zucchini,
1	teaspoon vanilla		unpeeled
		1	cup chopped pecans

Beat eggs. Add sugar and oil. Stir in flour, mixing well. Add vanilla, cinnamon and baking powder and beat into batter. Stir in zucchini and nuts by hand. Pour into 2 greased and floured 8½x4½x2½-inch loaf pans. Bake at 350 degrees for 40 to 50 minutes or until toothpick inserted in center comes out clean.

Yield: 2 loaves   Carol Giles

Batter can be divided into smaller loaf pans. Decrease baking time depending on size of pans used. This freezes well. Good for teacher or neighbor gifts or just for family to enjoy.

 ## Angel Biscuits

5	cups all-purpose flour	1	cup shortening
¼	cup sugar	2	cups buttermilk
3	teaspoons baking powder	1	package dry yeast
1	teaspoon soda	2	tablespoons warm water
1	teaspoon salt		

Sift and measure flour. Sift again with dry ingredients, using large bowl. Cut in shortening. Add buttermilk and yeast dissolved in warm water. Mix well. Roll out on floured board. Cut and bake on a greased pan at 425 degrees for 15 minutes. Biscuits rise best if started in cold oven. Dough will keep well in refrigerator for up to 2 weeks. After cutting refrigerated dough, let stand at room temperature approximately 10 to 15 minutes before baking for best results.

Yield: 3 dozen   Joan Lawson

Cream Biscuits

2	cups all-purpose flour	2	teaspoons sugar
1	teaspoon salt	1	to 1½ cups heavy cream
1	tablespoon baking powder	⅓	cup butter, melted

Preheat oven to 425 degrees. Use an ungreased baking sheet. Combine the flour, salt, baking powder and sugar in a mixing bowl. Stir the dry ingredients with a fork to blend and lighten. Slowly add 1 cup of the cream to the mixture, stirring constantly. Gather the dough together; when it holds together and feels tender, it is ready to knead. If the dough is shaggy and falling away, slowly add more cream as needed. Place dough on lightly floured surface and knead one minute. Cut the dough as desired and dip into the melted butter so all sides are coated. Place on baking sheet 2 inches apart. Bake at 425 degrees for approximately 15 minutes or until lightly browned. Serve hot.

Yield: 1 dozen

Honey Kendrick

Mayonnaise Biscuits

2	cups self-rising flour	2	tablespoons mayonnaise
1	cup milk		

Combine all ingredients. Pour batter into greased and floured muffin tins one-half full. Bake at 400 degrees until golden brown.

Yield: 1 dozen

Pam Davis

Whipping Cream Biscuits

2	cups self-rising flour	1	cup whipping cream
1	teaspoon sugar		

Combine all ingredients and mix well. Dough will be stiff. Turn dough out onto lightly floured surface and knead 10 to 12 times. Roll dough out ¼-inch thick. Cut with 2-inch biscuit cutter. Put on a greased baking sheet. Bake at 450 degrees 10 to 12 minutes.

Yield: 1½ dozen

Sally Moritz

Cream Cheese Coffee Cake

2	**(8 ounce) cans crescent dinner rolls**	2	**(8 ounce) packages cream cheese, softened**
1	**cup sugar**	1	**egg, separated**
		1	**teaspoon vanilla extract**

Spread 1 package rolls flat in 13x9x2-inch baking pan. Cream ¾ cup sugar, cream cheese, egg yolk and vanilla extract until smooth. Spread over rolls. Top with remaining layer of crescent rolls. Beat egg white until frothy and spread over dough. Sprinkle with remaining ¼ cup sugar. Bake at 350 degrees for 30 to 35 minutes. Do not cover after baking.

Yield: 10 servings   Marcia Felts

Easy Coffee Cake

½	**cup butter or margarine, melted**	1	**teaspoon ground cinnamon**
½	**cup firmly packed brown sugar**	2	**(8 to 10 ounce) cans refrigerated biscuits**
		⅓	**cup chopped pecans**

Combine butter, brown sugar and cinnamon. Dip each biscuit into this mixture. Overlap biscuits in an 8 or 9-inch round pan in a spiral fashion; fill the center of the pan with the remaining biscuits. Combine the remaining butter mixture with the pecans and pour over the coffee cake. Bake at 350 degrees for 10 minutes.

Yield: 6 to 8 servings   Vickie Wilkinson

To reheat, cover with foil to retain moisture.

Poppy Seed Coffee Cake

⅓ cup poppy seeds	2 teaspoons baking powder
1 cup buttermilk	1 teaspoon baking soda
1 cup butter or margarine, softened	½ teaspoon salt
	1 teaspoon vanilla extract
1½ cups sugar	⅓ cup sugar
4 eggs	1 teaspoon cinnamon
2½ cups all-purpose flour	confectioners' sugar

Combine poppy seeds and buttermilk; soak overnight in refrigerator. Preheat oven to 350 degrees. Cream butter and 1½ cups sugar until light and fluffy. Add eggs 1 at a time, beating after each addition. Combine flour, baking powder, soda and salt. Add vanilla to buttermilk mixture. Add dry ingredients and buttermilk mixture alternately to creamed mixture, beginning and ending with dry ingredients. Spoon half the batter into a well-greased 10-inch tube or Bundt pan. Combine ⅓ cup sugar and cinnamon and sprinkle over batter. Top with remaining batter. Bake at 350 degrees for 1 hour or until knife inserted in center comes out clean. Cool in pan 10 minutes. Turn out and dust with confectioners' sugar.

Yield: 8 to 12 servings   Carolyn Eager

Caramel Nut Ring

½ cup margarine	2 tablespoons water
½ cup chopped pecans	2 (8 ounce) cans crescent dinner rolls
1 cup firmly packed brown sugar	

Melt margarine in small saucepan. Spray a 12-cup Bundt pan well with non-stick vegetable spray. Use 2 tablespoons of the melted margarine to coat bottom and sides of 12-cup Bundt pan. Sprinkle pan with 3 tablespoons of chopped pecans. Add remaining nuts, brown sugar and water to remaining margarine. Heat to a boil, stirring occasionally. Remove dinner rolls from package but do not unroll. Cut each can of rolls into 16 slices. Place in Bundt pan. Separate each slice slightly to allow sauce to penetrate. Spoon half the caramel nut sauce over slices. Repeat next layer with second can of rolls and top with remaining caramel sauce. Bake at 350 degrees for 25 to 30 minutes or until golden brown. Cool 3 minutes. Turn onto serving platter and slice. Freezes well.

Yield: 8 to 10 servings   Sharon Stalvey

Pecan Crescents

2 cups sifted all-purpose flour	1 cup frozen unsalted butter or margarine, cut into 1-inch pieces
¼ teaspoon salt	1 egg yolk, slightly beaten
	¾ cup sour cream

Pecan Filling:

Combine in a small bowl:

¾ cup sugar	¾ cup coarsely chopped pecans
1½ teaspoons ground cinnamon	

In a food processor fitted with steel blade, combine flour and salt. Add butter or margarine. Turn on and off to break butter or margarine into chunks the size of peas. In a small bowl, combine egg yolk and sour cream; add to the flour mixture. Process just until combined. Place dough on a lightly floured surface; gather into a ball. Divide dough into 4 pieces; pat into small circles. Wrap each piece in plastic wrap and refrigerate overnight. Prepare filling; set aside. Preheat oven to 375 degrees. Remove one circle of dough at a time from refrigerator. On a lightly floured surface, roll out dough into a 12-inch circle. Cut circle into 8 wedges. Sprinkle filling evenly over surface of dough. Roll up each wedge, starting at outside edge. Place on an ungreased baking sheet. Bend into crescent shapes. Repeat with remaining circles. Bake in preheated oven 20 to 25 minutes until brown and crispy. Cool on rack.

Yield: 32 crescents   Honey Kendrick

 *Corn Fritters*

1⅓ cups sifted all-purpose flour	1 egg, well-beaten
2 teaspoons baking powder	1 (8 ounce) can cream style corn
½ teaspoon salt	

Mix the dry ingredients together. Add egg and corn to dry ingredients. Drop by teaspoonful in deep hot cooking oil and drain on paper. Serve hot.

Yield: 4 to 6 servings   Tootsie Tillman

 *Hush Puppies #1*

1½ cups cornmeal
1 cup all-purpose flour
1 teaspoon sugar
1 teaspoon salt
¼ teaspoon soda

2 teaspoons baking powder
1 small onion, grated
1¼ cups buttermilk
1 egg

Mix together cornmeal, flour, sugar, salt, soda and baking powder. Add grated onion, buttermilk and egg. Drop by teaspoonful in hot grease.

Yield: 40 to 60   Martha Barham

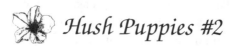 *Hush Puppies #2*

2 slices bacon
1 cup white, finely ground, cornmeal
1 teaspoon baking soda
2 tablespoons all-purpose flour

½ teaspoon salt
2 tablespoons brown sugar
1 small onion, grated
1 egg
buttermilk

Chop bacon into small pieces; fry in skillet over low heat until crisp. While bacon fries, sift dry ingredients into mixing bowl. Add bacon, bacon grease and grated onion. Mix well. Add unbeaten egg and stir it in. Then add only enough buttermilk so the batter can be loosely manipulated into balls with two teaspoons, like macaroons, and dropped into moderately heated deep fat. Vegetable oil may be used. Cooked hush puppies should be only about 1½-inches in diameter.

Yield: 30   Bobbie Lester

These go well with sausage for Sunday breakfast.

Blueberry Muffins

2 cups self-rising flour	½ cup milk
1¼ cups sugar	1¾ cups whole blueberries
2 eggs, slightly beaten	½ cup mashed blueberries
1 teaspoon vanilla extract	additional sugar
½ cup oil	

Combine flour and sugar in a large bowl; set aside. Combine eggs, vanilla, oil and milk. Make a well in the center of dry ingredients, pour in liquid ingredients. Stir until well mixed. Fold in all blueberries. Stir well, approximately 1 minute. Spoon batter half-full into muffin tins that have been sprayed with non-stick vegetable spray. Sprinkle lightly with additional sugar. Bake at 375 degrees for 25 minutes.

Yield: 2 dozen   Janice Worn

Microwave Cinnamon-Nut Muffins

2 cups all-purpose flour	½ cup milk
1 tablespoon baking powder	½ cup vegetable oil
½ teaspoon salt	3 tablespoons sugar
½ cup sugar	1½ teaspoons ground
½ cup chopped pecans	cinnamon
2 eggs, beaten	

Icing:

2 cups confectioners' sugar	1 teaspoon vanilla
1 to 2 tablespoons milk	

Combine flour, baking powder, salt, ½ cup sugar and pecans together. Stir well. Make a well in center of mixture. Combine eggs, milk and oil. Add to dry ingredients and stir until moistened. Spoon batter into paper-lined microwave muffin cups, filling half full. Combine 3 tablespoons sugar and cinnamon. Sprinkle approximately ½ teaspoon sugar/cinnamon mixture on each muffin. Microwave at medium high (70% power) for 2½ minutes, rotating once. Let muffins cool in pan for 1 minute. Mix together confectioners' sugar, milk and vanilla. Pour icing over each muffin and serve immediately.

Yield: 1½ dozen   Jane Stanaland

This is a quick breakfast idea for this coffee cake-like muffin. Busy mothers can have these made in no time.

Raisin Bran Muffins

3	cups granulated sugar	5	teaspoons baking soda
5	cups all-purpose flour	4	eggs, slightly beaten
1	(11 ounce) package raisin bran cereal	1	quart buttermilk
1	teaspoon salt	1	cup butter or margarine, melted

Mix sugar, flour, raisin bran, salt and baking soda together in a large bowl. Mix eggs, buttermilk and butter or margarine together. Fold into the dry ingredients. Place in airtight bowl in refrigerator and take out desired amount as needed. Batter will keep for two months. Pour batter half-full into greased muffin tins. Bake at 350 degrees for 10 to 15 minutes.

Yield: 48 muffins

Claire Buescher

Lemon Raspberry Streusel Muffins

2	cups all-purpose flour	½	cup oil
½	cup sugar	1	teaspoon grated lemon peel
2	teaspoons baking powder	2	eggs
½	teaspoon baking soda	1	cup fresh or frozen raspberries, thawed
½	teaspoon salt		
1	(8 ounce) carton lemon yogurt		

Preheat oven to 400 degrees. Grease 36 miniature muffin cups or 14 regular muffin cups, may use paper baking cups, if desired. In large bowl combine flour, sugar, baking powder, baking soda and salt and mix well. In small bowl, combine yogurt, oil, lemon peel and eggs. Mix well. Add to dry ingredients, stirring gently until moistened. Stir in raspberries. Fill muffin cups ¾ full.

Topping:

⅓	cup sugar	2	tablespoons butter or margarine
¼	cup all-purpose flour		

In small bowl, combine topping ingredients and mix until crumbly. Sprinkle over batter. Bake at 400 degrees for 11 to 13 minutes. If using larger muffin pan, bake at 400 degrees for 18 to 20 minutes. Cool 5 minutes and remove from muffin cups. Serve warm.

Yield: 36 miniature or 14 regular muffins

Tonya Smith

Cinnamon-Topped Oatmeal Muffins

1 cup self-rising flour	3 tablespoons vegetable oil
½ cup sugar	1 egg, beaten
1 cup quick-cooking or old-fashioned oatmeal	1 cup milk
	¼ teaspoon vanilla
½ cup raisins	

Preheat oven to 425 degrees. Sift together self-rising flour and sugar; stir in oats and raisins. Add oil, egg, milk and vanilla. Stir only until dry ingredients are moistened. Fill greased muffin cups approximately ⅔ full.

Topping:

4 tablespoons sugar	1 teaspoon cinnamon
4 tablespoons all-purpose flour	5 teaspoons melted butter or margarine

To make topping, mix sugar, flour, cinnamon and melted butter until crumbly. Sprinkle topping on muffin batter. Bake at 425 degrees for approximately 15 minutes.

Yield: 12 muffins   Carol Giles

King and Prince Oatmeal Raisin Muffins
(The King and Prince Beach Resort, St. Simons Island, Georgia)

1¼ cups rolled oats	¾ cup all-purpose flour
1 cup buttermilk	1 teaspoon baking powder
1 egg	½ teaspoon salt
¾ cup brown sugar	½ teaspoon baking soda
¼ cup butter, melted and cooled	½ cup raisins
	½ cup chopped pecans

Combine the rolled oats and buttermilk in mixing bowl and let it stand for 1 hour. Add eggs, brown sugar, and butter. Mix 30 seconds. Scrape down bowl. Add combined dry ingredients, raisins and pecans. Mix on low speed approximately 15 seconds or only until dry ingredients are moistened. Fill muffin tins half full. Bake at 350 degrees for 15 minutes.

Yield: 12 muffins   Janet Nichols

75

Little Applesauce Muffins

½	cup margarine	1	tablespoon baking powder
½	cup sugar	½	teaspoon salt
2	eggs	¼	cup margarine, melted
¾	cup applesauce	½	cup sugar
1¾	cups all-purpose flour	¼	teaspoon cinnamon

Cream ½ cup margarine and sugar. Beat in eggs. Stir in applesauce. Mix together flour, baking powder and salt. Stir into butter mixture until moist. Spoon into 36 tea muffin pans. Bake at 425 degrees for 15 minutes. While warm, dip tops into ¼ cup melted margarine and roll in mixture of ½ cup sugar and ¼ teaspoon cinnamon.

Yield: 36 muffins

Marcia Felts

Miniature Cinnamon Muffins

1½	cups all-purpose flour	½	cup sugar
1½	teaspoons baking powder	⅓	cup shortening
½	teaspoon allspice	1	egg
½	teaspoon salt	½	cup milk

Topping:

6	tablespoons butter, melted	½	cup sugar
1	teaspoon cinnamon		

Preheat oven to 350 degrees. Sift together flour, baking powder, allspice, and salt and set aside. Cream sugar and shortening. Add egg and milk. Mix well. Add dry ingredients to batter mixture. Stir until just combined. Spoon into well-greased miniature muffin tins, filling each cup ⅔ full. Bake at 350 degrees for 15 to 20 minutes. When muffins are done and still hot, turn out of tin. Dip each muffin in melted butter and roll in cinnamon and sugar mixture.

Yield: 48 muffins

Floye Luke

Velvet Corn Muffins

¾ cup unsalted butter, softened
¾ cup sugar
3 large eggs
½ cup all-purpose flour
1⅔ cups yellow cornmeal

4 teaspoons baking powder
½ teaspoon salt
2 cups milk
1 (8¾ ounce) can whole kernel corn, drained

Preheat oven to 425 degrees. Grease 2 dozen 2½-inch muffin tins. Beat butter with sugar in mixing bowl until light and fluffy. Beat in eggs one at a time, beating well after each addition. Combine flour, cornmeal, baking powder and salt in a medium bowl. With mixer at low speed, add dry ingredients to batter alternately with milk, beginning and ending with dry ingredients. Fold in corn. Spoon batter into prepared muffin pans, filling each cup ¾ full. Bake 20 minutes or until toothpick inserted in center comes out clean. Cool in pans on wire rack 10 minutes. Remove from pans.

Yield: 2 dozen   Honey Kendrick

Potato Refrigerator Rolls

2 (¼ ounce) packages of active dry yeast
1 cup very warm water
2 cups mashed potatoes, approximately 4 medium potatoes

1⅓ cups vegetable shortening
1½ cups sugar
3 teaspoons salt
2 cups potato water
3 eggs
4 to 6 cups all-purpose flour

Dissolve yeast in warm water. Dice potatoes and just cover with water. Cook for 30 minutes. Drain potatoes reserving 2 cups potato water. Thoroughly mash potatoes. Add shortening, sugar, salt and mashed potatoes to hot potato water. When cold, add yeast and eggs. Stir in enough flour to make a stiff dough. Turn onto slightly floured board. Dough will be sticky to work with. Flour hands and dough while kneading 4 or 5 times. Grease a large bowl and lightly grease dough. Place in bowl; cover lightly and refrigerate until ready to use. Roll out on floured board using flour on dough and rolling pin. Cut rolls and let rise 2 hours. Bake at 375 degrees for 10 to 15 minutes.

Yield: 2 dozen   Pat Chitty

Also can use this dough to make cinnamon rolls.

Cheesy Bacon Roll

3 tablespoons margarine	1 (10 ounce) package flaky
1 (10 ounce) jar pasteurized	biscuits
process cheese spread	6 to 7 pieces bacon, cooked
	and crumbled

Preheat oven to 350 degrees. Line a 9-inch cake pan with foil. Grease the foil well. Melt margarine and cheese in saucepan over low heat. Separate biscuits and cut into fourths. Pour cheese mixture into bottom of cake pan. Place cut biscuits over cheese. Bake at 350 degrees for 10 to 15 minutes. Invert cake pan on serving platter, peel off foil and sprinkle with crumbled bacon.

Yield: 6 to 8 servings

Debbie Davis

Savannah Beer Rolls

3½ cups biscuit baking mix	1 (12 ounce) can beer
3½ tablespoons sugar	

Mix all ingredients well and pour into a greased muffin pan. Bake at 400 degrees for approximately 15 minutes.

Yield: about 18 rolls

Julie Taylor

Tartlets

1 (1½ pound) loaf thin-sliced	½ cup butter or margarine,
sandwich bread	melted

Using a rolling pin, roll each bread slice to ¼-inch thick. Cut with a 2½-inch daisy shaped cutter. Lightly brush each side of bread with melted butter or margarine. Place in miniature muffin tins. Bake at 400 degrees for 8 to 10 minutes. Fill with favorite chicken salad or shrimp salad!

Yield: 22 shells

Vallye Blanton

Salads & Dressings

Scott/Green Home
Built 1906

Applesauce Salad

1	(16 ounce) can applesauce	1	cup chopped nuts
2	(3 ounce) packages cherry gelatin	1	cup cola flavored carbonated drink
1	(20 ounce) can crushed pineapple, undrained		

Heat applesauce. Dissolve gelatin in hot applesauce. Cool and add pineapple, nuts and cola. Pour into a 13x9x2-inch dish and refrigerate. Will congeal in 2 to 3 hours.

Yield: 12 to 15 servings   Sadie Shelton

To make a green salad, use lime gelatin and lemon-lime carbonated drink.

Blueberry Salad

2	(3 ounce) packages blackberry gelatin	1	(8 ounce) package cream cheese, softened
2	cups hot water	1	cup sour cream or plain yogurt
1	cup blueberry pie filling	½	cup sugar
1	(20 ounce) can crushed pineapple, undrained	1	teaspoon vanilla
		½	cup chopped nuts

Dissolve gelatin in hot water. Add pie filling and undrained pineapple. Pour into 13x9x2-inch dish and chill. Mix cream cheese, sour cream, sugar and vanilla. Mix well and spread on top of gelatin. Sprinkle with nuts.

Yield: 8 servings   Mary Corbett

Blueberry Salad

2	cups hot water	1	(16½ ounce) can
1	(6 ounce) package		blueberries, drained
	blueberry gelatin	½	cup chopped pecans
1	cup cold water	1	(8 ounce) package cream
1	(8¼ ounce) can crushed		cheese, softened
	pineapple, undrained	1	cup sour cream
		½	cup sugar

Boil 2 cups water. Stir in blueberry gelatin. Add 1 cup cold water, un-drained pineapple, and blueberries. Mix well. Add pecans. Pour into 13x9x2-inch dish and refrigerate until congealed. For topping, mix cream cheese, sour cream and sugar with electric mixer and chill for 2 to 3 hours; then spread over blueberry mixture and chill until serving time.

Yield: 8 servings   Kathy Lincoln

Blueberry-Pretzel Salad

2	cups crushed pretzels	1	(12 ounce) container frozen
¾	cup margarine, melted		whipped topping
3	tablespoons sugar	3	(3 ounce) packages grape
1	(8 ounce) package cream		gelatin
	cheese, softened	1	quart fresh blueberries
1	cup sugar	2	cups boiling water

Layer 1: Mix and press crushed pretzels, margarine and 3 tablespoons sugar into a 13x9x2-inch pan. Bake at 400 degrees for 9 minutes. Cool completely. Layer 2: Cream together cream cheese and 1 cup sugar. Fold in whipped topping. Spread over pretzel crust. Layer 3: Dissolve gelatin in boiling water. Add blueberries, pour on top of cream cheese mixture. Refrigerate 5 to 8 hours before serving.

Yield: 8 servings   Margaret Perryman

Buttermilk Congealed Salad

1   (20 ounce) can crushed
     pineapple, undrained
2   (3 ounce) packages
     strawberry gelatin

2   cups buttermilk
1   (12 ounce) container frozen
     whipped topping

Pour undrained pineapple into saucepan. Add gelatin and heat over low heat until dissolved. Remove from heat, add buttermilk. Pour into 13x9x2-inch dish. Refrigerate until partially set, then fold in whipped topping. Return to refrigerator until set and ready to serve.

Yield: 10 to 12 servings   Janice Baker

Cherry Salad

1   (6 ounce) package cherry
     gelatin
1¾ cups hot water

1   (15 ounce) can cherry pie
     filling
1   (8 ounce) can crushed
     pineapple, undrained

Dissolve gelatin in hot water; then add pie filling and pineapple. Pour into a 13x9x2-inch dish. Refrigerate until congealed then add topping.

Topping:

1   (8 ounce) carton sour
     cream
1   (8 ounce) package cream
     cheese, softened

½   cup sugar
½   teaspoon vanilla

Mix sour cream, cream cheese, sugar and vanilla. Spread on top of gelatin mixture.

Yield: 10 to 12 servings   Marcia Felts

Chinese Chicken Salad

½ pack won ton skins
¼ (2 ounce) jar sesame seeds
½ tablespoon margarine
3 chicken breasts, skinned, cooked and sliced

½ head lettuce, shredded
4 celery ribs, thinly sliced
½ cup fresh parsley, chopped
½ (2 ounce) package slivered almonds

Slice won ton skins into ½ inch strips and fry until golden. Drain, crumble and set aside. Toast sesame seeds in margarine and drain. Toss sesame seeds with remaining ingredients, except won tons.

Sauce:
2 tablespoons sugar
3 tablespoons white vinegar
1 teaspoon salt

¼ cup light oil
¼ teaspoon pepper

Boil sugar, vinegar and salt; add oil and pepper. Allow to cool in refrigerator then pour this over salad and toss well. Serve with crumbled fried won ton skins on individual servings.

Yield: 6 to 8 servings   Pat Chitty

Serve at bridge luncheon accompanied with Chinese snow peas cooked tender and a small fruit cup topped with peach yogurt.

Curried Chicken Salad

6	chicken breast halves	¾	cup sour cream
	salt and pepper to taste	1	teaspoon curry powder
	lemon juice	½	teaspoon cinnamon
1	cup seedless raisins	½	cup chopped celery
½	cup red wine	1	(2 ounce) package sliced
¾	cup mayonnaise		toasted almonds

Cook chicken until tender. Remove skin and meat from bone. Cut meat into bite-size pieces. Salt and pepper lightly. Sprinkle with lemon juice, cover and refrigerate overnight. Soak raisins in wine approximately 3 hours. To make dressing, combine mayonnaise, sour cream, curry powder and cinnamon. Mix well. Combine chicken, raisins and celery with dressing. Garnish with almonds.

Yield: 6 servings   Lynn Minor

Hawaiian Chicken Salad

1	whole chicken	1	cup diced celery
1	whole onion	1	(20 ounce) can chunk
1	bunch celery tops		pineapple, drained
1	teaspoon salt	1	teaspoon lemon juice
½	teaspoon black pepper	1	tablespoon grated onion
1	cup pre-cooked rice	4	teaspoons curry powder
1	cup mayonnaise	1	cup flaked coconut

Boil whole chicken, whole onion and celery tops together with salt and pepper to taste. Allow to cool. Cook rice and let cool. Dice chicken, disposing of onion and celery tops. Combine chicken and rice with mayonnaise, diced celery, pineapple, lemon juice, salt, pepper, onion, and curry in a bowl and refrigerate overnight. Add coconut just before serving.

Yield: 6 to 8 servings   Sue Ellen Clyatt

Southwestern Chicken Salad

4	chicken breast halves, skinned	⅛	teaspoon pepper
1	teaspoon salt	¼	cup chopped onion
¼	cup mayonnaise	4	(8-inch) flour tortillas
¼	cup sour cream	1	cup shredded longhorn cheese
1	(4 ounce) can chopped green chilies, undrained	3	cups shredded lettuce sour cream to garnish
1	teaspoon ground cumin	1	small tomato, diced
¼	teaspoon salt		picante sauce

Place chicken in Dutch oven; cover with water, and add 1 teaspoon salt. Bring to boil. Cover, reduce heat and simmer 30 minutes or until tender. Drain chicken, reserving broth for other uses. Bone chicken and shred into small pieces. Set aside. Combine mayonnaise and ¼ cup sour cream, stirring well. Add chilies, cumin, salt and pepper, stirring well. Combine chicken and onion; add to sour cream mixture, stirring to coat. Cover and refrigerate for 2 hours. Place tortillas on baking sheet; sprinkle cheese evenly over each tortilla. Bake at 300 degrees for 10 minutes or until cheese melts; transfer to individual serving plates. Arrange lettuce over tortillas, top each one with one forth chicken mixture. Garnish with sour cream and tomato. Serve with picante sauce.

Yield: 4 servings

Becky Stewart

Cranberry Salad

2	(3 ounce) packages raspberry gelatin	½	to 1 whole (16 ounce) can whole cranberry sauce
2	cups hot water	½	cup chopped celery
1	(8 ounce) can crushed pineapple, undrained	1	cup chopped pecans

Dissolve gelatin in hot water. Set aside until mixture thickens slightly. Thoroughly mix pineapple, cranberry sauce, celery and pecans. Stir into gelatin. Pour into 13x9x2-inch serving dish. Chill overnight.

Yield: 8 to 10 servings

Pam Edwards

Keeps for over a week in refrigerator.

Holiday Cranberry Salad

1 (8 ounce) can crushed pineapple, undrained	1 (16 ounce) can whole cranberry sauce
1 (3 ounce) package strawberry gelatin	½ cup cold liquid (pineapple juice and water)
1 cup boiling water	2 teaspoons lemon juice
	½ cup chopped nuts, optional

Drain pineapple, using juice plus water to make ½ cup cold liquid. Dissolve gelatin in hot water. While still warm, stir in cranberry sauce and mix until melted. Stir in cold liquid, lemon juice, pineapple and nuts, if used. Pour into 1½-quart mold and chill until set.

Dressing:

2 tablespoons mayonnaise	½ teaspoon sugar
2 tablespoons sour cream	

Blend mayonnaise, sour cream and sugar well. Spoon dressing on individual servings.

Yield: 6 to 8 servings · Cheryl Gaston

May use individual molds and garnish with mint leaves or parsley.

Peach Salad

1 (6 ounce) package peach gelatin	2 cups buttermilk
3 tablespoons sugar	1 (8 ounce) container frozen whipped topping
1 (8¼ ounce) can crushed pineapple, undrained	½ cup chopped nuts

Heat gelatin, sugar and pineapple until gelatin and sugar dissolve. Let mixture cool. Then fold in buttermilk, whipped topping and nuts. Place in 13x9x2-inch dish. Refrigerate until congealed.

Yield: 8 to 10 servings · Floye Luke

Lemon-Lime Congealed Salad

1   (3 ounce) package lemon
    gelatin
1   (3 ounce) package lime
    gelatin
1   (10 ounce) can lemon-lime
    carbonated drink
1   (8 ounce) can crushed
    pineapple, undrained
1   (10 ounce) can grapefruit,
    drained
½   cup chopped pecans
1   unpeeled apple, diced

Dissolve gelatin in 2 cups boiling water. Add lemon-lime drink and stir. Let thicken in refrigerator. Mix undrained pineapple, drained grapefruit, pecans and apple. Stir into thickened mixture. Place mixture in 13x9x2-inch dish. Refrigerate to congeal.

Yield: 10 to 12 servings   Lee Limbocker

Strawberry Pretzel Salad

1   cup sugar
1   (8 ounce) package cream
    cheese, softened
2   cups frozen whipped
    topping
1   (6 ounce) package
    strawberry gelatin
2   cups water
2   (10 ounce) packages frozen
    strawberries

Cream sugar and cream cheese together. Add whipped topping. Spread over cooled crust and refrigerate for approximately 30 minutes. Dissolve gelatin in 2 cups boiling water. Add frozen strawberries and allow to thicken in refrigerator. Pour on top of cream cheese layer and congeal.

Crust:
¾   **cup margarine**   2   **cups crushed pretzels**

Melt margarine and mix with pretzels. Spread evenly in 13x9x2-inch baking dish. Bake at 350 degrees for 10 minutes. Cool.

Yield: 8 to 10 servings   Libby George

Fiesta Coleslaw

1½ cups mayonnaise	1 (7 ounce) jar diced
½ cup chili sauce	pimentos, drained
1 (7 ounce) jar green olives,	½ head cabbage, shredded
drained and cut in half	2 green peppers, chopped
	2 onions, chopped

Combine mayonnaise and chili sauce until blended. Add olives and pimentos. Pour over cabbage, peppers and onions. Toss until all ingredients are mixed.

Yield: 4 servings   Vickie Wilkinson

Mexican Coleslaw

½ cup plain low-fat yogurt	1 (15 ounce) can black beans,
½ cup tomato salsa	drained
4 teaspoons reduced calorie	½ cup shredded carrots
mayonnaise	½ cup diced red onion
2 teaspoons red wine vinegar	¼ cup chopped fresh flat-leaf
2 teaspoons fresh lime juice	parsley, optional
2½ cups shredded green	
cabbage	

Combine yogurt, salsa, mayonnaise, vinegar, and lime juice. Pour mixture over cabbage, beans, carrots, red onions and parsley. Toss until cabbage is thoroughly coated with dressing mixture. Better if refrigerated for approximately 2 hours before serving.

Yield: 6 to 8 servings   Judith Joseph

Good with chicken fajitas and Spanish rice.

Chilled Fruit Salad

1 (20 ounce) can peach pie
  filling
1 (10 ounce) carton frozen
  strawberries, thawed and
  drained

1 (15 ounce) can chunk
  pineapple, drained
1 large banana, sliced

Mix peach pie filling, strawberries and pineapple in bowl. Cover and chill. Add banana 1 hour before serving.

Yield: 8 servings   Brenda Davis

Fresh Fruit In Champagne

1 watermelon
1 cantaloupe
1 honeydew melon
1 fresh pineapple

1 bunch seedless green
  grapes
  champagne

Cut watermelon in half lengthwise and clean out one half of the melon. Using fruit scoop, make watermelon, cantaloupe and honeydew melon balls. Cut pineapple in small bite-size pieces. Place all cut fruit and grapes in hollowed-out watermelon half. Pour champagne over fruit. Refrigerate until served.

Yield: 10 to 12 servings   Sally Moritz

Frozen Fruit Salad

¾ cup sugar
½ teaspoon salt
1 (16 ounce) carton sour
  cream
2 tablespoons lemon juice
4 bananas, mashed

1 (6 ounce) jar cherries
½ cup chopped pecans
1 (8½ ounce) can crushed
  pineapple, undrained
  lettuce leaves

Combine sugar, salt, sour cream and lemon juice. Add mashed bananas to mixture. Add cherries, pecans and pineapple. Spray mold with non-stick vegetable spray or place liners in muffin tin. Pour salad in tin and freeze. Serve frozen on lettuce leaves.

Yield: 12 servings   Vallye Blanton

Curry Rice Salad

1	(6 ounce) jar artichoke hearts, drained; reserve liquid	¾	teaspoon curry powder
3	green onions, thinly sliced	⅓	cup mayonnaise
1	small green pepper, diced	1	(6 ounce) box long grain and wild rice
8	large green olives with pimentos, sliced		olives for garnish

Mix artichokes (whole or quartered), onions, green pepper, and olives. Mix curry powder with mayonnaise and artichoke liquid. Prepare rice according to box directions and cool, then add to artichoke mixture. Garnish with olives. Serve cold.

Yield: 6 servings

Sharon Coleman

Wild Rice And Artichoke Salad

2	cups chicken broth	⅓	cup chopped stuffed green olives
1	cup uncooked wild rice		
⅓	cup chopped green onions	1	(6 ounce) jar marinated artichoke hearts, drained and chopped
⅓	cup chopped green peppers		
⅓	cup chopped celery		salt and pepper to taste
½	cup mayonnaise		olives for garnish

Bring broth to a boil. Add rice, cover and simmer over low heat for 20 minutes or until tender. Remove from heat and cool. Combine rice with remaining ingredients. Chill well. Garnish with additional sliced olives.

Yield: 8 to 10 servings

Teresa Steinberg

This salad tastes even better if made a day in advance. White rice may be substituted for wild rice.

Celebration Salad

1	large head Romaine lettuce, torn	1	(11 ounce) can mandarin oranges, drained
8	cherry tomatoes, halved	3	ounces blue cheese, crumbled
1	small red onion, sliced		
6	slices bacon, cooked and crumbled		

Layer ingredients. Toss with dressing when ready to serve.

Dressing:

¾	cup vegetable oil	1	teaspoon salt
¼	cup apple cider vinegar	4	teaspoons sugar
1	clove garlic, minced		black pepper to taste

Combine in jar. Shake well.

Yield: 8 servings

Melissa Carter

Java Salad

1	(8 ounce) bottle Green Goddess dressing	⅔	cup chopped celery
3	cups cooked rice, hot	¼	cup chopped chutney
¼	cup raisins	1	(2 ounce) jar pimentos, chopped
1	teaspoon minced onions	¼	cup chopped green pepper
2	cups cooked, chopped, chicken	¼	cup dry cashews
		6	to 8 lettuce leaves

Stir dressing in hot rice. Add raisins and onions. Let chill for two hours. Remove from refrigerator and add chicken, celery, chutney, pimento, green pepper and cashews. Serve on lettuce.

Yield: 4 to 6 servings

Sharon Coleman

Delicious accompanied with fresh fruit! May also be served with avocado slices. If bottled Green Goddess dressing unavailable, see recipe in dressings section; or, use buttermilk Ranch dressing.

Judy's Luncheon Salad

Dressing:

½ cup salad oil	2 teaspoons sugar
2 tablespoons white wine vinegar	1 teaspoon dry mustard
2 tablespoons lemon juice concentrate	½ teaspoon salt

Mix salad oil, wine vinegar, lemon juice, sugar, dry mustard, and salt in jar. Shake well then refrigerate several hours or overnight.

1 head romaine lettuce	3 oranges, peeled and
1 green pepper	sectioned or 1 (11 ounce)
1 small red onion	can mandarin oranges
3 medium bananas, sliced	

Tear lettuce into bite-size pieces. Slice green pepper lengthwise then into thirds. Slice onion thinly and separate into rings. Just before serving place lettuce, green pepper and onion in salad bowl. Add bananas and oranges on top. Shake dressing. Pour on top and toss to cover fruit and vegetables.

Yield: 8 to 10 servings   Carol Giles

Lettuce, green pepper and onions can be prepared ahead and stored in plastic bags. This salad is nice served with quiche.

 # Marinated Shrimp Salad

1 pound cooked shrimp	½ cup raw cauliflower
1 (3 ounce) can sliced broiled mushrooms	flowerets
	¼ cup mayonnaise
¼ cup seasoned Italian dressing	½ teaspoon salt
	⅛ teaspoon curry powder
1 cup diced celery	

Place shrimp and mushrooms in bowl, add Italian dressing and mix. Cover and let stand in refrigerator for at least 2 hours. Add celery and cauliflower. Stir in mayonnaise, salt and curry powder. Serve on lettuce.

Yield: 4 servings   Barbara Parks

Crabmeat-Shrimp Pasta Salad

3	cups water	1	tablespoon chopped fresh parsley
1	pound unpeeled medium-sized fresh shrimp	¼	cup mayonnaise
2	cups seashell macaroni	¼	cup Italian salad dressing
1	cup thinly sliced celery	1	tablespoon lemon juice
½	medium green pepper, finely chopped	½	teaspoon crushed dried whole oregano
½	medium red pepper, finely chopped	¼	teaspoon salt
½	small purple onion, chopped		dash of pepper
2	green onions, chopped	1	(8 ounce) can lump crabmeat, drained

Bring water to a boil; add shrimp and cook 3 to 5 minutes. Drain well; rinse with cold water. Chill. Peel and devein shrimp; set aside. Cook macaroni according to package directions, omitting salt; drain. Rinse with cold water, and drain again. Add celery, green pepper, red pepper, purple onion, green onions and parsley; blend well. Combine mayonnaise, salad dressing, lemon juice, oregano, salt and pepper. Add to macaroni mixture. Stir in crabmeat and shrimp. Chill before serving.

Yield: 7 servings   Suzanne Sullivan

Congealed Salad With Crabmeat And Asparagus

1	envelope unflavored gelatin	2	cups mayonnaise
2	tablespoons water	¼	cup vinegar
3	(3 ounce) packages lime gelatin	2	cups shredded Cheddar cheese
1	teaspoon salt	4	to 5 drops hot sauce
3	cups water	1	pound fresh crabmeat, drained and flaked
2	(15 ounce) cans cut asparagus, undrained		lettuce leaves

Combine unflavored gelatin and 2 tablespoons water; let stand 5 minutes. Combine unflavored and flavored gelatin, salt and 3 cups water in saucepan; bring to boil. Remove from heat; chill until consistency of unbeaten egg white. Drain asparagus, reserving juice from 1 can. Combine the reserved juice, mayonnaise, vinegar, cheese, hot sauce and crabmeat. Fold into the chilled gelatin mixture. Pour half of gelatin mixture into a 13x9x2-inch casserole dish. Top with drained asparagus and remaining gelatin mixture. Chill until firm. Cut into squares, and serve on a bed of lettuce.

Yield: 12 servings

Martha Grow

Baked Seafood Salad

¾	pound shrimp	1	tablespoon lemon juice
2½	cups water	1	tablespoon Worcestershire
1	cup drained and flaked		sauce
	crabmeat	½	teaspoon salt
1	cup thinly sliced celery	⅛	teaspoon pepper
½	cup chopped pecans or	⅓	cup bread crumbs
	sliced almonds		celery leaves for garnish
1	cup mayonnaise		

Boil shrimp in water 3 to 5 minutes. Devein, peel and chill. Combine all but 4 to 6 shrimp, crabmeat, celery, nuts, mayonnaise, lemon juice, Worcestershire sauce, salt and pepper. Place in 9x9x2-inch baking dish or 4 shells. Bake at 350 degrees for 20 minutes. Top with bread crumbs and bake an additional 5 minutes to brown top. Garnish with remaining shrimp and celery leaves.

Yield: 4 to 6 servings   Zan Martin

South Georgia Taco Salad

1	large onion, finely chopped	1	head lettuce, washed and
1	tablespoon oil		torn in small pieces
1	pound lean hamburger,	1	(8 ounce) package shredded
	browned and drained		cheese for tacos
1	(1¼ ounce) package taco	1	large tomato, diced
	seasoning mix	1	(10 ounce) package plain
1	cup salsa		taco chips
1	cup water	1	(8 ounce) bottle Catalina
			dressing

Place onion and oil in large skillet and sauté over medium heat until clear. Add hamburger, taco mix, salsa and 1 cup water. Simmer, uncovered, over low heat until thickened. Cool to room temperature. Prepare lettuce and toss in cheese and tomato. In large bowl, mix hamburger mixture and lettuce mixture. Immediately prior to serving, crush taco chips and add to lettuce mixture. Blend in enough Catalina dressing to moisten all ingredients well. (Too much dressing will cause sogginess.)

Yield: 20 to 25 servings   Mary Beth Meyers

Suzanne Hartin's Congealed Almond Cheese

1	(8 ounce) package cream cheese	1	envelope unflavored gelatin
1	(3 ounce) package cream cheese	¼	cup water
½	cup butter	1	cup slivered almonds
½	cup sour cream	1	teaspoon grated lemon rind
2	tablespoons sugar	½	cup golden raisins
		½	teaspoon almond extract

Combine cream cheese and butter. Beat with electric beater. Add sour cream and sugar and mix. Combine gelatin and water in small saucepan. Cook over low heat until gelatin dissolves. Cool. Add gelatin mix to cream cheese mixture. Stir in almonds, lemon rind, raisins, and almond extract. Place in 1-quart mold and chill overnight. Do not freeze.

Yield: 4 cups   Susan Golden

Broccoli Salad

3	cups chopped fresh broccoli	1	cup mayonnaise-type salad dressing
1	cup chopped purple onions		
8	slices bacon, cooked and crumbled	1	tablespoon vinegar
		1	tablespoon sugar
½	cup raisins, optional	1	cup grated Cheddar cheese

Mix broccoli, onions, bacon and raisins in a bowl. Mix salad dressing, vinegar and sugar in a separate bowl. Blend. Add salad dressing mixture to broccoli mixture and stir. Sprinkle with grated cheese and chill.

Yield: 4 to 6 servings   Jadan Pitcock

Broccoli-Cauliflower Salad

1	bunch broccoli	½	cup mayonnaise
½	head cauliflower	2	tablespoons sugar
1	small purple onion, finely chopped	1	tablespoon red wine vinegar
1	cup grated sharp Cheddar cheese	8	slices bacon, fried and crumbled

Wash broccoli and cauliflower and break into small flowerets. In large bowl, mix broccoli, cauliflower, onion and cheese. Blend mayonnaise, sugar and vinegar. Pour over broccoli-cauliflower mixture and toss until all ingredients are well-coated. Refrigerate for at least 1 hour before serving, add crumbled bacon and toss well.

Yield: 8 servings   Sharon Stalvey

"Napa" Cabbage Salad

1	Chinese "Napa" cabbage or Bokchoy	2	bunches green onions

Wash, drain and cut up cabbage and onions. Place in plastic bag and refrigerate until ready to use.

2	(3 ounce) packages chicken flavored Ramen noodles	1	(1 ounce) box or jar sesame seeds
2	(2 ounce) packages slivered almonds		

Toast noodles, almonds and sesame seeds on cookie sheet at 350 degrees for 10 to 15 minutes. Cool, then place in jar or zip lock bag.

Dressing:

1	cup vegetable oil	3	tablespoons vinegar
½	cup sugar	1	packet of chicken flavor from Ramen noodles
½	teaspoon salt		

Dissolve sugar over low heat. Mix everything when ready to serve.

Yield: 8 to 10 servings   Denise Rountree

Layered Cabbage Salad

1	medium head cabbage, chopped	1½	cups frozen green peas, thawed
1	pound bacon, cooked and crumbled	1	small onion, chopped
1½	cups shredded mozzarella or Swiss cheese	1	bunch broccoli flowerets

Place cabbage in 3 quart bowl. Layer bacon, cheese, peas, onion, and broccoli.

Dressing:

1½	cups mayonnaise	½	cup sugar
½	cup plain yogurt	½	cup Parmesan cheese
½	teaspoon salt	¼	teaspoon black pepper

Mix all ingredients together and pour over layered salad. Cover with plastic wrap and refrigerate for 24 hours. Toss before serving.

Yield: 8 to 10 servings   Sally Kurrie

24 Hour Layered Vegetable Salad

1	head lettuce	¼	cup finely chopped green onions
1	(5 ounce) package frozen English peas, thawed	½	cup finely chopped green pepper
3	to 4 stalks broccoli	1½	ounces real bacon bits
¼	to ½ head cauliflower	6	ounces Cheddar cheese, grated
1	pint mayonnaise		

Tear lettuce into bite-size pieces. Place in bottom of 3 quart bowl. Add uncooked peas. Break broccoli and cauliflower into flowerets. Add broccoli, cauliflower, onions and green peppers on top of peas. Spread mayonnaise across the top, making sure edges are sealed. Sprinkle bacon and cheese on top of mayonnaise. Seal with plastic wrap, then cover with aluminum foil. Chill in refrigerator 24 hours. Before serving, toss until evenly mixed.

Yield: 12 to 16 servings   Brenda Davis

English Pea Salad

1   (17 ounce) can English
    peas, drained
3   to 4 green onions, chopped

4   slices bacon, cooked and
    crumbled
2   tablespoons mayonnaise

Mix peas, onions and bacon in bowl. Add mayonnaise to desired consistency.

Yield: 4 servings   Karen Bishop

Frozen peas, thawed, can be substituted for canned English peas.

New Potato Salad

½   cup mayonnaise
¼   cup finely chopped onions
1½ tablespoons Dijon mustard
¼   teaspoon black pepper

3   to 4 cups cooked and
    quartered new potatoes
¾   cup quartered cucumber
    slices
¼   cup red pepper strips

In large bowl mix mayonnaise, onion, mustard and pepper. Combine potatoes with mayonnaise mixture and add cucumber and red pepper. Mix well and refrigerate.

Yield: 6 servings   Terry Thomson

Sweet and Sour Sauerkraut Salad

2   (16 ounce) cans sauerkraut
1   (4 ounce) jar chopped
    pimentos, undrained
1   large green pepper, thinly
    sliced

1   medium onion, thinly sliced
1   cup sugar
⅔   cup vegetable oil
½   cup cider vinegar
1   tablespoon celery seed

Drain and rinse sauerkraut about 3 times. Add undrained pimento, pepper and onion. In saucepan, mix sugar, oil, vinegar and celery seed. Bring to boil. Pour over sauerkraut mixture. Chill several hours or overnight.

Yield: 10 to 12 servings   Pam Mackey

Easy Tomato Aspic

1	(15 ounce) can stewed tomatoes	3	or 4 drops hot pepper sauce
1	(3 ounce) package lemon flavored gelatin	1	(12 ounce) carton cottage cheese
		4	lettuce leaves

Put tomatoes in blender and chop. In saucepan, heat tomatoes and add lemon gelatin. Stir to dissolve. Stir in hot pepper sauce and pour into 8x8x2-inch glass dish to chill. When congealed, cut into squares and serve with cottage cheese on lettuce leaves.

Yield: 4 servings   Marcia McRae

 # Herbed Tomato Platter

6	ripened medium tomatoes, peeled	1	teaspoon salt
⅔	cup salad oil	¼	teaspoon coarsely ground black pepper
¼	cup vinegar	½	teaspoon dried basil
¼	cup chopped parsley	½	teaspoon thyme
¼	cup sliced green onions	½	teaspoon marjoram
1	clove garlic, minced		

Place tomatoes in deep bowl. Combine remaining ingredients and pour over tomatoes. Cover and chill, baste occasionally. Before serving baste well again. Place on serving platter and pour some of the dressing over tomatoes, if desired.

Dutch Cucumbers: (Served With Herbed Tomato Platter)

2	cups thinly sliced cucumbers	¼	cup sugar
1	cup thinly sliced onions	¾	teaspoon salt
½	cup vinegar		generous sprinkling of coarsely ground black pepper
½	cup cold water		

Place cucumbers and onions in deep bowl. Combine vinegar, water, sugar, salt and pepper in a small bowl and stir until well blended. Pour over cucumbers. Chill and baste often. Drain and place on separate serving platter.

Yield: 6 to 8 servings   Mary Young Oliver

 *Perfect Tomato Aspic*

¼ cup cold water	1 (4½ ounce) bottle olives,
1 envelope unflavored gelatin	sliced or chopped
2 cups tomato juice	2 or 3 celery ribs, finely
1 beef bouillon cube	chopped
juice of ½ lemon	6 to 8 leaves of lettuce
	mayonnaise for garnish

Pour cold water into bowl and sprinkle gelatin on top to dissolve. Heat tomato juice to boiling, then add bouillon cube to dissolve. Pour tomato juice over gelatin. Add lemon juice, olives and celery. Mix well and place in 8x8x2-inch glass dish. Refrigerate until congealed. Serve on lettuce with a spoonful of mayonnaise on top.

Yield: 6 to 8 servings   Ginna McTier

Marinated Zucchini Salad

Marinade:

⅔ cup salad oil	¾ teaspoon salt
¼ cup vinegar	¾ teaspoon dry mustard
1 small clove garlic, minced	dash freshly ground black
1 teaspoon sugar	pepper

Salad:

1 (16 ounce) can sliced carrots, drained	2 cups thinly sliced zucchini
	6 to 8 leaves Bibb lettuce
1 (14 ounce) can artichoke hearts or hearts of palm, drained	2 ounces blue cheese, crumbled

To make marinade, combine salad oil, vinegar, garlic, sugar, salt, dry mustard and black pepper. Shake well. Pour over carrots, artichoke hearts and zucchini. Chill overnight. To serve, drain vegetables, arrange on lettuce leaves and top with crumbled blue cheese.

Yield: 8 servings   Vickie Wilkinson

Vegetable Salad

6	medium tomatoes, diced	1½	cups tarragon vinegar
2	cups unpeeled, sliced cucumbers	1	cup water
		½	cup sugar
2	medium onions, sliced	2	teaspoons basil
1	cup thinly sliced carrots	1	teaspoon salt
1	cup thinly sliced celery	½	teaspoon pepper

Place tomatoes, cucumbers, onions, carrots, and celery in airtight container. Combine vinegar, water, sugar, basil, salt, and pepper. Pour over vegetables. Seal and chill at least 4 hours or overnight.

Yield: 8 to 10 servings   Vallye Blanton

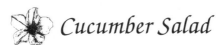 Cucumber Salad

1	(6 ounce) package lime gelatin	1	pinch salt
		4	tablespoons lemon juice
½	cup boiling water	1	large cucumber, grated
1	cup cottage cheese	1	large onion, grated
1	cup mayonnaise		

Dissolve gelatin in boiling water. Allow to cool. Add cottage cheese, mayonnaise, salt, lemon juice, cucumber and onion. Refrigerate until congealed.

Yield: 4 to 6 servings   Lamb Lastinger

Thousand Isles Dressing

½	medium red onion	2	teaspoons pimento
4	stalks celery	2	hard boiled eggs
4	sweet pickles	1	quart mayonnaise
½	green pepper	1	cup ketchup
2½	sprigs parsley		

Chop vegetables very fine. Mix together mayonnaise and ketchup then blend with chopped vegetables.

Yield: 1 quart   Julie Budd

French Dressing

1 cup salad oil	⅓ cup ketchup
½ cup wine vinegar	salt and pepper to taste
½ cup sugar	

Mix the above ingredients and blend well. Pour over chilled greens.

Yield: 2 cups   Patti Wright

Especially good on spinach.

Fresh Salad Dressing

½ cup vegetable oil	½ teaspoon salt
3 tablespoons wine vinegar	½ teaspoon dry mustard
3 tablespoons lemon juice	½ teaspoon pepper
1 teaspoon sugar	1 clove garlic, pressed

Mix all ingredients together and shake well. Refrigerate overnight. Serve over green salad.

Yield: 1 cup   Pat Chitty

Green Goddess Dressing

1 egg yolk	1 tablespoon lemon juice
2 tablespoons tarragon vinegar	1 teaspoon onion salt
1 tablespoon anchovy paste	dash of garlic salt
½ teaspoon salt	2 tablespoons chopped chives
1 cup salad oil	2 tablespoons chopped parsley
¼ cup cream	

Mix egg yolk, vinegar, anchovy paste and salt in bowl. While beating, add oil, 2 tablespoons at a time. Stir in cream, lemon juice, onion salt, garlic salt, chives and parsley. Pour in jar and refrigerate. Dressing keeps well in refrigerator.

Yield: 1 quart   Mary Young Oliver

 *Fruit Salad Dressing*

5	tablespoons vinegar	1	teaspoon paprika
⅓	cup honey	¼	teaspoon salt
1	teaspoon celery seed	1	tablespoon lemon juice
½	cup sugar	1	cup salad oil
1	teaspoon dry mustard	1	teaspoon grated onion

Combine vinegar, honey, celery seed, sugar, dry mustard, paprika, salt and lemon juice. Blend in blender or use an electric mixer on medium. Gradually add salad oil and continue blending; then stir in grated onion. Store in refrigerator until used.

Yield: 2 cups   Elizabeth Mixson

Creamy Buttermilk Dressing

1	pint buttermilk	½	teaspoon pepper
1	pint mayonnaise	½	teaspoon garlic powder
½	tablespoon salt	1	tablespoon minced onion
4	teaspoons monosodium glutamate	1	tablespoon dried parsley

Mix all ingredients together except mayonnaise. Blend well. Then add mayonnaise. Will keep in refrigerator up to 3 weeks.

Yield: 1 quart   Patti Wright

Great dip for marinated chicken wings or raw vegetables.

Spinach Salad Dressing

1	tablespoon sugar	⅔	cup warm water
1½	tablespoons minced onion	1	teaspoon Worcestershire sauce
4	tablespoons Dijon mustard		
1½	tablespoons salt	2	cups vegetable oil
⅔	cup vinegar	4	drops hot sauce

Mix sugar, onion, mustard, salt, vinegar, and water. Then add Worcestershire, vegetable oil and hot sauce. Serve over salad.

Yield: 2½ cups   Pam Mackey

Strawberry Cream Dressing

½ cup mayonnaise
1 (8 ounce) package cream
   cheese, softened
1 (3 ounce) package cream
   cheese, softened

1 (8 ounce) carton sour
   cream
1 cup fresh strawberries
½ cup powdered sugar

Place all ingredients in a food processor fitted with the steel blade. Process until smooth and creamy. Serve over fresh fruit. Covered and refrigerated, dressing will keep up to 3 days.

Yield: 2½ cups

Honey Kendrick

Variation: Substitute for fresh strawberries 1 (10 ounce) package frozen strawberries that have been thawed and drained. Decrease sugar, if desired.

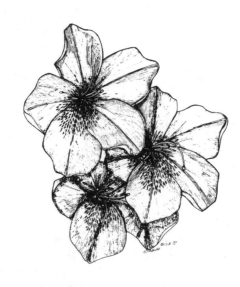

Eggs, Cheese & Pasta

Langdale, Vallotton, Chapman, Linahan
and Greneker Law Office
Rose Home
Built 1899

Breakfast/Brunch Casserole

1½ dozen eggs
¼ cup milk
¼ cup butter
1 (10¾ ounce) can cream of
  mushroom soup
1 cup grated sharp Cheddar
  cheese, divided

¼ cup sherry
1 pound sausage, cooked and
  drained, or 1 pound
  chopped ham
½ pound mushrooms, sliced
  and sautéed

Combine eggs and milk, blending well. Scramble egg mixture in butter until soft. Combine soup, ¾ cup cheese and sherry in medium saucepan. Heat until cheese melts. In a greased, 2-quart baking dish, layer scrambled eggs, sausage or ham, and mushrooms. Pour soup mixture over mushrooms. Top with remaining ¼ cup cheese. Cover with aluminum foil and refrigerate overnight. Bake, uncovered, at 275 degrees for 50 minutes.

Yield: 9 to 12 servings   Vickie Wilkinson

This recipe doubles easily to serve 18 to 24 people and is great for a crowd.

Breakfast Pie

1 (6 ounce) can crescent rolls
10 slices bacon
2 tomatoes
5 slices American cheese

3 eggs, separated
¾ cup sour cream
½ cup all-purpose flour
  salt and pepper to taste

Roll out crescent rolls and layer in bottom of pie plate. Cook bacon, tear into bite-size pieces and place on top of rolls. Slice tomatoes and place on top of bacon. Place cheese slices on top of tomatoes. Beat egg whites. Combine egg yolks, sour cream, flour, salt and pepper. Fold in egg whites. Pour over cheese layer. Bake at 350 degrees for 35 to 40 minutes.

Yield: 6 to 8 servings   Vallye Blanton

Tempting Breakfast Pie

1 cup corn flakes, crumbled	½ cup cottage cheese
1 tablespoon bacon drippings	⅓ cup milk
5 eggs	1 green onion, thinly sliced
2½ cups frozen hash-brown	1 teaspoon salt
potatoes	8 slices bacon, cooked crisp
½ teaspoon pepper	and crumbled
1½ cups shredded Swiss cheese	

Mix crumbled corn flakes with drippings and set aside. In medium size bowl, beat eggs until foamy. Stir in hash browns, pepper, Swiss cheese, cottage cheese, milk, green onion and salt. Pour into greased 9-inch pie pan. Sprinkle with corn flake mixture and bacon. Cover and refrigerate overnight. Bake, uncovered, at 325 degrees for approximately 45 minutes or until knife inserted in center comes out clean.

Yield: 10 to 12 servings   Claire Hiers

Breakfast Pizza

1 (16 ounce) package mild	5 eggs
pork sausage	¼ cup milk
2 (6 ounce) cans crescent rolls	½ teaspoon salt
1 cup frozen hash browns,	⅛ teaspoon pepper
thawed	2 tablespoons grated
1 cup shredded Cheddar	Parmesan cheese
cheese	

Brown sausage, drain excess fat. Separate dough into 8 triangles. Place in 12-inch pizza pan with points to the center. Press over bottom and up sides to form crust. Seal triangles together. Spoon sausage over crust. Sprinkle with potatoes and top with Cheddar cheese. Beat eggs, milk, salt and pepper. Pour onto crust. Sprinkle Parmesan cheese over the mixture. Bake at 375 degrees for 25 to 30 minutes.

Yield: 6 to 8 servings   Barbara Bankston

Canterbury Farm Ham And Egg Bake

1	cup chopped, cooked ham	3	tablespoons all-purpose flour
1	large onion, chopped		
5	tablespoons butter, divided	2	cups milk
1	cup sliced fresh mushrooms	1½	cups grated Cheddar cheese
20	eggs, lightly beaten	2	cups soft breadcrumbs
¼	teaspoon ground cayenne pepper	¼	cup chopped parsley or chives

Preheat oven to 325 degrees. Sauté chopped ham and onion in 3 table-spoons butter in 12-inch skillet until onion softens but does not brown, approximately 5 minutes. Add mushrooms and sauté until slightly soft-ened. Put into bowl. Combine eggs with cayenne pepper in skillet; cook over medium heat stirring until scrambled but still very runny. Remove from heat. Fold in ham mixture. Spoon into greased 13x9x2-inch baking dish. Melt remaining 2 tablespoons butter in medium size saucepan over medium heat. Stir in flour until blended; cook 1 minute. Slowly stir in milk until blended. Cook, stirring until thin and bubbly, approximately 3 min-utes. Stir in cheese until melted and smooth. Do not boil. Cheese can be melted in microwave to save time. Pour cheese sauce over ham mixture. Sprinkle breadcrumbs over sauce. Cover pan tightly and refrigerate over-night. Bake, uncovered, at 325 degrees for 40 minutes or until bubbly, top is set and lightly browned. Sprinkle with herbs.

Yield: 12 servings   Carolyn Eager

Creamed Eggs Chartres

1 cup finely shredded white onion	⅛ to ¼ teaspoon cayenne pepper
⅓ cup butter	4 hard boiled eggs, peeled and sliced, reserving 4 center slices for garnish
¼ cup all-purpose flour	
1 egg yolk	
2 cups milk	1 tablespoon paprika
¼ teaspoon salt	2 tablespoons Parmesan cheese

In skillet over medium heat, sauté onion in butter until transparent. Stir in flour, cook 3 to 5 minutes. Add egg yolk to milk, then blend into flour and onion mixture. Add salt and cayenne pepper and cook, stirring constantly until thick. Remove from heat, add sliced eggs. Mix lightly. Pour into two 8-ounce casseroles and sprinkle lightly with paprika and Parmesan cheese mixed together. Bake, uncovered, at 350 degrees until heated thoroughly. Garnish with egg slices.

Yield: 2 servings   Geneva M. Morris

This is a favorite of Brennan's in New Orleans.

Cheese and Sausage Grits

1 (16 ounce) package mild sausage, browned hot pepper sauce to taste	2 cups boiling water
	1 cup grated extra-sharp Cheddar cheese
⅓ clove garlic, minced	¼ cup butter, melted
½ teaspoon salt	2 large eggs, well-beaten
⅛ teaspoon pepper	1 (8 ounce) can mild green chilies, seeded and chopped
1 cup instant grits	

Brown sausage and drain. Add hot pepper sauce, garlic, salt and pepper to sausage. Set aside. Cook grits in 2 cups boiling water. Stir all remaining ingredients together, mixing well. Pour mixture into a greased 13x9x2-inch baking dish. Bake, uncovered, at 350 degrees for 1 hour.

Yield: 10 servings   Elaine Bridges

Garlic Grits

1	onion, chopped	2	cloves garlic, pressed
1	teaspoon salt	4	eggs
1	cup quick grits		milk
¾	cup butter, divided	1	cup crushed corn flakes
1	(8 ounce) block sharp Cheddar cheese, grated		

Bring 4 cups of water to a boil and add onion, salt and grits. Cook 2½ to 5 minutes. In separate pan, melt ½ cup butter and add cheese and garlic over medium heat. Beat eggs, then add enough milk to eggs to make one cup. Add eggs to cheese mixture, stirring constantly. Then add cheese mixture to grits. Mix well. Pour into greased 13x9x2-inch casserole. Melt remaining ¼ cup of butter. Add corn flakes to butter. Sprinkle on grits. Bake at 350 degrees for 45 minutes.

Yield: 15 to 20 servings   Jana Yates

Eggs Continental

¾	cup fine soft breadcrumbs	2	tablespoons minced parsley or chives
4	hard-boiled eggs, sliced		
3	slices cooked bacon, diced	¼	teaspoon salt
¼	pound fresh mushrooms, sliced	¼	teaspoon paprika
1	(8 ounce) carton sour cream	½	cup grated Cheddar cheese

Line shallow individual casseroles or an 8-inch pie pan with bread-crumbs. Place sliced eggs in a layer over the crumbs. Meanwhile, fry the bacon until crisp. Approximately 5 minutes before the bacon is done, add the mushrooms and sauté until just softened. Drain off fat, add bacon and mushrooms to sour cream, parsley or chives, salt and paprika. Mix thoroughly and spread over eggs. Top with grated cheese and sprinkle with paprika. Bake at 350 degrees for 15 to 20 minutes, or until cheese is melted and sauce is bubbly.

Yield: 6 to 8 servings   Mary Dasher

Eggs à la Princess Caramon

12	hard-boiled eggs	1½	cups finely chopped, fresh
12	tablespoons butter, divided		mushrooms
4	tablespoons all-purpose	2	tablespoons fresh parsley
	flour	1	teaspoon dried tarragon
1½	cups half-and-half	1	teaspoon dry mustard
1	teaspoon salt	1	cup heavy cream
½	teaspoon white pepper	½	cup shredded Gruyère or
½	teaspoon finely chopped		Swiss cheese
	garlic	4	tablespoons grated Romano
2	tablespoons minced green		cheese
	onions	2	tablespoons breadcrumbs

Preheat oven to 350 degrees. Cut eggs in half lengthwise. Place cooked egg whites aside and mash yolks in a bowl. Melt 3 tablespoons butter in a saucepan, stir in flour, and cook for 2 minutes; do not brown. Remove from heat and whisk in half-and-half. Return to heat and cook, stirring until sauce thickens and comes to a boil. Lower heat and cook approximately 5 minutes. Season with salt and white pepper. Remove from heat and stir 4 tablespoons of the white sauce into mashed egg yolks. In a skillet, melt 3 tablespoons butter over high heat. Add garlic, onions and mushrooms. Toss over high heat until mixture looks dry, approximately 5 to 10 minutes. Add to egg yolk mixture, along with parsley, tarragon and mustard. Beat in 4 tablespoons softened butter, and add more salt and pepper if needed. Stuff egg whites with this mixture. Thin remaining white sauce with heavy cream, bring to a boil and stir in Gruyère or Swiss cheese. Taste for seasoning. Spoon some of the sauce into an ovenproof serving dish. Arrange stuffed eggs on sauce and spoon more sauce over eggs, covering completely. Sprinkle with grated Romano, breadcrumbs and drizzle with 2 tablespoons melted butter. Bake at 350 degrees for 20 minutes. Serve immediately.

Yield: 8 servings   Elaine Bridges

Can be prepared ahead the day before, covered with plastic wrap and refrigerated.

Eggs McBrunch

2	tablespoons butter	¼	teaspoon salt
2	tablespoons all-purpose flour	¼	teaspoon dry mustard
		4	English muffins, split
1	cup milk	8	slices Canadian bacon, heated
1	cup grated sharp Cheddar cheese	8	poached eggs

In medium saucepan, melt butter over low heat. Stir in flour until well blended. Add milk gradually, stirring constantly until mixture begins to thicken. Blend in cheese, salt and mustard. Cook over low heat, stirring until mixture is smooth and bubbly. Toast English muffins. Put warmed Canadian bacon on top of each muffin half. Top with poached egg. Spoon cheese sauce over.

Yield: 8 servings   Elaine Bridges

Mexican Eggs

½	cup chopped green onions, reserve some for garnish	1	(8 ounce) can chopped chilies
¼	cup butter	1	(12 ounce) jar salsa, medium or hot
2	dozen eggs, beaten with small amount of milk salt and pepper to taste	¾	pound Cheddar cheese, grated
8	corn tortillas, cut in eighths	2	pints sour cream

Sauté onions in butter. Soft scramble eggs. Salt and pepper eggs. Layer in greased 13x9x2-inch baking dish in order: tortillas, eggs, onions, chilies, salsa and cheese. Cover with sour cream. Garnish with green onions. Bake at 300 degrees for 1 hour. Can be assembled the day before.

Yield: 16 servings   Jana Yates

Serve with garlic grits for brunch.

Aunt Jody's Quiche

1	(12 ounce) package crabmeat, drained, can substitute ham or lamb	1	9-inch deep dish pie crust
1	(4 ounce) can sliced mushrooms, drained	4	eggs
2	cups natural shredded Swiss cheese		dash of hot pepper sauce
1	cup New York shredded sharp Cheddar cheese	¼	teaspoon salt
		¼	teaspoon pepper
		½	pint whipping cream or half-and-half cream

Arrange thin layers of crabmeat, mushrooms and cheese in pie crust. Beat eggs with dash of hot pepper sauce, salt and pepper. Fold, don't whip, in the whipping cream and pour over meat, cheese and mushrooms in pie crust. Bake at 400 degrees for 15 to 20 minutes or until lightly browned on top.

Yield: 4 to 6 servings

Barbara Hornbuckle

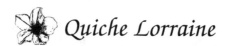 ## Quiche Lorraine

Line a 10-inch pie plate with pastry. Prick bottom and chill.

4	eggs		pepper to taste
2	cups thin cream	1	pound bacon
	pinch cayenne pepper	1	small onion, minced
	pinch sugar	1	cup grated Swiss cheese

Beat eggs and cream until blended. Add cayenne pepper, sugar and pepper and stir. Cook bacon and break into bits. Sauté onion. Place bacon and onion, then cheese, then egg mixture into pie shell. Bake at 450 degrees for 12 minutes. Reduce heat to 325 degrees and bake an additional 15 minutes.

Yield: 6 to 8 servings

Barbara Parks

Quiche Supreme

1	9-inch deep-dish pie shell	1	(8 ounce) block Cheddar cheese, shredded
3	tablespoons butter		
1	medium onion, chopped	3	eggs
1	cup sliced fresh mushrooms	½	cup milk
1	cup chopped fresh broccoli	1	tablespoon chopped parsley
		½	cup crumbled bacon

Bake pie shell for 10 minutes at 400 degrees. In butter, sauté onions, mushrooms and broccoli until soft. Spoon into baked pie shell. Sprinkle cheese over vegetables. Beat eggs in small bowl until frothy. Stir in milk and pour over vegetables and cheese. Top with parsley and bacon. Bake at 400 degrees for 15 minutes, then lower to 350 degrees and bake an additional 20 minutes. Let stand for 5 to 10 minutes.

Yield: 6 to 8 servings   Jana Yates

Swedish Oatmeal Pancakes

4	cups rolled oats	1	quart buttermilk
1	cup whole wheat flour	4	eggs, beaten
¼	cup sugar	½	cup butter, melted
2	teaspoons baking powder	2	teaspoons vanilla
	pinch of salt	2	teaspoons baking soda

Mix all ingredients. Let batter stand 30 minutes to 1 hour. Cook pancakes in butter. Serve with syrup.

Yield: 8 to 10 servings   Beth Sullivan

Sausage N' Cheese Tarts

½ pound bulk pork sausage
1¼ cups biscuit mix
¼ cup butter or margarine, melted
2 tablespoons boiling water
1 egg, slightly beaten
½ cup half-and-half

2 tablespoons thinly sliced green onions
½ cup shredded Cheddar or Swiss cheese
cherry tomato rose and fresh parsley sprigs for garnish, optional

Cook sausage over medium heat until browned, stirring to crumble; drain and set aside. Combine biscuit mix, butter and boiling water. Stir well. Press approximately 1 tablespoon of dough into bottom and sides of well-greased and floured muffin cups. Spoon sausage evenly into cups. Combine egg, half-and-half and green onions. Stir well. Spoon approximately 1 tablespoon egg mixture into each cup. Bake at 375 degrees for 20 minutes. Sprinkle cheese over each tart. Bake an additional 5 minutes. If desired, garnish platter with tomato rose and parsley.

Yield: 1 dozen

Patti Wright

Sausage and Egg Soufflé

8 slices of bread, crusts removed
1 pound pork sausage, browned and crumbled
2 cups shredded sharp Cheddar cheese

2 cups milk
8 eggs
½ teaspoon salt, if desired
½ teaspoon dry mustard coarsely ground black pepper

Preheat oven to 350 degrees. In a 13x9x2-inch pan layer bread, sausage and cheese. Blend together milk, eggs, salt, mustard, and pepper. Pour over mixture in pan. Cover and refrigerate overnight. Bake, uncovered, at 350 degrees for 45 minutes.

Yield: 6 to 8 servings

Carolyn Eager

118

Macaroni and Cheese

2   cups elbow macaroni
dash of salt
½   cup margarine
4   eggs, whipped

3   cups milk
2   cups grated, sharp Cheddar
cheese

Cook macaroni in salted water as directed on package. Drain in colander. Return macaroni to saucepan and add margarine. Then add whipped eggs and milk. Stir in cheese. Place in greased 2-quart casserole. Bake at 350 degrees for approximately 30 minutes or until liquid is firm but not dry.

Yield: 10 to 12 servings   Claire Buescher

Marvelous Macaroni and Cheese

1   (8 ounce) package elbow
macaroni
1   (10¾ ounce) can cream of
mushroom soup
¼   cup chopped onions

¼   cup chopped pimentos
¼   cup chopped green pepper
1   cup mayonnaise
1   (8 ounce) block sharp
Cheddar cheese, grated

Cook macaroni according to package directions and drain. Heat undiluted soup. Add onions, pimentos, and green pepper. Cook slowly 5 to 10 minutes. Add mayonnaise. In a greased 2-quart casserole dish make two layers of macaroni soup mixture and cheese. Bake at 350 degrees for 30 minutes.

Yield: 6 to 8 servings   Melissa Carter

Pasta Stuffed With Five Cheeses

1   (8 ounce) box jumbo pasta shells, approximately 32 shells
1   (8 ounce) package cream cheese
1   cup low-fat cottage cheese
1   cup shredded mozzarella cheese
1   egg, slightly beaten
¼   cup grated Parmesan and Romano cheese topping
2   tablespoons chopped fresh parsley
2   teaspoons dried whole basil
½   teaspoon dried whole oregano
½   teaspoon dried whole thyme
⅛   teaspoon lemon rind
    pinch of ground nutmeg
1   (14½ ounce) can stewed tomatoes, undrained
1   (8 ounce) can tomato sauce
1   cup white wine
1   (8 ounce) can mushroom stems and pieces, drained
1   teaspoon dried whole oregano
1   teaspoon dried whole thyme
1   clove garlic, minced
    parsley sprigs, optional

Cook pasta shells according to package directions; drain and set aside. Combine cream cheese with cottage cheese, mozzarella cheese, egg, Parmesan and Romano cheese, parsley, basil, oregano, thyme, lemon rind and nutmeg, mixing well. Stuff cheese mixture into shells. Arrange stuffed shells in a lightly greased 12x8x2-inch baking dish. Bake, covered, at 350 degrees for 25 minutes or until thoroughly heated. Puree stewed tomatoes; combine tomatoes with tomato sauce, white wine, mushrooms, oregano, thyme and garlic in a saucepan. Simmer 25 minutes or until sauce is thickened. Spoon sauce onto plates. Arrange pasta shells on sauce. Garnish with parsley, if desired.

Yield: 6 servings

Patti Wright

 ## Casserole Marie-Blanche

1 cup cream-style cottage cheese	⅓ cup chopped chives
1 cup sour cream	¾ (8 ounce) package very thin noodles, cooked and drained
½ teaspoon salt	
½ teaspoon red pepper	1 tablespoon butter

Combine cottage cheese, sour cream, salt, pepper and chives, then add noodles. Pour into buttered 2-quart casserole and dot top with 1 tablespoon butter. Bake at 350 degrees approximately 20 minutes or until bubbles. This is served with steak, roast beef or ham.

Yield: 4 to 6 servings   June Purvis

Fettuccine Alfredo

1 (16 ounce) package fettuccine	2 cups whipping cream
¾ cup butter	¾ cup grated Parmesan cheese, divided
¼ teaspoon garlic powder	¼ cup sour cream

Cook pasta according to package directions, omitting salt. Drain well and return to hot pan. Melt butter in a small saucepan. Stir in garlic powder. Add to fettuccine in Dutch oven. Gradually add whipping cream, ½ cup Parmesan cheese and sour cream. Cook over low heat, stirring constantly, until thoroughly heated. Remove from heat. Transfer to a serving dish and sprinkle with remaining cheese. Serve immediately.

Yield: 6 to 8 servings   Honey Kendrick

Noodles Alfredo

1 (16 ounce) package broad noodles, cooked and drained	¾ cup light cream, warmed
½ cup butter	1½ cups grated Parmesan cheese chopped parsley chives

Place noodles in large serving dish. Melt butter. Pour butter, cream and grated cheese over noodles. Mix well. Toss to coat and sprinkle with parsley and chives.

Yield: 6 to 8 servings   Jan Anderson

For variety, add cooked broccoli, spinach or toasted cashews.

Linda's Vegetable Pasta

1 bunch broccoli, cut in bite-size pieces	½ cup frozen green peas, thawed
2 small zucchini, sliced	¼ cup chopped fresh parsley or 1½ tablespoons dried parsley
½ pound asparagus, cut in 1-inch pieces	
1 (16 ounce) package linguine	1½ teaspoons salt
1 large clove garlic	¼ teaspoon ground black pepper
1 basket cherry tomatoes, halved	¼ teaspoon crushed red pepper
¼ cup olive oil	
¼ cup chopped fresh basil or 1 teaspoon dried basil	¼ cup butter
½ pound mushrooms, sliced ½-inch thick	¾ cup heavy cream
	⅔ cup grated Parmesan cheese

Steam broccoli, zucchini and asparagus in steamer until crisp and tender. Drain and place in large bowl. Cook linguine and drain. Return linguine to pot with lid on. In frying pan, sauté garlic and tomatoes in olive oil. Stir in basil and mushrooms. Cook 5 minutes. Stir in peas, parsley, salt, black and red pepper. Cook an additional 3 to 5 minutes. Add mixture to steamed vegetables in large bowl. In same frying pan, melt butter. Stir in cream and cheese. Cook over medium heat, stirring constantly until mixture is smooth. Be careful not to boil. Add to linguine in large pan or bowl. Toss to coat. Stir in vegetables. If needed, heat gently until hot.

Yield: 6 with salad and bread; 8 as side dish   Jan Fackler

Vegetables

The Landmark
Fender/Price Home
Built 1903

Cinnamon Apple Casserole

6	medium apples, peeled, cored and cut into wedges	4	lemon slices
1¼	cups brown sugar, divided	2	tablespoons cinnamon
4	to 6 tablespoons butter or margarine	4	slices white bread with crusts removed and cut into quarters

Mix apple wedges and 1 cup of brown sugar in large mixing bowl. Layer half of apples in an ungreased 1½-quart casserole dish. Dot with 1 table-spoon of butter and 2 lemon slices. Make a second layer of apples and dot with another tablespoon butter and remaining lemon slices. Sprinkle with cinnamon, using more or less to taste. Bake, uncovered, at 350 degrees for approximately 30 minutes, or until tender. Melt remaining butter, dip bread in butter and arrange on top of apples. Sprinkle with remaining ¼ cup of brown sugar, more or less to taste. Return to oven at 350 degrees until golden brown and toasted. Check before 10 minutes as this will brown quickly.

Yield: 4 to 6 servings   Mary Corbett

This is delicious with turkey, ham and game. Also makes a great brunch accompaniment.

Zapped Apples

4	large apples	ground cinnamon to taste
1	cup raisins	ground nutmeg to taste
⅔	cup brown sugar	apple juice

Remove core without cutting through bottom skin and peel small strip at top of each apple. Place apples in an ungreased 9x9x2-inch microwave dish and fill apples with raisins. Mound brown sugar on top and sprinkle with cinnamon and nutmeg. Drip apple juice into each apple. Cover with vented plastic wrap. Microwave on high for 8 to 10 minutes. Pour pan juices over apples and serve.

Yield: 4 servings   Barbara Hornbuckle

Hurry-Up Asparagus Casserole

1 **(15 ounce) can asparagus spears, drained**	1 **(4 ounce) jar pimentos, drained**
1 **(17 ounce) can English peas, drained**	1 **(10¾ ounce) can cream of mushroom soup**
1 **(4 ounce) can mushrooms, drained**	1 **cup grated sharp Cheddar cheese**

Mix asparagus, English peas, mushrooms, pimentos and mushroom soup together and pour into greased 9x9x2-inch casserole dish. Top with cheese. Bake, uncovered, at 350 degrees until bubbly.

Yield: 6 to 8 servings   Floye Luke

Canned French-fried onion rings makes a good, crunchy topping.

Almond Asparagus Casserole

6 **to 8 ounces slivered almonds**	1 **(10¾ ounce) can cream of mushroom soup, undiluted**
2 **tablespoons butter**	4 **hard-boiled eggs, chopped**
1 **(10½ ounce) can asparagus tips, drained**	20 **to 30 round buttery crackers, crumbled**

Preheat oven to 350 degrees. Sauté almonds in butter until golden. In medium mixing bowl, combine asparagus tips and soup. Add eggs. Stir crackers and almonds into asparagus mixture, reserving 2 tablespoons of each for topping. Pour into lightly greased 1½-quart baking dish. Bake, uncovered, for 40 to 45 minutes or until bubbly. Remove and sprinkle with reserved crackers and almonds. Return to oven and broil just until crackers are lightly browned.

Yield: 4 to 6 servings   Mary Beth Meyers

Fabulous Baked Beans

½	pound bacon	1	(16 ounce) can butterbeans, undrained
1	large onion, chopped	1	cup ketchup
1	(16 ounce) can kidney beans, drained	1	teaspoon vinegar
1	(16 ounce) can baked beans, undrained	¾	cup brown sugar

Chop bacon and fry in Dutch oven. Remove bacon and drain all but 2 tablespoons of oil. Sauté onion in Dutch oven. Add all three beans together with the ketchup, vinegar and brown sugar to Dutch oven. Add crumbled bacon and simmer until warm.

Yield: 10 to 12 servings   Marcia Tillman

 # Mrs. Everett's Baked Beans

1	(16 ounce) bag dried great Northern beans	3	tablespoons bacon drippings

Soak beans in cold water overnight. Next day boil in salted water with bacon drippings. When beans are tender, drain off most of the liquid and add:

1	cup chili sauce	1	heaping cup brown sugar
1	cup ketchup	1	teaspoon paprika
1	medium onion, grated	2	tablespoons Worcestershire sauce
1	tablespoon prepared mustard	6	to 8 bacon strips

Place in greased 13x9x2-inch baking dish, except bacon. Cover top with strips of bacon. Bake, uncovered, at 250 degrees for 3 hours.

Yield: 10 to 12 servings   Tootsie Tillman

Key West Black Beans

1	pound black turtle beans	1	teaspoon salt
1	quart cold water	1	tablespoon sugar
6	cloves garlic, minced	1	tablespoon vinegar
2	green peppers, slivered	5	to 6 green onions, chopped
2	large onions, minced		apple cider vinegar,
⅔	cup olive oil		½ teaspoon per serving
2	bay leaves		

Soak beans overnight. Rinse. Place in 6-quart Dutch oven, cover with cold water and boil 1 hour. Add garlic, peppers, onions, olive oil, bay leaves and salt. Cover and cook slowly 4 hours or until beans begin to thicken. Add sugar and vinegar just before serving. Remove bay leaves. Serve over bed of rice. To each serving add chopped green onions and apple cider vinegar according to taste.

Yield: 6 to 8 servings   Carol Giles

These beans are best if cooked the day before. Good accompaniment to smoked pork chops, ham or sausage.

Best Broccoli Casserole

1	large bunch fresh broccoli, chopped	1	(2 ounce) jar diced pimentos, drained
1	cup sour cream	1	(2 ounce) package slivered almonds
1	(10¾ ounce) can cream of mushroom soup	1	(8 ounce) block sharp Cheddar cheese, grated
1	(4 ounce) can mushrooms, drained		

Parboil broccoli and drain. Combine sour cream, cream of mushroom soup, mushrooms, pimentos and almonds in large mixing bowl. Add cooked broccoli and mix well. Pour into greased 2-quart baking dish. Cover top with grated cheese. Bake, uncovered, at 350 degrees for 20 to 25 minutes.

Yield: 6 to 8 servings   Stuart Lynn Simpson

 ## Layered Green Bean Casserole

2 (15 ounce) cans whole green beans, undrained
1 teaspoon or 1 cube chicken bouillon
½ cup thinly sliced onions
2 tablespoons parsley flakes
6 tablespoons butter, divided
2 tablespoons all-purpose flour
1 cup sour cream
grated rind of 1 lemon

Cook beans with bouillon for approximately 30 minutes. Drain and set aside. Cook onions and parsley in 3 tablespoons butter on low heat for approximately 5 minutes. Pour onion mixture into an ungreased 9x9x2-inch casserole dish. Melt remaining 3 tablespoons butter. Add flour, sour cream and lemon rind. Toss beans in this mixture. Place in casserole on top of onions.

Topping:
¾ cup crumbled saltines
¾ cup grated sharp Cheddar cheese
6 tablespoons butter, melted

Toss together saltines, cheese and butter. Sprinkle on top. Bake, uncovered, at 325 degrees for 30 minutes.

Yield: 6 to 8 servings   Jan Carter

Baked Broccoli Continental

2 pounds fresh broccoli
½ cup sliced ripe olives
¼ cup pimento strips
½ cup Parmesan cheese
¼ cup Italian breadcrumbs
¼ cup butter or margarine, melted
1 tablespoon lemon juice

Parboil broccoli and drain. Arrange broccoli, olives and pimento in 2-quart shallow baking dish. Combine cheese and breadcrumbs. Sprinkle over broccoli mixture. Combine butter and lemon juice. Pour over broccoli mixture. Bake, uncovered, at 350 degrees for 30 minutes or until hot.

Yield: 6 to 8 servings   Suzanne Sullivan

Broccoli And Wild Rice Bake

2	(10 ounce) package frozen chopped broccoli	1	single-serving size envelope instant cream of chicken soup mix
1	(6¾ ounce) package quick-cooking long grain wild rice mix	2	cups milk
		¾	cup soft breadcrumbs
1	(1 ounce) envelope sour cream sauce mix	1	tablespoon margarine, melted

Cook broccoli according to package directions. Drain and set aside. Prepare rice mix according to package directions. Combine sauce and soup mixes. Stir in milk. In 2-quart greased casserole combine rice and sauces. Fold in broccoli. Mix breadcrumbs with melted margarine and sprinkle over top of casserole. Bake, uncovered, at 350 degrees for 35 to 40 minutes.

Yield: 8 to 10 servings   Debbie Davis

 ## Cabbage And Tomatoes Au Gratin

½	cup chopped onion	½	teaspoon sugar
4	tablespoons butter	¼	teaspoon pepper
3	tablespoons all-purpose flour	6	cups finely shredded cabbage
2	cups canned tomatoes	3	slices bread, cubed
2	teaspoons Worcestershire sauce	¼	pound pasteurized process cheese, cubed
¾	teaspoon salt		

Sauté onion until tender in 3 tablespoons of butter. Blend in flour. Stir until smooth. Add tomatoes, Worcestershire sauce, salt, sugar and pepper. Cook cabbage in a small amount of salted water for 5 minutes. In a skillet, brown bread cubes in 1 tablespoon of butter. In a 2-quart casserole dish, layer cabbage, tomato mixture, bread and cheese, twice, ending with bread and cheese. Bake, covered, at 375 degrees for 30 minutes.

Yield: 10 to 12 servings   Mary Young Oliver

Sherried Carrots

3	cups grated carrots	½	teaspoon salt
2	tablespoons margarine, melted	2	tablespoons dry sherry
1	tablespoon lemon juice	1	tablespoon chopped chives

Preheat oven to 350 degrees. Place grated carrots in a 9x9x2-inch casserole dish. Mix together margarine, lemon juice, salt and sherry. Pour over carrots. Sprinkle with chives. Bake, covered, for 30 minutes.

Yield: 6 servings   Suzanne Sullivan

Marinated Carrots

2	(12 ounce) packages fresh, peeled carrots	½	cup vegetable oil
1	small green pepper, cut into rings	1	cup sugar
1	medium onion, sliced	¾	cup vinegar
1	(10¾ ounce) can tomato soup	1	teaspoon prepared mustard
		1	teaspoon Worcestershire sauce
			salt and pepper to taste

Slice and boil carrots in salted water until fork-tender. Don't overcook. Drain and cool. When cool, alternate layers of carrots, green pepper rings and onion slices in 13x9x2-inch dish. Beat together tomato soup, oil, sugar, vinegar, mustard, Worcestershire sauce, salt and pepper. Pour over layered vegetables. Cover and refrigerate. Can be prepared a week in advance, but prepare at least a day ahead.

Yield: 20 servings   Elaine Bridges

Crusty-Top Cauliflower

1	large cauliflower	¾	cup shredded medium or
½	cup mayonnaise		sharp Cheddar cheese
2	tablespoons Dijon mustard		

Remove large outer leaves and stalk of cauliflower, leaving head whole. Wash cauliflower. Place in large saucepan with enough water to steam. Cover and cook 15 to 20 minutes until tender. Drain well. Place whole cauliflower in a greased 9x9x2-inch baking dish. Combine mayonnaise and mustard in a small bowl. Stir well and spread over cauliflower. Sprinkle with cheese. Bake, uncovered, at 350 degrees for 10 minutes or until cheese is melted and bubbly.

Yield: 6 to 8 servings   Honey Kendrick

Baked Corn Pudding

2	(10 ounce) packages frozen cut corn, thawed and drained	1	tablespoon grated onion
		¼	teaspoon pepper
3	eggs, beaten	2	cups half-and-half
¼	cup all-purpose flour	1	(2 ounce) jar diced pimentos, drained
1	tablespoon sugar		
1	teaspoon salt	2	tablespoons margarine, melted

Combine all ingredients. Mix well. Pour mixture into a greased 2-quart baking dish. Place baking dish in a large baking pan and fill with 1 inch hot water. Bake, uncovered, at 325 degrees for 1 hour and 15 minutes or until knife inserted in center comes out clean.

Yield: 8 servings   Linda McCrary

Corn Bake

2	(10 ounce) packages frozen cream-style corn or 1 (28 ounce) can cream-style corn	½	teaspoon dried parsley salt and pepper to taste
1	(6 ounce) can evaporated milk	1	cup shredded Cheddar cheese
1	egg, beaten	½	cup herb-seasoned breadcrumbs
2	tablespoons chopped onion	1	tablespoon margarine, melted
¼	cup chopped green pepper		paprika
	fresh parsley for garnish		

If using frozen corn, cook in 1 cup of boiling water 3 to 4 minutes. Combine corn with milk, egg, onion, green pepper, parsley, salt and pepper. Add ¾ cup of cheese. Mix well. Turn into greased 1½-quart casserole dish. Toss breadcrumbs with margarine. Add remaining ¼ cup cheese. Sprinkle over corn. Top with paprika and bake, uncovered, at 350 degrees for 25 to 30 minutes. Garnish with fresh parsley.

Yield: 4 to 6 servings   Julie Taylor

Corn Soufflé

3	tablespoons butter	1¼	cups milk
3	tablespoons all-purpose flour	2½	cups cooked fresh corn or 1 (16 ounce) can cream-style corn
1	teaspoon salt		
1	tablespoon sugar	2	eggs, well-beaten

Melt butter. Add flour, salt and sugar. Stir to a smooth paste. Add milk. Cook and stir constantly until mixture thickens and comes to a boil. Remove from heat. Stir in corn and eggs. Pour into greased 10x6x2-inch baking dish and place in pan of hot water. Bake, uncovered, at 350 degrees for 1 hour, or until set. If using a glass dish, decrease heat to 325 degrees.

Yield: 6 to 8 servings   Debbie Langdale

 ## Eggplant Soufflé

1	large or 2 medium eggplants		juice of 1 small onion
2	eggs	3	tablespoons butter or margarine
¼	cup milk salt, pepper, Worcestershire sauce and nutmeg to taste	1	cup finely crushed round buttery crackers

Peel and slice eggplant and soak in salt water about 45 minutes. Drain and boil in fresh water. When tender, drain well and mash fine. Beat eggs and combine with milk. Add egg mixture, seasonings and onion juice to eggplant. Grease 9x9x2-inch casserole dish with 1 tablespoon butter or margarine and top with crushed crackers, dotted with remaining 2 tablespoons butter or margarine. Bake, uncovered, at 350 degrees for 30 to 40 minutes, or until knife put into center comes out dry.

Yield: 6 to 8 servings   Mary Young Oliver

Favorite Eggplant Casserole

1	medium eggplant, peeled	½	cup grated sharp or medium Cheddar cheese
2	eggs		
1	(10¾ ounce) can cream of mushroom soup, undiluted	1	cup breadcrumbs
		1	small onion, finely chopped or minced
½	medium green pepper, chopped	1	teaspoon salt or seasoned salt
1	(2 ounce) jar chopped pimentos	½	teaspoon pepper

Cook eggplant in boiling salted water until soft. Drain and mash. Transfer to large mixing bowl. Add eggs and beat well. Add soup, green pepper, pimentos, cheese, breadcrumbs, onion, salt and pepper. Mix well. Pour into a greased 2-quart baking dish. Bake, uncovered, at 350 degrees for 30 minutes.

Yield: 4 to 6 servings   Marcia McRae

Cranberry Apple Bake

2 cups fresh cranberries	1 tablespoon water
1 cup sugar	4 to 5 baking apples

Place cranberries, sugar and water in saucepan. Boil 7 to 10 minutes. Slice apples and layer on bottom of greased 13x9x2-inch baking dish. Pour cranberries on top of apples.

Topping:

½ cup brown sugar	1½ to 2 tablespoons all-purpose flour
¼ cup butter, melted	1 cup old fashioned oatmeal

Mix topping ingredients together and sprinkle on top of cranberries. Bake, uncovered, at 325 degrees for 35 to 40 minutes or until brown.

Yield: 8 to 10 servings   Jan Girardin

Curried Fruit

1 (15 ounce) can peaches	⅓ cup margarine
1 (15 ounce) can pears	3 teaspoons curry powder
1 (15 ounce) can sliced pineapples	¾ cup light brown sugar
1 (15 ounce) can apricots, optional	1 (6 ounce) jar maraschino cherries

Drain and dry fruit (except cherries). Arrange fruit in greased 13x9x2-inch baking dish ending with pineapples on top. Melt margarine and add curry powder and sugar. Spoon over fruit. Bake, uncovered, at 350 degrees for 1 hour. Cool in refrigerator overnight. Remove from refrigerator; add cherries. Bake, uncovered, at 325 degrees for 30 minutes.

Yield: 10 to 12 servings   Lee Limbocker

Mint Julep Fruit Cup

⅓ cup sugar	4 cups mixed fresh fruit such as: orange sections, seedless grapes, sliced strawberries, and sliced peaches
⅔ cup water	
½ cup bourbon	
2 tablespoons minced fresh mint leaves or 1 teaspoon dried mint leaves	

In a small saucepan, combine the sugar and water. Bring the mixture to a boil, stirring until sugar is dissolved. Simmer for 4 minutes. Let the sugar syrup cool. In a large bowl stir together the sugar syrup, bourbon, mint leaves and fruit. Chill for 2 hours or overnight, stirring several times. Garnish the fruit with mint sprigs.

Yield: 4 servings

Honey Kendrick

Sherried Fruit

1 (16 ounce) can peach halves or slices	1 (10 ounce) jar cherries
1 (16 ounce) can pears	¼ cup butter
1 (20 ounce) can pineapple, rings or chunks	½ cup sugar
1 (16 ounce) can peeled apricots	1 cup sherry, not cooking sherry
1 (15 ounce) jar apple rings	2 tablespoons all-purpose flour

Drain all fruit and place in greased 13x9x2-inch dish. In double boiler, mix butter, sugar, sherry and flour. Cook until a runny cream texture. Pour sauce over fruit. Refrigerate overnight. Bake, covered, at 250 degrees for 20 minutes.

Yield: 10 to 12 servings

Floye Luke

Grand Marnier Grapes

8	cups seedless red or green grapes	2	tablespoons Grand Marnier or brandy
2½	cups sour cream	½	to ¾ cup brown sugar

Wash and dry grapes. Mix grapes with sour cream and Grand Marnier or brandy. Chill. Sprinkle brown sugar over grape mixture about 15 minutes before serving.

Yield: 8 to 12 servings   Martha Grow

May also be served without liqueur or brandy!

Sautéed Mushrooms

1	pint fresh mushrooms, sliced or whole	2	tablespoons Worcestershire sauce
2	tablespoons butter	1	tablespoon soy sauce

Sauté mushrooms in butter. Add Worcestershire sauce and soy sauce. Cover and cook 5 minutes.

Yield: 4 servings   Donna Thornton

Great over steaks.

Marinated Vidalia Onions

4	Vidalia onions	½	teaspoon celery salt
2	cups water	½	teaspoon paprika
1	cup sugar	½	teaspoon Beau Monde
½	cup white vinegar		seasoning
½	cup mayonnaise		juice of ½ lemon
½	teaspoon parsley flakes		

Slice onions and separate into rings. Mix water, sugar and vinegar and bring to a boil. Pour hot mixture over onions and soak overnight. Drain well and toss with mixture of mayonnaise, parsley flakes, celery salt, paprika, Beau Monde and lemon juice.

Yield: 6 to 8 servings   Ellen Clary

A summer cookout is not complete without Marinated Vidalia Onions.

Vidalia Onion Pie Supreme

3 cups thinly sliced Vidalia onions or sweet onions
3 tablespoons margarine or butter, melted
1 9-inch deep dish pie shell
½ cup milk
1½ cups sour cream, divided
3 tablespoons all-purpose flour
1 teaspoon salt
2 eggs, well beaten
2 to 3 slices crisp-fried bacon strips, crumbled

Cook onion in margarine until lightly browned. Spoon into pie shell. Combine milk and 1¼ cups sour cream and pour over onions. Blend flour and salt with remaining ¼ cup of sour cream and combine with beaten eggs. Pour egg mixture into pie shell. Bake, uncovered, at 325 degrees for 30 minutes or until firm in center. Garnish with bacon.

Yield: 6 to 8 servings

Janice Baker

Golden Baked Vidalia Onions

4 Vidalia onions, trimmed salt and pepper to taste
¼ cup butter
4 teaspoons Worcestershire sauce
2 teaspoons ground cumin
4 teaspoons brown sugar
½ cup chicken stock
½ cup dry white wine

With a sharp knife, cut out a 1-inch cavity in the top of each onion. Reserve the pieces removed. Sprinkle each onion with salt and pepper to taste and divide the butter, Worcestershire sauce, cumin and brown sugar among the cavities. Arrange the onions in a greased 9x9x2-inch baking dish. Add the broth, wine and reserved onion pieces to the dish. Bake, uncovered, at 425 degrees, basting occasionally, for 45 to 60 minutes, or until golden and tender when pierced with a fork.

Yield: 4 servings

Honey Kendrick

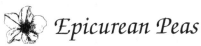 *Onion Pie*

1	cup round buttery cracker crumbs	¾	teaspoon salt
¼	cup butter, melted		dash of coarse ground black pepper
2	cups thinly sliced white onions	¼	cup grated sharp Cheddar cheese
2	tablespoons butter		paprika
2	eggs		parsley for garnish
¾	cup milk		

Mix cracker crumbs with ¼ cup melted butter. Press into 8-inch pie plate. Sauté onion in 2 tablespoons butter until translucent. Spoon into crust. Beat eggs with milk, salt and pepper. Pour over onions. Sprinkle with cheese and paprika. Bake, uncovered, at 350 degrees for 30 minutes. Test with knife. When knife comes out clean, it's ready. Garnish with parsley.

Yield: 6 to 8 servings   Kathy Owens

A nice accompaniment with steaks.

Epicurean Peas

4	slices bacon	1	(15 ounce) can English peas, drained
1	medium onion, chopped		
1	tablespoon all-purpose flour	2	tablespoons butter
			salt to taste
1	cup thin cream or milk	¼	teaspoon pepper
		1	(4 ounce) can mushrooms

Cook bacon, remove from pan and crumble. Brown onion in bacon drippings. Stir in flour and milk until thickened. Add peas, butter, salt, pepper, mushrooms and bacon. Put in greased 9x9x2-inch casserole dish. Bake, uncovered, at 350 degrees for approximately 20 minutes.

Yield: 4 to 6 servings   Lee Griffin

Cheese Scalloped Potatoes

6   medium baking potatoes,   ½   cup milk
    peeled and sliced   dash of salt and pepper
1   (10¾ ounce) can Cheddar
    cheese soup

Layer potatoes in the bottom of a greased 1-quart casserole dish. Mix
soup, milk, salt and pepper together and pour over the potatoes. Bake,
covered, at 350 degrees for 45 minutes. Uncover and bake an additional
10 minutes or until browned.

Yield: 4 servings   Floye Luke

Party Potatoes

8   to 10 medium potatoes,   4   tablespoons butter or
    peeled   margarine
1   (8 ounce) carton sour   ⅓   cup chopped chives
    cream   salt and pepper to taste
1   (8 ounce) package cream   paprika
    cheese, softened

Boil potatoes until tender and then drain. Beat sour cream and cream
cheese together. Add hot potatoes and beat until smooth. Add butter or
margarine, chives, salt and pepper to taste. Pour into a well-greased
2-quart casserole. Dot with extra butter and sprinkle paprika on top. Bake,
uncovered, at 350 degrees for 25 minutes.

Yield: 8 to 10 servings   Patti Wright

 # Potatoes With Cheese

6   large potatoes   2   tablespoons grated onion
1   (12 ounce) block Cheddar   salt and pepper to taste
    cheese

Boil potatoes whole, not peeled. When tender, drain and cool. Peel and
grate potatoes. Grate cheese. Toss onion and potatoes together. Grease a
1½-quart casserole and arrange alternate layers of cheese and potatoes
with salt and pepper. Bake, uncovered, at 350 degrees for 40 minutes.

Yield: 6 to 8 servings   Betty Webb

Poppy Seed Potatoes

8	to 10 red potatoes	1¾	cups shredded Cheddar
1	cup sour cream		cheese, divided
1	bunch green onions,	1	to 2 tablespoons poppy
	chopped		seeds

Cook potatoes in salted water until tender. Peel potatoes, then cube or shred. Mix potatoes, sour cream, chopped onion, ¾ cup cheese and poppy seeds. Place in 2-quart casserole. Sprinkle remaining 1 cup cheese over top. Bake, uncovered, at 350 degrees for 30 to 40 minutes.

Yield: 6 to 8 servings   Becky Crosby

Can be made a day ahead and refrigerated.

Potato Onion Casserole

4	Idaho potatoes	salt and pepper to taste
6	small white onions	1 bay leaf
4	tablespoons olive oil	1½ cups fresh or canned
½	cup shredded fresh basil or	chicken broth
	1 teaspoon dried basil	

Preheat oven to 450 degrees. Peel potatoes and cut into very thin slices, approximately 4 cups. Cut onions into thin slices, approximately 2½ cups. Grease bottom of 2½-quart casserole with 1 tablespoon olive oil. Alternate layers of potatoes and onions with remaining 3 tablespoons olive oil, basil, salt and pepper. Top with bay leaf. Pour chicken broth over potatoes. Bake, covered, for approximately 30 minutes. Uncover and bake an additional 30 minutes or until potatoes are tender. Remove bay leaf and serve.

Yield: 6 to 8 servings   Suzanne Sullivan

Red new potatoes are also very tasty in this recipe.

 *Potato Topper*

1 cup shredded sharp Cheddar cheese	¼ cup butter or margarine, softened
½ cup sour cream	2 tablespoons chopped green onion

Blend all ingredients. Serve at room temperature over hot baked potatoes.

Yield: 1 cup

Tilda Stubbs

Sweet Potato Soufflé

2 cups cooked, mashed sweet potatoes	1 pinch of salt
1 cup sugar	1 teaspoon vanilla
2 eggs	½ cup butter, melted

Mix sweet potatoes, sugar, eggs, salt, vanilla and butter. Pour in 12x9x2-inch casserole dish.

Topping:

1 cup brown sugar	⅓ cup butter
⅓ cup all-purpose flour	1 cup chopped pecans

Mix brown sugar, flour, butter and nuts and sprinkle over sweet potato mixture. Bake, uncovered, at 350 degrees for 30 minutes.

Yield: 8 servings

Mary Perry

Crunchy Sweet Potato Soufflé

3	cups cooked, mashed sweet potatoes	2	eggs
1	cup sugar	¼	cup margarine, melted
½	teaspoon salt	⅓	cup milk
		1	teaspoon vanilla

Mix together sweet potatoes, sugar, salt, eggs, margarine, milk and vanilla. Pour into a greased 12x9x2-inch baking dish.

Topping:

⅓	cup self-rising flour	1	cup chopped pecans
1	cup brown sugar	2	tablespoons margarine, melted
1	cup grated coconut		

Combine topping ingredients and sprinkle over soufflé. Bake, uncovered, at 375 degrees for 30 minutes.

Yield: 8 servings   Barbara Bankston

This soufflé may be prepared, then frozen and ready to bake when needed. Great at Thanksgiving and Christmas dinners!

Working Girl's Potato Casserole

2	pounds frozen hash browns	1	pint sour cream
½	cup butter, melted	10	ounces sharp Cheddar cheese, grated
1	teaspoon salt		
¼	teaspoon pepper	2	cups corn flakes, crushed, mixed with ¼ cup melted butter
½	cup chopped onion		
1	(10¾ ounce) can cream of chicken soup		

Thaw potatoes and mix with butter, salt, pepper, onion, soup, sour cream and cheese. Place in a greased 13x9x2-inch casserole dish and cover with crushed buttered corn flakes. Bake, covered, at 350 degrees for 45 minutes.

Yield: 6 to 8 servings   Cheryl Gaston

143

Brown Rice Parmesan

1 cup uncooked brown rice	2 tablespoons butter
½ teaspoon salt	½ cup Parmesan cheese
½ cup chopped onion	4 slices bacon

Cook rice as package directs, but reduce salt to ½ teaspoon. Sauté onion in butter until tender. Combine onion, cheese and cooked rice. Stir well. Cook, drain and crumble bacon. Sprinkle bacon over rice.

Yield: 4 servings

Vallye Blanton

Best Ever Consommé Rice

¾ cup margarine	3 (10½ ounce) cans beef or
1½ medium onions, chopped	chicken consommé
1½ cups uncooked long grain rice	1 (4 ounce) can sliced mushrooms

Melt margarine and stir in chopped onions. Cook until translucent. Add rice and stir. Add consommé and mushrooms. Pour into a greased 2-quart casserole dish. Bake, uncovered, at 325 degrees for 1 hour.

Variation:

½ pound small shrimp, cleaned and cooked	¾ medium green pepper, chopped
	1 (2 ounce) jar pimentos

Add cooked shrimp, green pepper and pimentos before baking.

Yield: 8 servings

Patti Wright

The shrimp variation would be great for luncheons.

Janice's Green Rice

1	cup uncooked rice	1	medium onion, chopped
2	cups water	⅓	cup cooking oil
1	teaspoon salt	½	to ¾ cup grated Cheddar
1	egg		cheese
½	cup evaporated milk		garlic salt and pepper to
1	(10¾ ounce) can cream of		taste
	mushroom soup	¾	cup dried parsley
1	(4 ounce) can mushrooms,		
	sliced or pieces and stems		

Cook rice in 2 cups boiling, salted water. Combine egg, evaporated milk, mushroom soup, mushrooms, onion, oil, cheese, garlic salt, pepper and parsley. Mix in the cooked rice. Place in a greased 13x9x2-inch casserole dish. Bake, covered, at 350 degrees for 1 hour.

Yield: 8 to 10 servings   Carol Giles

Oven Cooked Rice With Mushrooms

½	cup margarine	1	(10½ ounce) can beef
1	cup uncooked long grain		bouillon
	rice	1	(10½ ounce) can French
1	(7 ounce) can mushrooms;		onion soup
	sliced, pieces or whole,		
	undrained		

Melt margarine in frying pan. Pour in rice and cook until chalky but not brown, approximately 5 minutes. Add mushrooms, bouillon and onion soup. Pour into greased 2-quart casserole dish. Bake, covered, at 350 degrees for 1 hour. Stir once during cooking.

Yield: 4 servings   Brenda Davis

Southern Dressing

2	cups cornmeal	1	cup chopped celery
1	tablespoon sugar	¾	cup chopped green onion
1	tablespoon baking powder	2	(14½ ounce) cans chicken broth
1	teaspoon salt		
2	eggs, beaten	1	(10¾ ounce) can cream of chicken soup
1	(12 ounce) can evaporated milk		
		¾	cup sliced almonds
¼	cup vegetable oil	1	teaspoon poultry seasoning
3	tablespoons butter or margarine, melted	¼	teaspoon pepper
		1	teaspoon salt
2	cups sliced fresh mushrooms		dash of parsley flakes

Combine cornmeal, sugar, baking powder and salt. Add eggs, evaporated milk and oil, mixing well. Place a greased 10-inch cast iron skillet in 350 degree oven for 5 minutes. Remove and spoon batter into skillet. Bake at 350 degrees for 35 to 40 minutes or until light golden brown. Cool, crumble in large bowl. In skillet, melt 3 tablespoons butter or margarine. Sauté mushrooms, celery, and green onion until tender. In a large bowl, combine sautéed vegetables with cornbread. Add chicken broth, cream of chicken soup, almonds, poultry seasoning, pepper, salt and parsley flakes, mixing well. Spoon into a greased 13x9x2-inch baking dish. After preheating, bake, uncovered, at 350 degrees for 45 minutes.

Yield: 6 to 8 servings   Pat Chitty

To make ahead, prepare dressing and cover and refrigerate overnight. To bake, let stand 30 minutes and bake, uncovered, at 350 degrees for 55 minutes.

Spinach and Artichoke Casserole

3	(10 ounce) packages frozen chopped spinach
1	(16 ounce) can artichoke hearts, halved or quartered
1	small onion, minced
½	cup margarine, melted
½	cup sour cream
2	(3 ounce) packages cream cheese, softened
	Parmesan cheese to taste
1	teaspoon lemon juice
	garlic salt to taste
1	cup (or more) round buttery cracker crumbs

Cook and drain spinach. Line bottom of greased 13x9x2-inch casserole dish with artichoke hearts. Sauté onions in margarine. Add spinach, sour cream, cream cheese, Parmesan cheese, lemon juice and garlic salt. Spread over artichokes. Top with cracker crumbs and more Parmesan. Bake, uncovered, at 350 degrees for approximately 20 minutes or until bubbly.

Yield: 6 to 8 servings   Sharon Coleman

Spinach Soufflé

1	(10 ounce) package frozen chopped spinach
3	eggs
1	(12 ounce) carton low-fat cottage cheese
4	ounces sharp Cheddar cheese, grated
3	tablespoons all-purpose flour
2	tablespoons butter or margarine

Thaw spinach and drain well. Squeeze out all liquid. Whip eggs in mixing bowl until frothy. Add cottage cheese, spinach, Cheddar cheese and flour. Mix well. Pour into a greased, round 2-quart baking dish. Dot top with butter or melt butter and stir into spinach mixture. Bake, uncovered, at 350 degrees for 45 minutes to 1 hour. Will be golden when done. May be mixed ahead and baked later.

Yield: 6 to 8 servings   Carol Giles

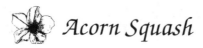 *Acorn Squash*

1	acorn squash	1	tablespoon butter
2	tablespoons chopped onion		salt and nutmeg to taste
2	tablespoons brown sugar		

Cut acorn squash in half and remove seeds. Fill each squash half with 1 tablespoon of onion, 1 tablespoon brown sugar and ½ tablespoon butter. Sprinkle with salt and nutmeg to taste. Place a small amount of water in bottom of a 9x9x2-inch baking pan and bake, uncovered, at 350 degrees for 1 hour and 15 minutes or until tender.

Yield: 2 servings

Marsha Rudolph

Miss Morris' Squash Dressing

3	pounds fresh yellow squash, chopped	1	cup sour cream
2	carrots, chopped	½	teaspoon salt
2	large onions, chopped	½	teaspoon pepper
1	cup chopped celery	2	cups herb-seasoned stuffing mix
1	(10¾ ounce) can cream of chicken soup, undiluted	1	cup shredded Cheddar cheese

Boil squash until tender and drain. Boil carrots, onions and celery in ¼ cup water until tender and drain. Add carrots, onion, celery, soup, sour cream, salt and pepper to squash. Fold in herb stuffing mix. Place mixture in buttered 10x10x2-inch casserole dish. Top with shredded cheese. Bake, uncovered, at 350 degrees for 35 to 40 minutes.

Yield: 6 to 8 servings

Sue Clary

Carrots, onions, and celery can be cooked in microwave. To prevent sogginess, do not cook squash in microwave. Squash, carrots, onions and celery can also be shredded in a food processor for a different texture.

Layered Squash Casserole

½ cup margarine, melted
1 (8 ounce) package herb-
   seasoned stuffing mix, may
   use unseasoned stuffing
2 (15 ounce) cans squash,
   reserving liquid from 1 can
2 carrots, grated

1 (10¾ ounce) can cream of
   chicken soup
1 medium onion, chopped
   salt and pepper to taste
1 (8 ounce) carton sour
   cream
1 (4 ounce) jar chopped
   pimentos

Mix margarine with stuffing. Line bottom of 13x9x2-inch casserole dish with ½ of stuffing. In large bowl, combine squash, carrots, soup, onion, salt, pepper, sour cream and pimentos. Pour into stuffing-lined dish. Cover with remaining stuffing. Bake, uncovered, at 350 degrees for 30 minutes.

Yield: 10 to 12 servings   Melissa Carter

Mexican Squash Soufflé

1 pound crookneck, yellow,
   summer squash
1 medium onion, chopped
1 clove garlic, chopped
2 tablespoons butter
1 (4 ounce) can green chilies,
   chopped

1 teaspoon salt
¼ teaspoon black pepper
1 egg, beaten
½ cup heavy cream
¼ cup dry white wine
⅓ cup grated sharp Cheddar
   cheese

Preheat oven to 350 degrees. Wash squash and slice thinly. Place squash in a heavy skillet with just enough water to prevent scorching and cook, covered, until barely tender. Drain well, mash slightly. In a skillet, sauté onion and garlic in butter until tender. Turn heat off and add chilies, salt, pepper and squash. Stir in egg, cream and wine. Pour into greased 1-quart casserole dish. Bake, uncovered, for 30 to 35 minutes until set. Sprinkle cheese over top the last 10 minutes of baking.

Yield: 4 servings   Jan Fackler

This casserole can be prepared a day ahead and taken out to room temperature before baking, approximately 2 hours depending on the shape of your dish.

Baked Cheese Stuffed Tomatoes

6	medium tomatoes	½	teaspoon dried marjoram
2	cups grated Swiss cheese	1	teaspoon dry mustard
½	cup light cream	1½	teaspoons salt
2	egg yolks, slightly beaten	⅓	cup packaged breadcrumbs
2	tablespoons chives	2	tablespoons butter, melted
3	tablespoons grated onion		

Halve tomatoes crosswise. Scoop out pulp. Combine pulp with cheese, cream, egg yolks, chives, onion, marjoram, mustard and salt. Mix well. Spoon into tomato shells. Toss crumbs with butter and sprinkle over tomatoes. Bake, uncovered, in a greased 13x9x2-inch casserole dish at 350 degrees for 25 minutes.

Yield: 6 servings   Vallye Blanton

Elaine's Herbed Tomatoes

8	medium ripe tomatoes	⅓	cup minced fresh parsley
1¼	teaspoons salt	⅓	cup minced chives
¼	teaspoon pepper	¾	cup salad oil
¾	teaspoon dried thyme leaves	⅓	cup tarragon vinegar

Peel whole tomatoes and place in bowl. Sprinkle with salt, pepper, thyme, parsley and chives. Combine oil and vinegar. Pour over tomatoes. Cover and chill for 2 to 24 hours, occasionally spooning dressing over tomatoes. Drain tomatoes prior to serving. Sprinkle additional parsley over tomatoes before serving.

Yield: 8 servings   Floye Luke

These tomatoes are attractive served in pyramid fashion in a compote-type serving dish.

 ## Escalloped Tomatoes

1	small onion, chopped	1	(28 ounce) can tomatoes
¼	cup butter	1	teaspoon salt
1¼	cups dry bread cubes	⅛	teaspoon pepper
½	cup brown sugar		

Sauté onion in butter, using an iron frying pan. Add bread cubes and sugar. Cook slowly. Stir in tomatoes and seasoning. Place mixture in buttered 9x9x2-inch pan. Bake, uncovered, at 350 degrees for 45 minutes.

Yield: 4 to 6 servings   Helen Smith

Tomato Provençal

4	slices bacon, diced	½	teaspoon seasoned salt
1	clove garlic, minced	10	tomatoes, fresh or canned
1	medium onion, chopped	6	tablespoons grated Parmesan cheese
¼	pound fresh mushrooms, sliced	1	tablespoon butter or margarine
1	tablespoon all-purpose flour		

Fry bacon. Remove from pan. Sauté garlic, onion and mushrooms. Stir in bacon, flour and salt. Slice tomatoes and place half of slices in greased 10x6x2-inch baking dish. Spoon half of bacon mixture over tomatoes. Sprinkle 3 tablespoons of cheese over bacon mixture. Repeat layers. Dot with butter. Bake, uncovered, at 350 degrees for 20 minutes.

Yield: 10 to 12 servings   Floye Luke

Good served with grits or rice. Also good served for breakfast or brunch.

Helen's Kentucky Vegetable Casserole

1 (15 ounce) can French-style
  green beans, drained
1 (15 ounce) can shoe peg
  corn, drained
1 (8 ounce) can sliced water
  chestnuts, chopped
1 small onion, chopped

1 (8 ounce) package shredded
  sharp Cheddar cheese
1 (10¾ ounce) can cream of
  mushroom soup
1 (8 ounce) carton sour
  cream

Mix green beans, corn, water chestnuts, onion, cheese, soup, and sour cream and pour into a greased 2-quart casserole dish.

Topping:

1 package finely crushed
  round buttery crackers

1 (2 ounce) package slivered
  almonds
¼ cup margarine

Sprinkle crushed crackers and almonds on top of vegetables. Place small pats of butter or margarine on top of crumbs and almonds. Bake, uncovered, at 350 degrees for approximately 30 minutes, or until brown and bubbly.

Yield: 6 to 8 servings

Peggy Gayle

Marinated Vegetables

1 (15 ounce) can tiny English
  peas, drained
1 (15 ounce) can white shoe
  peg corn, drained

1 (15 ounce) can tiny green
  butter beans, drained
½ cup chopped onion
½ cup chopped celery
½ cup chopped green pepper

Combine the above vegetables and marinate.

Marinade:

¾ cup apple cider vinegar
½ cup salad oil
¾ cup sugar

1 teaspoon salt
1 teaspoon pepper

Heat above ingredients and pour over vegetables. Refrigerate overnight.

Yield: 10 to 12 servings

Robin Coleman

152

Marinated Fresh Vegetables

1	small head fresh cauliflower	1	cup vegetable oil
1	bunch fresh broccoli flowerets	½	cup sugar
½	pound fresh mushrooms	½	cup white wine vinegar
2	medium green peppers, chopped	1	tablespoon dried Italian dressing mix
1	small red onion, sliced and separated into rings	2	teaspoons dry mustard
		1	teaspoon salt

Break cauliflower and broccoli into pieces. Combine cauliflower, broccoli, mushrooms, green pepper, and onion in large bowl. In another bowl mix oil, sugar, vinegar and seasonings. Pour over vegetables and toss. Cover and chill at least 3 hours or overnight. Toss several times during marinating.

Yield: 10 to 12 servings   Kim Strickland

Italian Zucchini Bake

½	pound fresh zucchini, sliced	¼	teaspoon pepper
2	tablespoons margarine	¼	teaspoon thyme
3	eggs, beaten	¼	teaspoon garlic salt
1	whole green onion, chopped	1	cup shredded mozzarella cheese
½	cup milk		paprika
1	teaspoon salt		

Place zucchini in 1½-quart casserole dish and dot with margarine. Bake, uncovered, at 400 degrees for 15 minutes or until zucchini is cooked but crisp. Combine eggs, onion, milk, salt, pepper, thyme, garlic salt and pour over zucchini. Sprinkle with cheese and paprika. Set casserole dish in a shallow pan filled with 1 inch of hot water. Bake, uncovered, at 350 degrees for 40 minutes or until inserted knife comes out clean.

Yield: 6 servings   Mary Young Boatenreiter

Great for Brunches! Zucchini Au Gratin

2	cups cooked zucchini	2	eggs, well-beaten	
⅓	cup chopped onion	¼	cup margarine, melted	
½	cup grated Cheddar cheese	½	cup crushed round buttery	
½	cup mayonnaise		crackers	

Mix zucchini, onion, cheese, mayonnaise, eggs, and margarine. Place in 9x9x2-inch buttered casserole dish. Top with cracker crumbs. Bake, uncovered, at 350 degrees for 30 minutes.

Yield: 4 to 6 servings   Suzanne Sullivan

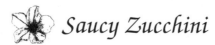 ## *Saucy Zucchini*

3	pounds fresh squash	1	(16 ounce) can tomatoes
1	medium onion, chopped		all-purpose flour or
¼	green pepper, chopped		cornstarch as needed
1	small clove garlic, chopped	½	cup grated Parmesan
1	tablespoon butter		cheese
1	tablespoon bacon drippings		

Slice squash into 1-inch rounds, then quarter slices. Parboil in salty water until tender. Do not overcook. Drain and pour into 2-quart baking dish. In saucepan, cook onion, green pepper and garlic over low heat in butter and bacon drippings until tender. Add tomatoes and heat thoroughly. Thicken with flour or cornstarch. Pour sauce over squash and top with grated Parmesan cheese. Bake, uncovered, at 375 degrees for 30 minutes or until bubbly.

Yield: 6 to 8 servings   Marie Burns

Beef

The Fairgate
Roddey/Mixon/Dover Home
Built 1922

 *Beef Burgundy*

2	pounds round steak, cut into 1x2-inch strips	1	(14½ ounce) can beef bouillon
1	clove garlic, minced	1	cup Burgundy wine
3	medium onions, chopped	1	(4 ounce) can mushrooms, drained
½	cup margarine		
1	tablespoon all-purpose flour	½	teaspoon thyme
			salt and pepper to taste

Brown steak, garlic and onions in margarine in a Dutch oven. Add the remaining ingredients. Cover and simmer slowly for approximately 3 hours. Serve over rice.

Yield: 6 to 8 servings   Suzanne Sullivan

 *Beef Kebobs*

2	pounds beef tenderloin	2	to 3 medium tomatoes, cut in wedges
½	cup salad oil		
½	cup wine vinegar	½	pound large whole mushrooms
2	tablespoons soy sauce		
4	tablespoons minced green onions	4	to 6 fresh or canned onions, halved
1	clove garlic, minced	4	to 6 fresh or canned small potatoes, quartered
½	teaspoon pepper		
1	tablespoon sugar	6	to 8 strips thickly sliced bacon, cut in 2-inch strips
2	to 3 medium green peppers, cut in 1-inch pieces		

Cut beef into large cubes. Prepare marinade by mixing oil, vinegar, soy sauce, green onions, garlic, pepper and sugar together. Marinate beef for 12 hours. Remove meat from marinade. On skewers, alternate beef, green pepper, tomatoes, mushrooms, onion, potatoes (onions and potato should be parboiled if using fresh) and bacon. Bacon should be placed on both sides of meat to give it a good flavor. Use any, or all, of the above suggested vegetables. Cook on charcoal grill, turning often.

Yield: 4 servings   Jane McLane

Double for 8 to 10 people.

Beef Tips On Noodles

1½ to 2 pounds stew beef
2   tablespoons oil
1   (10¾ ounce) can cream of
     mushroom soup
1   envelope dry onion soup
     mix

1   (4 ounce) can sliced
     mushrooms, undrained
     black pepper to taste
1   (10¾ ounce) soup can of
     water
1   (8 ounce) package medium
     egg noodles

Cut meat into cubes. Place meat in skillet and brown well in hot oil. Mix drained meat, soups, mushrooms, pepper and can of water. Pour in 3-quart casserole dish. Bake, covered, at 350 degrees for 1 hour. Cook egg noodles according to package directions. Serve beef mixture over noodles.

Yield: 4 servings   Kim Strickland

Big Daddy Rodger's Chili

1   or 2 (12 ounce) cans flat
     beer, optional
½   pound bacon, cooked and
     drained
1   tablespoon parsley flakes
2   (4 ounce) cans mushrooms
3   pounds ground beef,
     browned and drained
1   (8 ounce) can of Parmesan
     cheese

2   (15 ounce) cans kidney
     beans
4   (10¾ ounce) cans tomato
     soup or 2 (10¾ ounce)
     cans tomato soup and 2
     (16 ounce) cans tomatoes
3   tablespoons chili powder
2   tablespoons garlic powder
2   tablespoons salt

If using beer, open before cooking and let stand 2 to 3 hours at room temperature. Crumble bacon and combine all ingredients except beer in large pot and cook over medium-low heat for 2 to 3 hours or until thickened and flavors are combined. Before serving, add beer to desired consistency.

Yield: 8 servings   Claire Buescher

 *Chili*

3	pounds onions, chopped	2	(10¾ ounce) cans tomato soup
2	cloves garlic, minced	2	(16 ounce) cans tomatoes
¼	cup margarine		salt and pepper to taste
2	pounds ground beef		chili powder to taste
2	(15 ounce) cans kidney beans		

In large skillet or Dutch oven, cook onions and garlic in margarine until tender and slightly brown. Add ground beef and cook until brown. Add kidney beans, soup, and tomatoes. Season with salt, pepper and chili powder to taste. Simmer, covered, for 3 to 4 hours.

Yield: 6 to 8 servings   Suzanne Sullivan

Chili Con Carne

1½	pounds ground beef	4	(15 ounce) cans dark kidney beans
1	pound hot bulk pork sausage	3	to 4 tablespoons chili powder
2	cups chopped onion	1	tablespoon salt
4	(16 ounce) cans chopped tomatoes		

Brown ground beef, pork sausage and onion in Dutch oven. Crumble meats with fork. Drain meat and return to Dutch oven, adding chopped tomatoes and kidney beans. Season with chili powder and salt. Simmer, covered, over low heat for 3 hours or until desired consistency.

Yield: 6 to 8 servings   Floye Luke

Pat's Texas Chili Cook Off Winner

6 slices bacon	1 (28 ounce) can tomatoes, drained; reserve liquid
1½ to 2 pounds ground chuck	
1 tablespoon bacon drippings	1 teaspoon liquid smoke
1 medium onion, chopped	1½ teaspoons chili powder
¼ large green pepper, chopped	1 (14 ounce) can tomato sauce
1 clove garlic, crushed	1 (8 ounce) can tomato sauce
1 teaspoon salt	¼ cup ketchup
¼ teaspoon pepper	¼ cup brown sugar
2 tablespoons vinegar	4 mild hot peppers, chopped
2 (15 ounce) cans red kidney beans, drained	

Cook bacon crisp, drain on paper towel and crumble. Brown ground chuck in reserved bacon drippings. Add bacon, onion, green pepper and garlic. Cook 1 to 2 minutes over medium to low heat. Put into slow cooker. Add salt, pepper, vinegar, kidney beans, tomatoes, liquid smoke, chili powder, tomato sauce, ketchup, brown sugar and chopped peppers. Cook over low heat 6 to 8 hours. To make spicier chili, use more chili powder or hot peppers. Use drained tomato juice if it gets too thick.

Yield: 6 to 8 servings   Pat Chitty

Can also be cooked in a Dutch oven over low heat for 2½ to 3 hours.

Grilled Sirloin

4 pounds sirloin, 3-inches thick	¼ cup red wine vinegar
	1 clove garlic, minced
¼ cup lemon juice	3 teaspoons salt
¼ cup vegetable oil	¼ teaspoon pepper
2 tablespoons oregano	

To make marinade, mix all ingredients except sirloin. Place beef in container and marinate for 24 hours. Place on hot grill and cook on high for approximately 35 minutes for rare to medium meat, turning once.

Yield: 8 servings   Janice Worn

Marinated Southern Beef Tenderloin

1   ounce Worcestershire sauce   6   ounces soy sauce
2   ounces bottled brown   beef tenderloin,
     bouquet sauce   approximately 10 pounds

Mix all ingredients together except beef. Marinate beef overnight in a marinating container. Bake at 450 degrees for 20 minutes. After 20 minutes, turn oven off and leave meat in oven an additional 15 minutes.

Yield: 20 to 25 servings   Patti Wright

This marinade can be enjoyed with steaks or any beef.

Hamburger Casserole

1½   pounds ground beef   1   (3 ounce) package cream
2   (8 ounce) cans tomato sauce   cheese
1   teaspoon salt   1   cup sour cream
¼   teaspoon pepper   1   medium onion, chopped
¼   teaspoon garlic powder   1   cup grated Cheddar cheese
1   (8 ounce) package medium
      old-fashioned egg noodles

Brown beef and drain. Add tomato sauce, salt, pepper, garlic powder and simmer for 15 minutes. Cook noodles according to package directions. While noodles are cooking, mix the cream cheese, sour cream and chopped onion. Drain noodles and mix all ingredients except Cheddar cheese. Spread in a buttered 13x9x2-inch casserole dish and sprinkle grated cheese on top. Bake, uncovered, at 350 degrees for 30 to 35 minutes.

Yield: 8 servings   Marcia Felts

Hamburger Supreme

1	pound ground beef	½	teaspoon salt
½	cup chopped onion	¼	teaspoon pepper
1	(10¾ ounce) can cream of mushroom soup	2	cups cooked vermicelli
½	cup milk	1	(8 ounce) package grated sharp Cheddar cheese

Brown meat; add onion. Cook until tender. Stir in soup, milk and seasonings. Layer half of noodles, meat sauce and cheese in a greased 2-quart casserole. Repeat layers of noodles and meat sauce. Reserve remaining cheese. Bake at 350 degrees for 20 minutes. Sprinkle with remaining cheese. Return to oven and bake until cheese melts.

Yield: 6 servings   Mary Powell

Freezes well.

Mexican Lasagna

1½	pounds ground beef	1	(8 ounce) carton cottage cheese
1	medium onion, chopped	8	corn tortillas, cut in fourths
1	clove garlic, minced	1	(8 ounce) package grated Monterey Jack cheese
1	(1¼ ounce) package taco seasoning mix	1	(8 ounce) package grated Cheddar cheese
2	(16 ounce) cans tomatoes, partially drained	1	(4½ ounce) can sliced black olives
1	egg, beaten		

In Dutch oven, brown meat with onion and garlic. Add taco mix and tomatoes until well blended. Combine egg and cottage cheese until thoroughly mixed. In a 13x9x2-inch baking dish, layer a third of meat, half of tortillas, cottage cheese mixture, Monterey Jack cheese, a third of meat, remaining tortillas, remaining meat, Cheddar cheese and olives. Bake at 350 degrees, uncovered, for one hour.

Yield: 8 to 10 servings   Jeanne Cowart

Corn tortillas can be substituted with 3 to 4 large flour tortillas.

 *Lasagna*

Meat Sauce:

¾ large onion, chopped
¼ cup salad oil
2 pounds ground beef
2 cloves garlic, minced

2 tablespoons dried parsley
1 (28 ounce) can tomatoes
2 (6 ounce) cans tomato paste
   salt and pepper to taste

Sauté onion in oil. Add meat and brown. Add remaining ingredients and cook, covered, slowly for 2 hours.

Cheese Sauce:

6 tablespoons butter
1 small onion, finely chopped
6 tablespoons all-purpose flour

3 cups milk
1 cup grated Parmesan cheese
2 egg yolks

Melt butter and sauté onion until transparent. Stir in flour. Add milk and cook until thickened, stirring constantly. Remove from heat and stir in cheese until well blended. Add hot mix to yolks.

1 (8 ounce) box lasagna noodles, cooked according to package directions
6 (6 ounce) packages mozzarella cheese, cut in thin strips

1 (3½ ounce) package pepperoni, skinned and thinly sliced

Line buttered 15x10x12-inch casserole dish with noodles, layer of meat sauce, layer of mozzarella cheese, layer of pepperoni and layer of cheese sauce. Repeat layers until all ingredients are used. Top with mozzarella cheese. Bake at 375 degrees, uncovered, for 30 minutes or until bubbly.

Yield: 8 to 10 servings   Virginia Beckmann

 ## Meat Loaf

¼ cup milk	lemon pepper marinade,
1 slice bread or 6 saltines	several good sprinkles
1 pound ground chuck or	1 egg, beaten
ground round steak	1 small onion, finely chopped
1 tablespoon Worcestershire	1 (10½ ounce) can beef
sauce	consommé
	salt and pepper to taste

Pour milk over bread or crackers. Mix together with remaining ingredients, reserving some of the consommé to be used for basting. Pour contents into 8½x4½x2½-inch loaf pan. Bake, covered with foil, at 325 degrees for 45 minutes. Baste occasionally with consommé. Remove foil and bake an additional 15 minutes.

Yield: 4 to 6 servings   Suzanne Sullivan

Mom's Best

1½ pounds ground beef	2 (8 ounce) cans crescent
¼ cup chopped onion	dinner rolls
¾ to 1 cup commercial	6 slices processed cheese
barbecue sauce	sesame seeds

Brown meat and onion; drain. Stir in barbecue sauce; set aside. Unroll crescent dough into 4 long rectangles on ungreased cookie sheet. Overlap long sides, firmly press perforations and edges to seal. Pat to form 15x13x2-inch rectangle. Spread meat mixture lengthwise down center of dough. Top meat with cheese slices. Fold shorter sides of dough 1-inch over filling. Bring long sides of dough rectangle over filling, overlapping edges. Pinch edges to seal. Sprinkle with sesame seeds. Bake at 375 degrees for 20 to 25 minutes or until golden brown.

Yield: 6 to 8 servings   Kathy Lincoln

Smoked Beef Brisket

1 (5 to 6 pound) beef brisket	seasoned salt and pepper
1 (10 ounce) bottle	to taste
Worcestershire sauce	garlic salt to taste

Marinate brisket in Worcestershire sauce, seasoned salt, pepper and garlic salt for 24 hours. Drain, reserving marinade. Place beef in 11x7x2-inch dish. Bake, uncovered, for 30 minutes at 450 degrees. Reduce heat to 225 degrees and bake an additional 5 hours. Let cool.

Sauce:

reserved marinade	⅓ cup Worcestershire sauce
1 cup ketchup	1 tablespoon lemon juice
¾ cup brown sugar	

Add enough water to reserved marinade to make two cups. Add ketchup, brown sugar, and Worcestershire sauce to marinade. Boil for 1 minute, then reduce heat and simmer 5 minutes. Add lemon juice and remove from heat. Slice meat. Pour sauce over meat. Reheat in oven and serve.

Yield: 6 servings   Tonya Smith

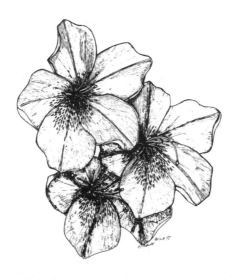

Spaghetti Sauce

3	pounds ground beef		salt and black pepper to
2	large onions, chopped		taste
2	large green peppers,	2	bay leaves
	chopped	1	teaspoon basil
2	to 3 cloves garlic, minced	1	tablespoon Italian
¼	cup margarine		seasoning
2	(6 ounce) cans tomato paste	1	(4 ounce) can mushrooms,
1	(28 ounce) can tomatoes		optional
1	tomato can water		pimento stuffed olives to
1	teaspoon celery salt		taste, optional
3	tablespoons Worcestershire		
	sauce		

Brown ground beef and drain. Sauté onions, green peppers and garlic in ¼ cup margarine in large Dutch oven. Add ground beef, tomato paste, tomatoes, water, celery salt, Worcestershire sauce, salt, pepper, bay leaves, basil, Italian seasoning, mushrooms and olives, if desired. Simmer slowly 4 to 5 hours. Serve over cooked, drained vermicelli and serve with Parmesan cheese.

Yield: 12 servings   Suzanne Sullivan

Upside Down Pizza

2	pounds ground beef	1	cup sour cream
1	medium onion, chopped	2	cups grated mozzarella
2	(8 ounce) cans tomato sauce		cheese
1	(1¼ ounce) package	1	(8 ounce) package crescent
	spaghetti sauce mix		rolls

Brown ground beef and onion together; drain. Stir in tomato sauce and spaghetti sauce mix. Place in 13x9x2-inch dish. Spread sour cream on top. Sprinkle with mozzarella cheese. Unroll crescent rolls and lay across top. Bake at 350 degrees for 20 minutes.

Yield: 8 servings   Marcia Felts

Mushrooms may be substituted for the onions.

This recipe, which was submitted by Lisa Felts, daughter of Marcia Felts, was featured in the August, 1991 edition of Southern Living.

Spaghetti Sauce with Meat

1¼ pounds lean ground beef
3 tablespoons salad oil
1 medium onion, chopped
1 clove garlic, pressed
2 (15 ounce) cans whole tomatoes, undrained
2 (6 ounce) cans tomato paste
1 teaspoon parsley flakes
1 cup red wine
¾ cup water

1 large bay leaf
2 tablespoons Worcestershire sauce
1 tablespoon sugar
1½ teaspoons salt
½ teaspoon pepper
1 teaspoon oregano leaves
1 teaspoon basil leaves
¼ teaspoon chili powder

In a 4 to 5-quart Dutch oven, brown meat in oil. After browning, skim most of oil off. Add chopped onion and garlic and cook until tender. Add tomatoes, tomato paste, parsley, wine, water, bay leaf, Worcestershire sauce, sugar, salt, pepper, oregano, basil, chili powder and stir until tomato paste is blended. Simmer, uncovered, for 1 hour. Stir occasionally. Remove bay leaf before serving.

Yield: 8 servings   Pat Chitty

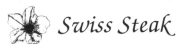

Swiss Steak

2 pounds round steak
  salt and pepper to taste
  all-purpose flour, as needed
  shortening, as needed
½ cup chopped celery
1 clove garlic, minced

2 tablespoons margarine
1 (6 ounce) can tomato paste
1 cup water
3 tablespoons wine vinegar
1 tablespoon sugar
¼ to ½ cup sherry wine

Cut steak into pieces. Salt, pepper and flour steak. Brown steak in skillet in shortening as for country fried steak. Sauté celery and garlic in margarine. Add tomato paste, water, vinegar, sugar and wine to make sauce. Place browned steak into 10½-inch frying pan or 4 to 5-quart Dutch oven in which above sauce has been made. Cook slowly 1½ to 2 hours, stirring occasionally.

Yield: 6 to 8 servings   Suzanne Sullivan

Pepper Steak With Mushrooms

1½ to 2 pounds partially frozen round steak

4 tablespoons oil, divided

1 medium onion, sliced and separated into rings

1 green pepper, cut into bite-size pieces

1 clove garlic, minced

1 pound sliced fresh mushrooms or 1 (4 ounce) can sliced mushrooms

2 tablespoons all-purpose flour

2 beef bouillon cubes

1½ to 2 cups boiling water

1 (16 ounce) can tomatoes

1 tablespoon Worcestershire sauce

salt and pepper to taste

1 (12 ounce) package egg noodles

Thinly slice partially frozen steak on diagonal. Heat 2 tablespoons oil in large skillet or Dutch oven. Add half of meat, brown, remove from pan and set aside. Then brown remaining meat, remove and set aside. Add 2 tablespoons more oil to pan. Add onion, green pepper, garlic and mushrooms. Sauté 5 minutes. Stir in flour and cook 1 minute. Dissolve bouillon in boiling water and pour into skillet with tomatoes and Worcestershire sauce. Bring to boil, stirring constantly. Reduce heat and simmer covered for 3 minutes. Stir in browned meat. Season with salt and pepper to taste. Cook and stir until hot, approximately 3 minutes. Cook egg noodles according to package directions. Serve meat mixture over egg noodles with a salad and toasted French bread.

Yield: 6 to 8 servings   Carol Giles

Meat mixture can be made ahead and reheated before serving.

 ## Savory Pepper Steak

¼ cup all-purpose flour
½ teaspoon salt
⅛ teaspoon pepper
1½ pounds round steak, ½-inch thick, cut in strips
¼ cup cooking oil
1 (8 ounce) can tomatoes, drained, reserving liquid
1¾ cups water
½ cup chopped onion
1 clove garlic, minced

1 beef flavored bouillon cube or 1 teaspoon beef flavored bouillon
1½ teaspoons Worcestershire sauce
2 large green peppers, cut in strips
½ pound fresh mushrooms, sliced; optional
¼ cup sherry wine, optional

Combine flour, salt and pepper and dredge meat. Use large skillet and brown meat in hot oil. Drain tomatoes, reserving liquid. Add tomato liquid, water, onion, garlic and bouillon to meat in skillet. Cover and simmer for approximately 1¼ hours or until meat is tender. Uncover and stir in Worcestershire sauce and pepper strips (also mushrooms and wine, if used). Cover and simmer for 5 minutes. If necessary, thicken gravy with a mixture of a small amount of flour and cold water. Add drained tomatoes and cook approximately 5 additional minutes. Serve over hot cooked rice.

Yield: 6 servings   Joanne Youles

Darn Good Stew

2 pounds lean chuck, cut in cubes
2 cups tomatoes, fresh or canned
1 (8 ounce) can tomato sauce
2 medium onions, quartered and sliced
1 clove garlic, minced
1 tablespoon sugar

1 pound whole fresh mushrooms
1 cup sliced celery
3 carrots, sliced
3 to 6 large red new potatoes, diced
3 tablespoons minute tapioca
1 tablespoon salt

Combine all ingredients, except mushrooms, in 4 to 5-quart Dutch oven. Bake, covered, at 250 degrees for 4½ hours. Add mushrooms and bake an additional ½ hour. Delicious!

Yield: 6 to 8 servings   Suzanne Sullivan

French Beef Stew

3   **pounds chuck steak, cut in**
    1-inch cubes

Marinade:

1½ **cups dry white wine**
¼   **cup brandy or gin**
2   **teaspoons salt**

¼   **teaspoon pepper**
2   **cups sliced carrots**
2   **cups sliced onions**

Combine the marinade ingredients in a bowl with the steak and refrigerate 5 hours or overnight.

Additional Ingredients:

1   **tablespoon all-purpose**
    flour
1½ **cups sliced fresh**
    mushrooms

1½ **cups peeled, seeded, diced**
    tomatoes
    bacon or salt pork, few
    pieces

Turn the marinade and beef into a 3-quart stewpot. Bring to a simmer and sprinkle with flour. Cook, uncovered, 1 to 2 minutes, stirring until blended. Add mushrooms, tomatoes and bacon or salt pork. Bring to a simmer again and cook, covered, for two hours. Serve with white or yellow rice, pasta or potatoes.

Yield: 6 servings   Chris Roan

 # *Stay-Abed Stew*

1   **(8½ ounce) can tiny English**
    peas
3   **ribs celery, sliced**
3   **carrots, pared and sliced**
1   **large onion, chopped**
1½ **pounds stew beef**

2   **raw potatoes, pared and**
    cubed
1   **teaspoon salt**
¼   **teaspoon pepper**
1   **(10¾ ounce) can tomato**
    soup
1   **bay leaf**

Combine all ingredients except tomato soup and bay leaf. Mix in 3-quart casserole that has tight lid. Add 1 can tomato soup, thinned with ½ can of water. Add 1 bay leaf on top of mixture and remove when done. Bake, covered, at 275 degrees for 5 hours.

Yield: 4 to 6 servings   Tilda Stubbs

Virginia's Beef Stew

2	(10¾ ounce) cans cream of mushroom soup		dash of pepper
1	(10¾ ounce) can golden mushroom soup	3	dashes onion powder
1	package dry onion soup mix	3	to 4 pounds stew beef
½	cup water	6	large potatoes, cut in quarters
1	teaspoon parsley flakes	5	or 6 large carrots, cut in chunks

Mix soups, soup mix, water and seasonings in a 4 to 5-quart Dutch oven or 13x9x2-inch casserole dish. Place meat and vegetables in soup mixture. Bake, covered, at 275 degrees for 5½ hours. The soups make gravy.

Yield: 8 servings   Carol Giles

Tex-Mex Special

1	(1¼ ounce) package taco seasoning mix	1	cup shredded Cheddar cheese
1	pound ground beef	1	(8 ounce) carton sour cream
½	(8 ounce) package dip size corn chips	1	(8 ounce) jar mild taco sauce

Preheat oven to 350 degrees. In 10-inch skillet, prepare taco seasoning mix as label directs with ground beef for tacos. Line 9-inch pie plate with corn chips, pushing some chips up the edge of the pie plate. Spoon ground beef mixture into corn chip crust. Sprinkle with shredded cheese. Spread sour cream over cheese. Bake, uncovered, at 350 degrees for 20 minutes or until heated through. In small saucepan, heat taco sauce over medium heat until hot. Spoon sauce around edge of pie.

Yield: 4 main dish servings   Cay Simmons

Taco Pie

1	pound ground beef	1	9-inch baked deep dish pie shell
1	medium onion, chopped		
1	(1¼ ounce) package taco seasoning mix	2	cups shredded cheese: Monterey Jack, Cheddar, or both
¾	cup water		
1	(15 ounce) can refried beans	1	cup corn chips, crushed
1	(8 ounce) jar taco sauce, divided	1	(8 ounce) carton sour cream
		2	cups shredded lettuce
		1	medium tomato, chopped

Cook ground beef and onion until browned. Drain. Add taco seasoning and water to beef, mix, and bring to a boil. Reduce heat and simmer 20 minutes. Combine beans and ⅓ cup taco sauce. Spoon ½ bean mixture in bottom of pie shell. Top with ½ meat, ½ cheese, and all of the corn chips. Then repeat with beans, meat and top with cheese. Bake at 400 degrees for 20 to 25 minutes. Serve with remaining taco sauce, sour cream, lettuce, and tomatoes as toppings.

Yield: 4 to 6 servings   Kim Strickland

Taco Casserole

1	pound ground beef	1	(15 ounce) can red kidney beans, undrained
1	(1¼ ounce) package taco seasoning mix		
1	(8 ounce) can tomato sauce	1	(10½ ounce) bag whole tortilla corn chips
2	cups water	1	cup grated Cheddar cheese
½	cup uncooked minute rice		

Brown ground beef and drain. Add all other ingredients except tortilla chips and cheese. Simmer 15 minutes. Add whole corn chips. Pour into 2-quart baking dish and top with grated cheese. Bake, uncovered, at 400 degrees for 10 to 15 minutes.

Yield: 8 servings   Jan Blanton

Poultry

Durant/Plowden/Kendrick Home
Built 1885

Cook It Slow - Chicken With Almonds

1   (10¾ ounce) can cream of celery soup
1   (10¾ ounce) can cream of chicken soup
1   (10¾ ounce) can cream of mushroom soup

½   cup butter, melted
½   cup slivered almonds
1¼ cups uncooked rice
3   chicken breasts, halved
¼   cup grated Cheddar cheese

In a large bowl, mix together undiluted soups, melted butter, and almonds. Set aside 1 cup of this mixture to baste chicken. Add rice to remaining mixture and pour into 2-quart baking dish. Place chicken breasts on top of the mixture. Bake at 325 degrees for approximately 2 hours. Baste chicken several times while cooking. Near end of baking time, sprinkle with cheese and allow to brown lightly.

Yield: 6 servings   Susan Smith

Chicken and Asparagus Casserole

4   to 5 chicken breast halves, boned
    Worcestershire sauce
1   cup butter, melted and divided
    pepper to taste
½   cup mayonnaise
1   cup grated Cheddar cheese

½   cup diced onion
¼   cup sour cream
1   (10¾ ounce) can cream of chicken soup, undiluted
1   (14½ ounce) can asparagus
1   (8 ounce) bag herb-seasoned stuffing mix

Place washed chicken breasts in 13x9x2-inch baking dish. Cover chicken with Worcestershire sauce and ½ cup melted butter. Season with pepper to taste. Bake at 350 degrees for 40 minutes. Remove chicken and shred, reserving cooking juices in baking dish. Stir together mayonnaise, cheese, onions, sour cream, chicken soup, asparagus, ½ of cooking juices and shredded chicken in 2½-quart casserole. Combine remaining ½ cup melted butter and stuffing mix. Place on top of chicken mixture. Bake at 350 degrees for an additional 30 minutes.

Yield: 6 to 8 servings   Julie Taylor

Chicken Bacon Sandwich Filling

6	slices bacon, fried and crumbled	¼	cup mayonnaise
1	cup finely chopped cooked chicken	2	tablespoons finely chopped green onions
		¼	teaspoon salt

Mix bacon with chicken. Add mayonnaise, chopped onions, and salt. Stir well. Spread on bread for sandwiches.

Yield: 6 servings

Vallye Blanton

Tasty and Tender Barbecue Chicken

6	chicken breast halves, with bone	1	(12 ounce) can cola-flavored carbonated drink
1	(12 ounce) bottle chili sauce	1	individual package dry onion soup mix

Place chicken breasts in 13x9x2-inch baking dish. Combine chili sauce, cola and onion soup mix. Pour over chicken. Bake, covered tightly with foil, at 300 degrees for approximately 2 hours.

Yield: 6 servings

Honey Kendrick

This sauce also works well for brisket.

Lemon Barbecue Chicken

1	clove garlic, crushed	¼	teaspoon dried thyme
½	teaspoon salt	2	tablespoons grated onion
¼	cup vegetable oil		salt and pepper to taste
½	cup lemon juice	1	chicken, cut into pieces
½	teaspoon black pepper		flour

Mash garlic and salt together in bowl. Add vegetable oil, lemon juice, pepper, thyme and onion. Chill 24 hours. Salt and pepper chicken, dust lightly with flour. Brown pieces of chicken. Place chicken in 13x9x2-inch glass dish and pour sauce over. Bake, uncovered, at 375 degrees until chicken is done, approximately 1 hour. Turn chicken often or baste.

Yield: 4 servings

Ann Cooper

Especially nice for chicken but may be used with other types of meat.

Capital Chicken

1	fryer, cut up or 6 breast halves	1	cup water
4	tablespoons butter	½	cup cream
1	tablespoon cooking oil	1	teaspoon salt
1	(8 ounce) package fresh, sliced mushrooms	¼	teaspoon tarragon
		¼	teaspoon black pepper
1	tablespoon all-purpose flour	1	(15 ounce) can artichoke hearts, drained
1	(10¾ ounce) can cream of chicken soup	6	whole green onions, chopped
1	cup dry white wine	2	tablespoons parsley

Brown chicken 10 minutes in butter and oil until brown on all sides. Place chicken in 13x9x2-inch casserole dish. In same frying pan sauté mushrooms until tender, stir in flour, soup, wine, and water. Simmer, stirring approximately 10 minutes until thickened. Stir in cream, salt, tarragon and pepper. Pour over chicken. Bake, uncovered, at 350 degrees for 1 hour. Add artichokes, green onions and parsley. Bake approximately 5 more minutes or until fork tender.

Yield: 4 to 6 servings   Sharon Swindle

Cheese Chicken With Wine

8	chicken breast halves, boned	¼	cup white wine
8	slices Swiss cheese	1	cup herb-seasoned stuffing mix
1	(10¾ ounce) can cream of chicken soup	¼	cup margarine, melted

Place chicken topped with Swiss cheese in a greased 2-quart casserole dish. Mix together soup and wine; spoon over chicken and cheese. Crush the stuffing mix and sprinkle over the chicken. Spoon the melted margarine over the casserole. Bake at 350 degrees for 45 to 55 minutes.

Yield: 6 to 8 servings   Vickie Wilkinson

Chicken Breast Bake

1 section round buttery crackers

4 chicken breast halves, cooked and chopped

1 (10¾ ounce) can cream of chicken soup

½ (8 ounce) carton sour cream

4 tablespoons margarine, melted

Crush half of the crackers and place in a 9x9x1½-inch casserole dish. Mix chicken, soup and sour cream and pour over crackers. Finely crush remaining crackers and sprinkle over chicken mixture. Melt margarine and drizzle over the top. Bake at 350 degrees for 40 minutes.

Yield: 6 servings

Ellen Clary

Celebrate With Champagne Chicken

2 tablespoons all-purpose flour

½ teaspoon salt

⅛ teaspoon pepper

4 chicken breast halves, skinned and boned

2 tablespoons butter

1 tablespoon olive oil

¾ cup champagne

½ cup fresh, sliced mushrooms

½ cup heavy cream

Combine flour, salt and pepper in paper bag. Add chicken and shake. Heat butter and oil in large skillet. Add chicken. Sauté for 4 minutes over medium heat. Add champagne and cook for 12 minutes over medium heat. Remove chicken. Add mushrooms and cream to skillet. Cook over low heat, stirring constantly until thickened. Return chicken to skillet. Cook until heated thoroughly.

Yield: 4 servings

Pam Mackey

Chicken Chow Mein

4	large chicken breast halves salt and pepper to taste	1	cup chicken broth
2	large onions, chopped	10	stalks celery, chopped
1	(16 ounce) can bean sprouts, drained	1	pound fresh mushrooms, chopped soy sauce to taste
3	tablespoons all-purpose flour	¼	cup dry sherry, optional

Place chicken breasts in large saucepan and just cover with water. Salt and pepper to taste. Boil, uncovered, until tender, approximately 30 to 40 minutes. Remove chicken, cool and cut into small pieces. Save broth. Place onions, mushrooms and celery in the chicken broth, seasoning to taste with soy sauce. Cook approximately 20 minutes until tender. Mix flour well with ½ cup cold water. Stir into vegetable mixture. Add bean sprouts and chicken. Cook approximately 15 minutes to thicken. Can be served over rice or chow mein noodles. Freezes well.

Yield: 6 to 8 servings   Suzanne Sullivan

Easy Chicken And Dressing

2	cups crumbled cornbread muffins	2	tablespoons margarine, melted
2	cups cubed dry bread	1	egg
1	teaspoon salt	1	(10¾ ounce) can cream of chicken soup, divided
¼	teaspoon pepper		
3	tablespoons chopped onion	4	to 6 chicken breast halves, boned and skinned
2	tablespoons chopped celery		

Combine crumbled cornbread muffins, cubed dry bread, salt, pepper, onion, celery, margarine, and egg with ½ can cream of chicken soup mixed with ¼ cup hot water. Mix thoroughly. Place in center of 12x8x2-inch baking dish. Place pieces of chicken around outer edges. Pour remaining ½ can of soup mixed with ½ to ¾ cup hot water over dressing and chicken. Bake, covered with foil, at 325 degrees for 1½ hours.

Yield: 4 to 6 servings   Brenda Davis

Chicken Pasta

2	skinless boneless chicken breasts	½	cup chopped green pepper
3	teaspoons (total) Paul Prudhomme's Meat Magic	2	cups chicken stock
1	(6 ounce) package pasta; fettuccine or angel hair	2	tablespoons all-purpose flour
1	cup chopped white onion	3	cups thinly sliced fresh mushrooms
½	cup chopped celery	½	cup chopped green onion

Cut the chicken in small pieces and place in a small bowl with 2 teaspoons of Meat Magic. Cook pasta according to directions. Place skillet over high heat and add the white onions, celery, green pepper and the remaining teaspoon of Meat Magic. Cook over high heat, shaking pan but not scraping for five minutes. Add ½ cup of chicken stock, start scraping up the browned coating on the bottom of the pan and cook 4 minutes. Stir in the chicken mixture and cook 4 minutes. Add flour and cook 2 minutes. Add the mushrooms, ½ cup stock and scrape the bottom of the pan and cook 4 minutes. Add another ½ cup stock and stir and scrape for 5 minutes. Add the green onions and remaining ½ cup stock. Stir and scrape for additional five minutes. Serve over pasta.

Yield: 6 servings

Chris Roan

Cindy's Creamy Chicken

4	whole chicken breasts, or 1 whole chicken, cut up	1	(4 ounce) can mushrooms, drained
1	(10¾ ounce) can cream of mushroom soup	1	cup sour cream
		½	cup sherry
			paprika

Put chicken in a 13x9x2-inch baking dish. Mix soup, mushrooms, sour cream and sherry and pour over chicken. Sprinkle with paprika. Bake at 325 degrees for 1 to 1½ hours. Serve with rice and green vegetable and/or salad.

Yield: 6 to 8 servings

Carol Giles

Chicken Tetrazzini

1	(6 pound) hen or 5 pounds chicken breasts	2	(2 ounce) jars chopped pimentos
2	teaspoons salt	1	clove crushed garlic
½	teaspoon pepper	¼	teaspoon garlic salt
½	cup butter or margarine	1	teaspoon Worcestershire sauce
2	medium green peppers, chopped	3	teaspoons cooking sherry
¼	cup plus 1 tablespoon all-purpose flour	6	cups grated medium Cheddar cheese, divided
2	cups milk	1	cup sliced almonds
2	(10¾ ounce) cans cream of mushroom soup	1	(1 pound) package thin spaghetti noodles

Place hen or chicken breasts in a large Dutch oven and cover with water. Add salt and pepper. Bring to a boil. Cover and reduce heat; simmer approximately one hour or until tender. Remove hen or chicken from broth, reserving broth. Cool chicken; remove meat from bone. Dice meat. Melt butter in a medium saucepan over low heat. Add green peppers; sauté until tender. Add flour and stir until smooth; cook one minute, stirring constantly. Gradually stir in milk. Add soup, pimento, garlic, garlic salt, Worcestershire sauce, sherry, chicken and 4 cups of the grated cheese; stir well. Cook over medium heat 10 minutes, stirring occasionally. Add enough water to reserved broth to measure 5 quarts. Bring broth to a boil in a large saucepan or Dutch oven. Cook noodles in boiling broth until tender, approximately 8 minutes; drain and rinse. Lightly grease two 13x9x2-inch baking dishes; spread half of noodles evenly into baking dishes; spread half of chicken mixture evenly over noodles. Repeat layers once, using remaining noodles and chicken mixture. Sprinkle remaining cheese evenly over both casseroles; top with almonds. Bake at 350 degrees for 15 to 20 minutes or until thoroughly heated.

Yield: 16 to 20 servings   Linda Miller

These casseroles freeze beautifully before baking. Cover with aluminum foil; seal securely; label and freeze. To serve: thaw overnight in refrigerator. Bake at 350 degrees for 35 minutes or until bubbly. Remove foil during last 10 minutes of baking.

Verdie's Chicken Casserole

salt and pepper	2 (10¾ ounce) cans cream of
1 large hen	mushroom soup
1 whole onion	milk as needed
1 rib celery	4 ounces Cheddar cheese,
1 (¾ pound) box spaghetti	grated
1 large onion, diced	1 (2 ounce) jar pimento strips
1 large green pepper, diced	1 (2½ ounce) can ripe olives,
½ pound fresh mushrooms,	sliced
sliced	parsley for garnish
6 tablespoons margarine	

Salt and pepper hen. Boil hen with whole onion and celery. Remove meat from bone and cut into bite-size pieces. Cook ¾ pound spaghetti in chicken broth. Mix hen with spaghetti. Sauté onion, pepper and mushrooms in margarine. Add soup to vegetables. Stir in spaghetti mixture and chicken. Add milk until creamy but not soupy. Pour in 13x9x2-inch greased casserole. Sprinkle on top for garnish: grated cheese, pimento strips, olives and parsley. Bake, covered, at 350 degrees for 15 minutes. Bake, uncovered, an additional 15 minutes.

Yield: 8 to 10 servings   Patti Wright

Chicken Excelsior House

6 whole chicken breasts,	1 cup sour cream
halved and boned	¼ cup sherry
garlic salt to taste	1 (8 ounce) can sliced
½ cup butter or margarine,	mushrooms
melted	generous dash of cayenne
1 teaspoon paprika	pepper
3 tablespoons lemon juice	

Sprinkle chicken breasts with garlic salt. Melt butter or margarine; add paprika and lemon juice. Roll chicken breasts in the melted butter mixture and place on baking sheet. Bake at 375 degrees for 1 hour or until tender. Make a sauce of sour cream, sherry, mushrooms and cayenne pepper. Pour sauce over chicken and bake an additional 15 minutes.

Yield: 12 servings   Pam Mackey

Clay Pot Chicken With Garlic And Herbs

1	(4½ to 5 pound) roasting chicken	1	medium onion, sliced
	salt and pepper to taste	1	medium carrot, sliced
6	sprigs fresh or ½ teaspoon dried thyme	1	celery rib, sliced
		3	extra-large garlic bulbs
6	sprigs parsley	4	fresh or ½ teaspoon ground sage leaves
2	bay leaves	1	sprig fresh or ¼ teaspoon dried tarragon
1	tablespoon unsalted butter, softened		

Cover 2 to 3-quart clay pot with cold water and let soak for 15 minutes. Sprinkle inside of chicken with salt and pepper. Place 2 thyme sprigs (or pinch dried), 2 parsley sprigs and bay leaf into cavity and truss the bird. Rub the butter over the chicken and sprinkle with salt and pepper. Drain the clay pot and add the onion, carrot and celery. Set the chicken on top of the vegetables and scatter the unpeeled garlic cloves around the chicken. Scatter around the sage leaves, tarragon sprig and the remaining 4 sprigs of thyme, 4 sprigs parsley and bay leaf. Cover the clay pot and place it in a cold oven. Bake at 475 degrees for approximately 1 hour and 20 minutes or until juices run clear when a thigh is pierced. Uncover and cook for approximately 10 minutes longer to brown the breast. Transfer the bird and garlic cloves to a warmed platter, cover loosely with foil and let rest for about 15 minutes. Strain the basting juices into a sauceboat and keep warm. Carve the chicken and serve with garlic cloves on the side. Let each person squeeze the garlic from its skin onto toasted bread.

Yield: 4 servings   Kellie McTier

Southern Delight Chicken And Dumplings

1	(2½ pound) chicken, cut into fryer pieces	2	cups all-purpose flour
1	teaspoon salt	2	cups milk
1	teaspoon pepper	½	cup water

Cover chicken with water in a 4-quart saucepan, sprinkle with salt and pepper. Boil over medium heat for 30 minutes. Remove chicken from saucepan and reserve broth for dumplings. Allow chicken to cool and remove meat from bone. Mix flour, ½ cup milk and ½ cup water in a bowl. Transfer flour mixture into another bowl containing enough flour to coat dough. Knead dough until firm. Press flat on floured surface. Let stand approximately 10 minutes. Roll out with rolling pin until knife blade thin. Cut into 2-inch squares. Drop into boiling broth. Cook approximately 10 minutes on high heat. Reduce heat to low and return chicken to pot. Pour 1½ cups milk into mixture and stir. Remove from heat. Add additional salt and pepper if needed.

Yield: 12 servings

Claire Buescher

Chicken Fajitas Valdosta Style

1	tablespoon Italian salad dressing	1	(4 ounce) can sliced mushrooms
1	medium onion, sliced	1	tablespoon soy sauce
1	medium green pepper, cut into ½-inch strips	1	tablespoon lime juice
4	chicken breast halves, boned, sliced into ½-inch strips	8	flour tortillas
			salsa, optional
			sour cream, optional

In a large skillet, combine Italian salad dressing, sliced onions, and green pepper strips. Sauté over medium heat until onions begin to wilt. Add chicken strips, mushrooms, soy sauce, and lime juice. Simmer 15 minutes stirring often, until chicken is browned. Heat flour tortillas in microwave for 10 seconds. Place chicken mixture down center of tortilla and roll up. Top with salsa and sour cream if desired. Serve with refried beans and Spanish rice.

Yield: 4 to 6 servings

Judith Joseph

Chicken Country Captain

4	slices bacon	1	(16 ounce) can chopped tomatoes
¼	cup all-purpose flour	2	teaspoons curry powder
1	teaspoon salt	½	teaspoon dried thyme
½	teaspoon pepper	½	cup currants, (not raisins)
6	to 8 chicken breast halves, boned	1	cup chicken broth, heated
2	celery ribs, chopped	3	cups cooked rice
1	small onion, chopped	½	cup toasted almonds
1	green pepper, chopped		chutney to taste
2	cloves garlic, chopped		

In Dutch oven or large frying pan, fry bacon until crisp. Remove bacon, drain, crumble and reserve. Also reserve bacon drippings. In brown bag place flour, salt and pepper. Shake chicken in flour mixture. Brown floured chicken in bacon drippings. Remove chicken and set aside. In bacon drippings, sauté celery, onion, green pepper and garlic. Add tomatoes, curry powder and thyme. Bring to a boil. Reduce heat to low and cover. Simmer approximately 10 minutes. In 13x9x2-inch casserole dish, place chicken breasts, cover with tomato mixture. Bake, covered, at 275 degrees for 1½ to 2 hours or until chicken is very tender. In a small bowl, place currants in hot chicken broth and let stand until plump, approximately 30 minutes. Gently stir drained currants into chicken approximately 10 minutes before removing from oven. Serve Country Captain with rice. Pass bowls of toasted almonds, crumbled bacon and chutney for topping.

Yield: 6 to 8 servings   Honey Kendrick

 ## Summer Chicken

2	fryers, quartered	½	cup margarine
1	(10 ounce) bottle Durkee sauce		juice of 1½ lemons

Clean chicken, place skin side up in a 13x9x2-inch casserole dish. Heat Durkee sauce, margarine and lemon juice. Pour sauce over chicken to cover. Bake, uncovered, at 350 degrees for 1½ hours.

Yield: 6 to 8 servings   Jan Carter

 ## Cordon Bleu Chicken Breasts

4	large chicken breast halves, boned and skinned	4	slices provolone cheese
¼	pound paper thin cooked ham	2	tablespoons butter
		1	egg, slightly beaten
		¼	cup dry breadcrumbs

Flatten chicken breasts. Place a slice of ham and a slice of cheese on each piece. Roll up from narrow end and secure with toothpicks. Melt butter in shallow pan. Dip each breast in egg, then roll in breadcrumbs. Place in melted butter, turning gently to drench both sides. Bake at 375 degrees, turning after 15 minutes. Bake an additional 15 minutes.

Yield: 4 servings   Lena Bosch

Margaret's Mexican Chicken

8	chicken breast halves, boned and skinned	1½	teaspoons ground cumin
2	(4 ounce) cans whole green chilies, halved and seeded	¼	teaspoon salt
		¼	teaspoon garlic powder
3	ounces Monterey Jack cheese, cut in strips	¼	to ½ cup skim milk
		4	cups shredded lettuce
¾	cup fine, dry breadcrumbs	½	cup picante sauce
1	tablespoon chili powder	½	cup sour cream

Trim excess fat from chicken. Place chicken between 2 sheets of waxed paper; flatten to ¼-inch thick. Place green chili half and one strip of cheese on each breast; roll up lengthwise, tucking edges under. Secure with toothpicks. Combine breadcrumbs, chili powder, cumin, salt, and garlic powder. Dip chicken roll in milk; dredge in breadcrumb mixture. Place chicken in 13x9x2-inch casserole dish coated with cooking spray. Bake at 400 degrees for 30 minutes or until done. To serve, place each chicken roll on ½ cup shredded lettuce; top with 1 tablespoon picante sauce and 1 tablespoon sour cream. Serve immediately.

Yield: 8 servings   Sally Kurrie

Golden Brown Chicken Casserole

½	cup margarine	2	tablespoons Worcestershire
1	chicken, cut into fryer		sauce
	pieces and skinned	1	bay leaf
	salt and pepper to taste		dash of lemon juice
1	(4 ounce) can sliced	1	(10½ ounce) can beef
	mushrooms		consommé soup
1	tablespoon all-purpose		
	flour		

Melt margarine in skillet. Salt and pepper chicken, then brown well in melted margarine. Transfer chicken to 13x9x2-inch casserole dish. Brown mushrooms in same margarine, take out and place around chicken. Add flour to the butter and mix well. Add Worcestershire sauce, bay leaf, lemon juice and beef consommé. Pour over chicken and mushrooms. Bake at 350 degrees for 1 hour. Before serving, remove bay leaf. The chicken and mushrooms get brown and the gravy thickens. This gravy is excellent for rice or mashed potatoes.

Yield: 4 servings   Patti Wright

Mustard Grilled Chicken

¼	cup Dijon mustard	1	whole shallot, sliced in
¼	cup whole seed mustard		rings
¼	cup hot German mustard		freshly ground pepper to
	juice of ½ lemon		taste
¼	cup distilled white vinegar	4	chicken breast halves,
¼	cup olive oil		boned and skinned
½	cup unsweetened apple		
	juice		

Combine Dijon mustard, whole seed mustard, German mustard, lemon juice, vinegar, olive oil, apple juice, shallot rings, and pepper in a bowl. Whisk to emulsify. Place chicken in a marinating container. Pour mustard mixture over chicken and marinate for 2 to 4 hours. Grill 6 to 7 minutes per side over medium-hot coals. Do not overcook. Heat remaining marinade thoroughly to serve as a sauce over grilled chicken, if desired.

Yield: 4 servings   Donna Miller

Mustard Marinade Grilled Chicken Breasts

2 tablespoons Dijon mustard
2 tablespoons coarse ground mustard
4 chicken breast halves, boned and flattened
4 tablespoons margarine
½ cup white wine
1 teaspoon tarragon
¼ teaspoon garlic or small clove, crushed
¼ teaspoon white pepper

Spread mustard on both sides of chicken breasts and place in refrigerator approximately 2 hours. Dab excess mustard off with a paper towel before cooking. To prepare sauce, melt together margarine, white wine, tarragon, garlic and white pepper. Brush this sauce on chicken breasts while grilling over medium heat, turning every 10 minutes. Takes from 20 to 25 minutes depending on temperature of grill.

Yield: 4 servings

Pat Chitty

California Coast Monterey Chicken

4 whole chicken breasts, halved, skinned, and boned
1 (8 ounce) block Monterey Jack cheese
2 eggs, beaten
1½ cups dry breadcrumbs
⅔ cup butter, divided
1 chicken bouillon cube
1 cup boiling water
½ cup chopped onion
½ cup chopped green pepper
2 teaspoons all-purpose flour
1 teaspoon salt
¼ teaspoon pepper
3 cups cooked rice
1 (4 ounce) can sliced mushrooms

Flatten chicken breast halves to ¼-inch thick. Cut cheese into 8 equal portions. Place 1 portion in center of each breast. Fold chicken over cheese; secure with toothpicks. Dip each breast in egg and coat with breadcrumbs. Brown meat on all sides in ⅓ cup butter. Dissolve bouillon in water. Sauté onions and pepper in ⅓ cup butter. Stir in bouillon, flour, salt, and pepper. Thicken. Stir in rice and mushrooms. Put rice mixture in 13x9x2-inch casserole dish and place chicken on top. Bake at 400 degrees for 30 to 45 minutes or until done.

Yield: 6 to 8 servings

Debbie Davis

Chicken In A Paper Bag

1	whole chicken	garlic salt or powder
1	non-recyclable paper	seasoned salt, optional
	grocery bag	paprika
	onion salt	pepper
	celery salt or seed	

Wash chicken and pat dry. Sprinkle spices inside and on outside of chicken. Amount of spices will depend on individual taste. Place chicken, breast side up, in bag and put bag in broiler pan. Fold end of bag so it is loosely closed, but inside lip of pan to avoid juices spilling out. Bake at 400 degrees for 1½ hours.

Yield: 3 to 4 servings   Carol Giles

Chicken Scallopini In Lemon Sauce

2½	tablespoons all-purpose flour	6	tablespoons unsalted butter
⅛	teaspoon salt	¼	cup chicken broth
⅛	teaspoon white pepper	¼	cup white wine
⅛	teaspoon garlic powder	½	fresh lemon, thinly sliced
4	boneless chicken breast halves, pounded to ¼-inch thickness	1	tablespoon finely chopped parsley

Mix flour, salt, white pepper and garlic powder. Arrange chicken breasts close together on a cutting board or wax paper and lightly sprinkle with flour mixture. Turn and flour other side of breasts. Heat butter in a large, heavy skillet. Quickly brown the chicken breasts a few pieces at a time. Remove from the pan and keep warm. Add the chicken broth, wine, and lemon slices. Push the lemon slices down into the liquid. Reduce the heat to simmer, cover and cook over low heat for 5 minutes. Place chicken breasts on a heated platter, pour the sauce over the chicken, and sprinkle with parsley.

Yield: 4 servings   Judith Joseph

Delicious served with spaghetti sauce and pasta. Veal can be substituted for chicken.

189

Pleasing Party Chicken

8	chicken breast halves, boned and skinned	1	(10¾ ounce) can cream of mushroom soup
1	(2½ ounce) jar dried beef	1	cup sour cream
8	to 12 slices bacon		

Layer each chicken breast with dried beef then wrap with a slice of bacon. Place in 8x8x2-inch baking dish. Mix soup and sour cream and pour over chicken. Refrigerate until ready to bake. Bake, covered with foil, at 275 degrees for 2 hours. Remove foil and bake 1 more hour to let it brown slightly.

Yield: 6 to 8 servings   Kathy Lincoln

Perfect Chicken Pan Pie

1	chicken, cooked, boned and diced	1	(10¾ ounce) can cream of chicken soup
¾	cup frozen tiny peas, uncooked		salt and pepper to taste
¾	cup diced carrots, uncooked	½	cup margarine, melted
		1	cup self-rising flour
1¾	cups chicken broth	¾	cup milk

Place chicken in bottom of greased 13x9x2-inch casserole dish. Sprinkle peas and carrots over chicken. Mix chicken broth, soup and spices and pour over chicken and vegetables. In a separate bowl combine margarine, flour and milk. Whip with a whisk until smooth and pour over casserole. Bake at 350 degrees for 40 minutes or until brown.

Yield: 6 to 8 servings   Mary Powell

This is also great with leftover turkey breast!

Poppy Seed Chicken

2	pounds of chicken breasts	½	cup butter or margarine
1	(10¾ ounce) can cream of chicken soup	1½	cups round buttery crackers, crushed
1	(8 ounce) carton sour cream	2	tablespoons poppy seeds

Boil chicken breasts in water. Remove bones and place chicken in a 13x9x2-inch casserole dish. Mix soup and sour cream and pour this mixture over chicken. Melt butter. Mix in crushed crackers and poppy seeds with butter. Pour over casserole. Bake at 350 degrees for 30 minutes.

Yield: 5 to 6 servings   Vallye Blanton

Russian Chicken

1	(8 ounce) bottle Russian dressing, not creamy	1	small clove garlic
1	(12 ounce) jar apricot preserves	6	large chicken breast halves
⅔	cup water	1	(11 ounce) can mandarin oranges
1	envelope dry onion soup mix	1	(2¼ ounce) package sliced almonds

Combine dressing, preserves, water, soup mix and garlic. Remove chicken skin and place skin side down in a 13x9x2-inch casserole dish; pour ½ the sauce over chicken. Bake 1 hour at 350 degrees. Turn chicken over and pour remaining sauce. Bake an additional 30 minutes. Garnish with oranges and almonds. Serve with rice.

Yield: 6 servings   Lisa Harris

Melt-In-Your-Mouth Quick Chicken Pie

4 cups cooked, cubed chicken
1 (10¾ ounce) can cream of mushroom soup
1 (10¾ ounce) can chicken broth
½ teaspoon tarragon, optional

2 boiled eggs, sliced; optional
1½ cups self-rising flour
1½ cups buttermilk
½ cup butter or margarine, melted

Place chicken in lightly greased 13x9x2-inch baking dish. Blend soup with broth and tarragon. Pour over chicken. Arrange egg slices over chicken. Combine flour, buttermilk and butter; mix well. Pour evenly over chicken mixture. Bake, uncovered, at 350 degrees for 1 hour or until crust rises to top and is golden brown.

Yield: 6 servings

Mary Beth Meyers

Chicken And Spinach Casserole

3 (10 ounce) packages frozen spinach
6 chicken breast halves, skinned and boned
2 (10¾ ounce) cans cream of mushroom soup
1 cup mayonnaise

1 (8 ounce) carton sour cream
⅛ cup dry white wine
1 cup grated sharp Cheddar cheese
1 tablespoon lemon juice
1 teaspoon curry powder
salt and pepper to taste

Topping:
½ cup grated Parmesan cheese

½ cup soft breadcrumbs

Prepare spinach as directed on package. Boil chicken until done yet tender. Remove chicken from pot and dice. Place spinach followed by chicken in bottom of a 13x9x2-inch casserole dish. Mix all other ingredients, except topping, and pour over spinach and chicken. Mix topping and sprinkle over top. Bake at 350 degrees for 30 minutes.

Yield: 8 to 10 servings

Claire Buescher

May substitute 2 bunches fresh broccoli for spinach. This recipe is easily halved.

Baked Swiss and Herb Chicken

8	chicken breast halves, skinned and boned	¼	cup dry white wine
8	slices Swiss cheese	¾	cup herb-seasoned stuffing mix, crushed
1	(10¾ ounce) can cream of chicken soup	¼	cup butter, melted

Arrange chicken in greased 13x9x2-inch casserole dish. Top each chicken breast with cheese slice. Combine soup and wine. Spoon sauce over chicken. Sprinkle with stuffing. Drizzle butter over stuffing. Bake at 350 degrees for 45 to 55 minutes.

Yield: 6 to 8 servings   Pam Mackey

Chicken Valdostana

9	tablespoons butter	¼	cup heavy cream
1	pound mushrooms, trimmed and sliced	12	chicken cutlets
	salt and freshly ground pepper to taste	1½	teaspoons tarragon
¼	cup dry Madeira wine	1	pound Italian Fontina cheese, grated

Preheat oven to 375 degrees. Heat 3 tablespoons of the butter in a wide skillet. Add mushrooms and cook, stirring constantly, until tender and beginning to render juices. Add salt, pepper, Madeira, and cream. Stir. Cook over high heat until all liquid is absorbed. Set aside. Sprinkle the chicken cutlets with salt, pepper, and tarragon. Heat the remaining 6 tablespoons butter, divided, in 2 heavy skillets. Over moderate heat, sauté the cutlets for only a minute on each side. They should turn white. Do not brown and do not crowd in the pan. Place the cutlets in a single layer in a 13x9x2-inch baking dish. Spread the mushrooms over the chicken. Cover the chicken and mushrooms completely with the Fontina cheese. Place the baking dish in the preheated oven for 10 minutes until chicken is just done. Cut into one cutlet to check for doneness. If not quite done, return to the oven for another minute or so, or until the texture of the chicken is creamy. Do not overcook.

Yield: 6 servings   Martha Grow

Tarragon Chicken Casserole

1	2½ to 3 pound chicken, cut into pieces	1¼	teaspoons salt
1	or 2 medium onions, chopped	¼	teaspoon pepper
1½	teaspoons tarragon	1	(10¾ ounce) can cream of chicken soup, undiluted
¼	teaspoon poultry seasoning	¼	cup milk
		¼	cup slivered almonds

Place chicken in lightly greased 13x9x2-inch baking dish; do not over-lap. Sprinkle onion, tarragon, poultry seasoning, salt and pepper over chicken. Combine soup and milk, stirring well; spoon over chicken. Bake, uncovered, at 375 degrees for 40 minutes or until tender. Sprinkle with almonds and bake an additional 10 minutes.

Yield: 6 servings   Jan Anderson

Creamy Swiss Chicken Casserole

6	chicken breast halves, boned and skinned	¼	cup milk
6	(4 x 4 inch) slices Swiss cheese	2	cups herb-seasoned stuffing mix
1	(10¾ ounce) can cream of chicken soup, undiluted	¼	cup butter or margarine, melted

Arrange chicken breasts in lightly greased 12x8x2-inch baking dish. Top with cheese slices. Combine soup and milk; stir well. Spoon sauce over chicken; sprinkle with stuffing mix. Drizzle butter over crumbs; cover and bake at 350 degrees for 50 minutes.

Yield: 6 servings   Mary Powell

Turkey à la King

1	large green pepper, cut into bite-size pieces	1	(4 ounce) jar diced pimentos, drained
⅓	cup margarine or butter	1	envelope chicken flavored bouillon or 1 to 2 teaspoons of chicken bouillon granules
⅓	cup all-purpose flour		
1	teaspoon salt		
2	cups milk		
4	cups cubed cooked turkey	2	tablespoons dry sherry
2	(4½ ounce) jars whole mushrooms	1	(11 ounce) box heat and serve biscuits

In a skillet over medium heat, cook green pepper in butter for 5 minutes until tender. Stir in flour and salt until blended. Gradually stir in milk and cook, stirring until thickened. Add turkey, mushrooms with their liquid, pimentos, bouillon and sherry. Heat to boiling, stirring often. Reduce heat and simmer for 5 minutes. Split biscuits and spoon turkey mixture over.

Yield: 6 servings   Tootsie Tillman

 # Night Before Christmas Turkey

Wash, salt and pepper cavity of a 15 pound turkey thoroughly. Rub outside with cooking oil. Slide turkey into very large brown grocery sack, keeping sack away from top and sides of bird. Place in large shallow broiler pan with no more than 4-inch sides. Before sealing sack, pour ½ cup water into cavity. Seal end of sack. Bake in oven from 11:00 pm until 8:00 am at 250 degrees. Remove and tear away sack.

Yield: 18 to 22 servings   Jan Carter

Two Hour Turkey

10	to 12 pound turkey	1	celery rib, sliced
	salt to taste	1	onion, sliced
	lemon pepper to taste	1	cup white wine
1	medium onion	1	(13½ ounce) can chicken
	parsley stems		broth
2	teaspoons rosemary	½	cup tomato juice
1	carrot, sliced		

Preheat oven to 425 degrees. Line baking pan with doubled heavy duty foil so that turkey sits on shiny side of foil. Remove giblets and neck from cavity. Sprinkle salt and lemon pepper in cavity and under neck skin. Put medium onion under neck skin. Fold wings under back and pull neck skin under wings. Do not put salt on top. Put a handful of parsley stems and 1 teaspoon of rosemary in cavity. Put all giblets and neck, carrot, celery, onion, and remaining rosemary around turkey. (This can be done the night before cooking and refrigerated. Leave at room temperature one hour before baking.) Heat wine. Pour half inside turkey and half around turkey. Heat chicken broth and tomato juice. Pour around turkey. Cover turkey with single sheet of heavy duty foil. Twist top foil with bottom foil several times so it is air tight. Do not let foil touch top of turkey. Bake at 425 degrees for one hour on lowest rack of oven. Remove and slit top of foil lengthwise. Open foil and push to sides. Bake uncovered for one more hour. DO NOT BASTE. Follow directions and the turkey will be done. The foil acts like a pressure cooker. It is not only fast but the turkey will be moist and delicious.

Yield: 16 to 20 servings   Chris Roan

Pork

First United Methodish Church
Built 1905

Ham Pilaf

1	medium onion, chopped	¼	cup dry sherry
¼	cup chopped green pepper	¼	teaspoon Worcestershire
½	cup chopped celery		sauce
3	tablespoons corn oil		salt and pepper to taste
2	cups diced cooked ham	1	(4 ounce) can chopped
¾	cup rice, uncooked		mushrooms, drained
1¼	cups chicken broth	1	tablespoon chopped parsley

Sauté onion, green pepper and celery in oil for 5 minutes. Add ham and sauté 5 minutes more. Add rice and brown lightly, stirring well approximately 2 minutes. Add broth, sherry, Worcestershire sauce, salt and pepper. Bring contents to a boil. Remove from skillet and pour into a 2-quart casserole dish. Bake, covered, at 350 degrees for 30 minutes. Stir in mushrooms and parsley. Cover and bake an additional 10 minutes.

Yield: 6 to 8 servings   Mary Powell

Honey Glazed Baked Ham

1	(8 pound) whole, fully	2	teaspoons lemon juice
	cooked ham	1	teaspoon ground cloves
4	sticks cinnamon	1	teaspoon orange juice
10	to 12 whole cloves	¼	cup dark brown sugar
2	tablespoons prepared	¼	cup honey
	mustard		

Slowly boil ham with cinnamon sticks for 3½ hours. Marinate in stock for 4 hours. Remove ham. Place on broiler pan. Slice crisscross cuts on top side of ham. Stud with cloves. Mix mustard, lemon juice, cloves and orange juice. Stir in sugar and honey. Baste with ⅓ glaze. Bake, uncovered, at 325 degrees for 25 minutes. Baste with remaining glaze. Bake an additional 5 to 10 minutes.

Yield: 10 to 12 servings   Pam Mackey

Harris' Favorite Meat Loaf

Loaf:

2½ pounds ground beef
1¼ pounds ground pork
2 slices bread made into crumbs
⅓ cup oatmeal
4 eggs, beaten
2 teaspoons salt
1 tablespoon prepared mustard
1 cup tomato sauce
1 medium onion, diced
1 (5 ounce) can evaporated milk
coarse black pepper to taste

Preheat oven to 400 degrees. Mix all ingredients and shape into loaf. Place into greased 13x9x2-inch dish. Bake, uncovered, one hour and baste occasionally with juices in pan.

Sauce:

4 tablespoons dark brown sugar
1 cup tomato sauce
½ cup milk
4 tablespoons prepared mustard
4 tablespoons vinegar

Mix all ingredients and heat in small saucepan. Pour over each serving.

Yield: 6 to 8 servings   Denise Retterbush

Delicious with mashed potatoes, peas and carrots.

Marinated Pork Chops

1½ cups vegetable oil
¾ cup soy sauce
2¼ teaspoons salt
½ cup red wine vinegar
⅛ teaspoon garlic salt
¼ cup Worcestershire sauce
2 tablespoons dry mustard
1 tablespoon black pepper
1½ teaspoons parsley flakes
⅓ cup lemon juice
6 to 8 pork chops

Combine oil, soy sauce, salt, vinegar, garlic salt, Worcestershire sauce, mustard, pepper, parsley flakes and lemon juice. Pour enough mixture over pork chops to marinate and refrigerate for at least 2 hours. Grill pork chops. Baste while grilling.

Yield: 3½ cups   Vallye Blanton

Unused sauce keeps in refrigerator 2 weeks.

Neapolitan Pork Chops

6	loin pork chops, 1-inch thick	1	cup thinly sliced green pepper
2	tablespoons pure vegetable oil	1	cup thinly sliced onion
1	pound fresh button mushrooms	1	(16 ounce) can tomatoes
		½	teaspoon oregano
		1	teaspoon salt
		⅛	teaspoon pepper

Trim fat from chops. Brown on both sides in hot oil in skillet. Remove chops. In remaining oil, sauté mushrooms, green pepper, and onion until tender. Add tomatoes, oregano, salt and pepper. Simmer 5 minutes. Add pork chops, cover and simmer 1 hour or until chops are tender. If thicker sauce is desired, uncover and simmer 15 minutes longer. Serve over rice.

Yield: 6 servings   Peggy Gayle

Stuffed Pork Chops Calle

½	cup chopped onion	1	tablespoon Worcestershire sauce
½	cup chopped green pepper		dash hot pepper sauce
4	tablespoons butter	1	teaspoon crushed dill seed
1	(3 to 4 ounce) can mushrooms	2	cups cooked rice
2	teaspoons garlic salt	6	pork chops, 1½-inch thick with pocket for stuffing

Sauté onion and green pepper in butter until tender. Add mushrooms, salt, Worcestershire sauce, hot pepper sauce, dill seed and rice. Allow rice to brown slightly. Pack mixture in pocket of chops and secure with toothpick. Broil on both sides to brown. Place in 13x9x2-inch glass dish and bake, uncovered, at 400 degrees for 30 minutes.

Yield: 6 servings   Diane Smith

Smothered Pork Chops

6	pork chops	½	cup water
	salt and pepper to taste	1	tablespoon parsley flakes
1	(10¾ ounce) can cream of	1	teaspoon lemon juice
	chicken soup	1	tablespoon soy sauce
½	cup canned broken	2	tablespoons cornstarch
	mushrooms, pieces and	¼	cup cold water
	liquid		

Season pork chops with salt and pepper. Place in 13x9x2-inch glass dish. Combine soup, mushrooms, water, parsley, lemon juice, soy sauce and pour over pork chops. Bake, covered with foil, at 350 degrees for 45 minutes to 1 hour. Remove foil and drain gravy. Return pork chops to the oven for a few minutes. Thicken gravy by adding cornstarch dissolved in water.

Yield: 6 servings   Denise Rountree

Chicken may be substituted for the pork chops. This is good served with rice.

Pork Tenderloin

1½	pounds pork tenderloin	1	cup bread crumbs
1	cup all-purpose flour	1	teaspoon paprika
1	teaspoon seasoned salt	3	tablespoons oil
2	to 3 eggs		juice of 1 lemon
2	tablespoons milk		

Cut tenderloins into approximately 20 pieces. Using a mallet, pound each piece until it is wafer thin. Mix together flour and seasoned salt in a bowl. In another bowl, beat the eggs and milk until well mixed. In a third bowl, mix together bread crumbs and paprika. Coat each tenderloin piece in flour, then egg mixture, then bread crumbs. In a large skillet, cook cutlets in medium hot oil for 2 to 3 minutes on each side. Remove from pan to a platter. Squeeze fresh lemon juice on top.

Yield: 6 to 8 servings   Donna Clary

 ## Grilled Pork Chops

1 tablespoon soy sauce	1 clove garlic, crushed
1 tablespoon sugar	4 pork chops, 1-inch thick
2 tablespoons cider vinegar	

Mix soy sauce, sugar, vinegar and garlic. Pour over chops in 8x8x2-inch dish and let marinate several hours in refrigerator, turning once or twice. Cook on grill approximately 12 to 15 inches from coals so they will cook slowly for 45 minutes to 1 hour.

Yield: 4 servings   Suzanne Sullivan

 ## Sweet and Sour Pork

2 pounds lean pork	½ teaspoon salt
2 teaspoons cream sherry	½ cup oil
1 tablespoon soy sauce	1 clove garlic, crushed

Cut pork into 1-inch cubes. Remove all fat. Mix pork, sherry, soy sauce and salt. Set aside to marinate for 30 minutes to 1 hour. Heat oil and add crushed garlic. Fry the meat on both sides. Edges should be crisp. Drain on paper towel.

Sauce:

⅔ cup sugar	2 tablespoons soy sauce
¼ cup ketchup	2 tablespoons cornstarch
⅓ cup pineapple juice	⅓ cup water
⅓ cup cider vinegar	1 cup pineapple chunks

Heat sugar, ketchup, pineapple juice, vinegar and soy sauce in small saucepan. Dissolve cornstarch in water and add to sauce mixture. Cook over medium low heat 15 minutes, stirring frequently. Add pineapple chunks and fried pork to sauce and simmer approximately 30 minutes on low heat until pork is tender.

Yield: 6 to 8 servings   Suzanne Sullivan

Serve over hot rice and top with Chinese noodles.

Stromboli

1 (16-ounce) can refrigerated loaf bread dough
¼ pound thinly sliced ham
¼ pound sliced hard salami
½ teaspoon dried whole basil, divided
½ teaspoon dried whole oregano, divided
3 ounces sliced provolone cheese
1 cup shredded mozzarella cheese
2 tablespoons butter or margarine, melted
1 teaspoon cornmeal

Place bread dough on a lightly greased baking sheet. Pat into a 15x10-inch rectangle. Arrange ham slices lengthwise down center. Place salami on top. Sprinkle with ¼ teaspoon basil and ¼ teaspoon oregano. Arrange provolone cheese over herbs, and top with mozzarella cheese. Sprinkle with remaining herbs. Moisten all edges of dough with water. Bring each long edge to center and press edges together to seal. Seal the ends. Brush dough with 1 tablespoon butter. Sprinkle with cornmeal. Carefully invert. Brush top with remaining butter. Bake, uncovered, at 375 degrees for 20 to 22 minutes.

Yield: 4 servings

Patti Wright

Saint Paul's Rice

1 (16 ounce) package bulk sausage
½ cup rice
4½ cups water
1 (1.8 ounce) box chicken noodle soup mix
1 medium green pepper, chopped
1 medium onion, chopped
2 ribs celery, chopped
½ cup slivered almonds, divided

Cook sausage thoroughly and drain. Set aside. Combine rice, water and soup mix in large saucepan and boil for 7 minutes. Remove from heat. Add sausage, green pepper, onion, celery and ¼ cup almonds. Pour into buttered 8x8x2-inch casserole dish and top with remaining almonds. Bake, uncovered, at 350 degrees for one hour.

Yield: 6 servings

Mary Corbett

Sausage Casserole

1 (16 ounce) package bulk mild sausage	1 cup cooked rice
1 medium onion, chopped	1 (10¾ ounce) can cream of mushroom soup
1 medium green pepper, chopped	

Partially brown sausage, onion and green pepper. Drain and add rice and soup. Mix well and place in 8x8x2-inch casserole dish. Bake, uncovered, at 350 degrees for 30 minutes.

Yield: 3 to 4 servings   Lee Limbocker

Wild Rice and Sausage Casserole

1 (16 ounce) package bulk sausage	2 (4 ounce) cans sliced mushrooms, drained
1½ cups chopped celery	1 (6 ounce) package long grain and wild rice mix
3 cups chicken broth	dash dried whole thyme
1 (10¾ ounce) can cream of mushroom soup	1 (2 ounce) package sliced almonds, optional
1 (10¾ ounce) can cream of chicken soup	parsley, optional
1 (8 ounce) can sliced water chestnuts, drained	

Combine sausage and celery in a large skillet. Cook over medium heat until sausage is browned and celery is tender. Stir to crumble meat. Drain. Stir in chicken broth, mushroom soup, chicken soup, water chestnuts, mushrooms, rice and thyme. Mix well. Spoon into a lightly greased 3-quart casserole and sprinkle with almonds. Bake, uncovered, at 350 degrees for 1½ hours. Garnish with parsley if desired.

Yield: 12 servings   Elaine Bridges

Pork with Vegetables

2 tablespoons soy sauce	2 bunches green onions, cut
2 tablespoons sherry	into 2-inch pieces
2 tablespoons cornstarch	1 (8 ounce) package sliced
2 pounds pork tenderloin,	fresh mushrooms
thinly sliced	1 (8 ounce) can bamboo
3 tablespoons oil, divided	shoots
4 cups Chinese cabbage, cut	
into bite-size pieces, or	
1 (6 ounce) package frozen	
snow peas; or, use portion	
of each	

Combine soy sauce, sherry and cornstarch. Pour over sliced tenderloin and place in container to marinate. Refrigerate for 2 to 3 hours or overnight. Heat wok and add 1 tablespoon oil. Fry onion and Chinese cabbage, if used, for approximately 2 minutes. Remove from wok. Add remaining 2 table-spoons oil and fry tenderloin. When meat is done, add onions, Chinese cabbage, mushrooms, bamboo shoots and snow peas.

Gravy ingredients:

1 tablespoon soy sauce	1 teaspoon sugar
1 tablespoon sherry	1 tablespoon cornstarch
½ cup water	salt and white pepper to
1 chicken bouillon cube	taste

Combine all gravy ingredients, except cornstarch, and mix well. When vegetable/meat mixture is thoroughly heated, add cornstarch to gravy ingredients and pour over vegetable/meat mixture. Stir to thicken. Add salt and white pepper to taste. Serve over rice or cook thin noodles, drain and add to vegetable/meat mixture before serving.

Yield: 6 servings   Jan Carter

Seafood

West Hall
Valdosta State College
Built 1917

Linguine And Clam Sauce With Shrimp

5	tablespoons butter or margarine
2	(6½ ounce) cans clams, undrained
1	clove garlic, minced
5	tablespoons olive oil
2	tablespoons chopped parsley
¾	teaspoon salt
¼	teaspoon oregano
½	teaspoon basil
	pepper to taste
1	pound medium shrimp, deveined and chopped
1	(8 ounce) package linguine

Melt butter; add undrained clams. Add garlic, olive oil, parsley, salt, oregano, basil and pepper. Simmer 10 minutes. Add shrimp and cook on low until shrimp are done. Serve over linguine.

Yield: 4 to 6 servings   Robin Coleman

Baked Crab And Shrimp

1	medium green pepper, finely chopped
1	medium onion, finely chopped
1	cup celery, finely chopped
1	pound crabmeat
1	cup mayonnaise
½	pound shrimp, cooked and chopped
½	teaspoon salt
⅛	teaspoon pepper
1	teaspoon Worcestershire sauce
8	large scallop shells
1	cup buttered breadcrumbs, optional

Mix all ingredients and place in shells. Bake at 350 degrees or broil until slightly brown on top and thoroughly heated. Buttered breadcrumbs may be placed on top before baking if desired.

Yield: 8 servings   Kaye Smith

This recipe may be baked in a 13x9x2-inch baking dish or served as a cold seafood salad on a bed of lettuce.

Crêpes With Crabmeat And Ham

Crêpes:

2	eggs	¾	cup all-purpose flour
1	cup water	1	tablespoon oil

Mix all ingredients except oil. Heat oil in a 7 or 8-inch skillet, then pour off. Pour 2 tablespoons of batter in greased skillet. When edges begin to brown, flip crêpe over. Continue this process until batter is used.

Filling:

1	(6 ounce) can crabmeat	¼	teaspoon nutmeg
½	pound chopped ham	¼	teaspoon ginger
1	(8 ounce) can sliced water chestnuts, halved and drained	¼	teaspoon pepper salt to taste
1	cup chopped onions	6	tablespoons butter
4	tablespoons butter	½	cup all-purpose flour
½	cup dry sherry	2	cups milk

Combine crabmeat, ham, and water chestnuts. Cook onions in 4 tablespoons butter and add meat mixture. Add sherry and cook rapidly to reduce to half. Stir in seasonings. Make a sauce of butter, flour and milk and stir into meat mixture. Place a spoonful of filling on each crêpe. Roll up and place seam side down into a 13x9x2-inch baking dish. Pour remaining sauce on top of crêpes. Bake, uncovered, at 350 degrees for 20 minutes.

Yield: 4 to 6 servings   Pat Chitty

Karen's Crawfish Étouffé

1	pound crawfish tails	½	cup chopped celery
	salt, pepper, cayenne	1	clove garlic, chopped
	pepper and paprika to taste	¼	cup chopped fresh parsley
½	cup butter	¼	cup chopped green onion
1	onion, chopped		tops
1	green pepper, chopped		

Season tails with salt, pepper, cayenne pepper and paprika. Melt butter in skillet and add tails. Cook 3 minutes. Remove tails and set aside. To drippings, add onion, green pepper, celery and garlic. Cook until soft. Return tails and add 2 cups water. Simmer 40 minutes, adding a little more water if necessary. During last 10 minutes, add parsley and onion tops. Serve over rice with French bread.

Yield: 6 to 8 servings   Sarah Parrish

Oyster Casserole

3	cups crushed saltines	¾	cup half-and-half
¾	cup butter, melted	1	teaspoon Worcestershire
1	pint oysters, reserving		sauce
	¼ cup juice		salt and pepper to taste

Mix saltines and melted butter and place ⅓ of this mixture in greased 11x7x2-inch casserole dish. Then place ½ of oysters on saltine mixture. Repeat with ⅓ of saltines and remaining half of oysters in casserole dish. Mix half-and-half, Worcestershire sauce, oyster juice, salt and pepper. Pour over top of casserole. Add remaining ⅓ of saltines to top. Bake, uncovered, at 350 degrees for 40 minutes.

Yield: 8 servings   Floye Luke

Oysters Benedict

8	small slices baked ham	½	teaspoon salt
4	English muffins	⅛	teaspoon pepper
¼	cup butter	1	to 2 cups hollandaise sauce
2	dozen large oysters		

Sauté ham 2 to 3 minutes on each side. Split and toast the English muffins. Heat the oysters in the butter over low heat, just until the edges begin to curl. Season with salt and pepper. Cut the pieces of ham more or less to fit the toasted muffins. Put 3 oysters on each piece of ham on the muffins. Spoon 2 to 4 tablespoons hollandaise sauce over each.

Yield: 8 servings

June Purvis

Baked Stretch Shrimp

2	packages Italian dressing mix	½	cup butter
1	cup vegetable oil	1	to 2 ounces black pepper
½	cup vinegar		juice of 2 lemons
4	tablespoons water	5	pounds raw unshelled medium shrimp, washed

Make dressing using oil, vinegar and water according to package directions. Combine butter, pepper (adjust amount to taste), lemon juice and dressing. Pour sauce over shrimp in a 13x9x2-inch casserole dish. Bake, covered, at 350 degrees for one hour. If shrimp have been marinating in dressing very long prior to baking, reduce cooking time.

Yield: 8 servings

Beverly Moye

Serve shrimp with plenty of sauce in soup bowls, hot French bread and salad. Everyone shells his own shrimp and "sops" bread in sauce.

Shrimp Fricassee

½ cup butter or margarine	1 bay leaf
1 tablespoon all-purpose flour	dash of garlic powder
	parsley flakes
1 (16 ounce) can tomatoes, chopped	dash of salt
	chopped green pepper to taste, optional
1 tablespoon instant onion	
⅛ teaspoon thyme	1½ pounds cooked shrimp, peeled and deveined
¼ teaspoon celery salt	

Melt butter or margarine in 3-quart saucepan. Add flour and stir until mixed. Add tomatoes and seasonings and heat thoroughly. If green pepper is included, cook until done. Add cooked shrimp and heat thoroughly. Serve over yellow rice.

Yield: 4 to 6 servings

Janet Nichols

Marinated Shrimp

2 pounds shrimp, peeled	½ teaspoon basil
½ cup butter, melted	¼ teaspoon oregano
½ lemon, thinly sliced	¼ teaspoon red pepper
2 cloves garlic, chopped	1 teaspoon sugar
1 bay leaf	1 teaspoon salt
1 dash hot pepper sauce	½ teaspoon white pepper
¼ cup white wine	½ teaspoon black pepper
2 green peppers, sliced	2 onions, sliced
½ teaspoon thyme	2 ribs celery, cut into pieces

Rinse shrimp well. Mix all ingredients and pour over shrimp. Cover and refrigerate overnight. Place in shallow 3-quart baking pan with marinade. Bake, uncovered, at 425 degrees for 10 to 15 minutes.

Yield: 4 servings

Suzanne Sullivan

 Shrimp Casserole

2½ pounds large shrimp,
    shelled and deveined
3   tablespoons salad oil
1   tablespoon lemon juice
¾   cup rice, uncooked
¼   cup minced green pepper
¼   cup minced onion
2   tablespoons butter
1   teaspoon salt
⅛   teaspoon pepper
⅛   teaspoon mace
    dash of cayenne
1   (10¾ ounce) can tomato
    soup
1   cup heavy cream
½   cup sherry
¾   cup slivered, blanched
    almonds

Cook shrimp in boiling, salted water for 5 minutes. Drain. Cut in halves lengthwise. Sprinkle with salad oil and lemon juice. Cook rice. Sauté green pepper and onions for 5 minutes in butter. Mix all ingredients well and place in 13x9x2-inch casserole dish. Reserve a few shrimp and almonds for garnish. Bake, uncovered, at 350 degrees for 35 minutes. Place reserved shrimp and almonds on top. Bake an additional 20 minutes.

Yield: 6 to 8 servings   Myra Jane Bird

Shrimp Aux Champions

¼   cup butter, melted
2   cups shrimp, cooked and
    deveined
2¼ cups grated Cheddar cheese
3   tablespoons chili sauce
½   teaspoon Worcestershire
    sauce
½   teaspoon salt
    dash of pepper
1   (3 ounce) can sliced
    mushrooms, drained
2   tablespoons diced pimentos
½   cup heavy cream
1   (8 ounce) can sliced water
    chestnuts, drained
1   (16 ounce) box wild rice,
    cooked
4   slices bread, cubed and
    buttered for breadcrumbs

Preheat oven to 350 degrees. Combine butter, shrimp, 1½ cups Cheddar cheese, chili sauce, Worcestershire sauce, salt, pepper, mushrooms and pimentos. Add cream and water chestnuts while stirring. Add cooked rice to shrimp mixture. Place into 3-quart casserole dish. Top with ¾ cup cheese, then breadcrumbs. Bake, uncovered, at 350 degrees for 25 minutes.

Yield: 6 to 8 servings   Sheila Myddleton

214

Jeneane's Marinated Shrimp

2	pounds or more shrimp, boiled and peeled	1½	teaspoons salt
1	large onion, sliced and separated	1	tablespoon dried dill weed
1½	cups vegetable oil	¼	teaspoon monosodium glutamate
¾	cup vinegar		hot pepper sauce, a few drops
2	tablespoons capers and juice		

Layer shrimp and onions in large bowl. Mix remaining ingredients and pour over shrimp and onions. Cover and refrigerate at least 24 hours before serving.

Yield: 4 to 6 servings   Jeneane Grimsley

Shrimp, Mushroom And Artichoke Casserole

½	pound mushrooms, sliced	1½	pounds shrimp, cooked and peeled
2½	tablespoons butter		
1	(8 ounce) can artichoke hearts, drained		

Sauté mushrooms in butter. Layer artichokes, shrimp and mushrooms in a 2-quart casserole.

Sauce:

4½	tablespoons butter	1	tablespoon Worcestershire sauce
4½	tablespoons all-purpose flour		salt and pepper to taste
¾	cup milk	½	cup freshly grated Parmesan cheese
¾	cup heavy cream		
½	cup dry cooking sherry	1	teaspoon paprika

Melt butter, whisk in flour, milk and cream. Stir until thick. Add sherry, Worcestershire sauce, salt and pepper. Pour sauce over shrimp, artichoke hearts and mushrooms. Sprinkle Parmesan cheese and paprika over top. Bake, uncovered, at 375 degrees for 20 to 30 minutes.

Yield: 6 to 8 servings   Lisa Henry

Special Shrimp Creole

1	medium onion, chopped	1	(6 ounce) can tomato paste
1	medium green pepper, chopped	1½	teaspoons sugar
½	cup sliced fresh mushrooms	½	teaspoon Creole seasoning
2	to 3 cloves garlic, minced	⅛	teaspoon paprika
2	tablespoons butter or margarine, melted	2	bay leaves
1	(16 ounce) can stewed tomatoes	1½	pounds fresh medium shrimp, peeled
1	(16 ounce) can tomato sauce	4	to 5 lemon slices and parsley sprigs for garnish

Sauté onion, green pepper, mushrooms and garlic in butter in a large skillet. Stir in stewed tomatoes, tomato sauce, tomato paste, sugar, Creole seasoning, paprika and bay leaves. Bring to boil, reduce heat and simmer, uncovered, for 20 minutes. Add shrimp and simmer 10 to 12 minutes, stirring occasionally. Discard bay leaves. Serve over rice. Garnish with lemon slices and parsley.

Yield: 4 to 5 servings   Patti Wright

A green salad and croissants are all you need to complete this meal!

Beer Battered Shrimp Or Grouper

1	cup beer		dash of cayenne pepper
2	eggs		vegetable oil for deep frying
2	tablespoons vegetable oil	2	pounds shrimp or grouper
1¼	cups all-purpose flour		(white fish), cut into 2-inch
1	teaspoon salt		slices

Pour beer, eggs, oil, flour, salt and pepper into blender or mix by hand. Cover and blend until smooth. Let stand 5 minutes. Heat oil in deep frying pan. Dip shrimp or fish in batter, let excess drip off. Add to hot oil. Fry until golden brown, turning once. Drain. Serve with Fresh Tartar Sauce (see recipe under sauces) or cocktail sauce.

Yield: 4 to 6 servings   Pat Chitty

Rule of thumb is to estimate ½ pound of shrimp per person.

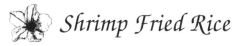

Shrimp Fried Rice

5	strips bacon	3	cups cooked rice
2	bunches green onions, chopped	1¼	pounds shrimp, cooked and chopped
1	medium green pepper, chopped		soy sauce to taste

Fry bacon in a large skillet until crisp. Remove bacon, reserving 2 tablespoons of drippings in skillet. Crumble bacon and set aside. Add chopped onions and green pepper to skillet. Sauté slowly for 15 minutes. Add rice and shrimp. Cook approximately 25 minutes, stirring or turning with large spoon. Sprinkle with soy sauce, approximately 4 times while cooking. When ready to serve, add crumbled bacon.

Yield: 4 servings   Emma Wainer

Shrimp Manalli

2½	pounds large raw shrimp, peeled and deveined	3	cloves garlic, chopped
1½	cups butter	1½	teaspoons fresh lemon juice
6	tablespoons Worcestershire sauce	2	teaspoons freshly ground pepper
6	drops hot pepper sauce		non-stick vegetable spray

Rinse shrimp. Do not dry. Melt butter in skillet. Add Worcestershire sauce, hot pepper sauce, garlic, lemon juice and pepper. Spray 13x9x2-inch baking dish with vegetable spray. Place shrimp in dish and cover with sauce. Marinate for 2 hours. Bake, uncovered, at 400 degrees for 30 minutes, then broil for 5 minutes.

Yield: 6 to 8 servings   Pam Mackey

Serve in bowls. Dip French bread in juices.

Bourbon Street Shrimp

¼	cup butter or margarine	1	teaspoon soy sauce
6	to 12 fresh mushrooms, sliced	¼	teaspoon pepper
1	(10¾ ounce) can cream of shrimp soup	1	cup sour cream
		1½	pounds shrimp, cooked and deveined

Melt butter or margarine and sauté sliced mushrooms until wilted, but still white. Stir in soup, soy sauce, pepper and sour cream. Cook, stirring on medium heat until mixture bubbles and becomes smooth. Fold in cooked shrimp and heat thoroughly. Serve immediately over hot rice.

Yield: 4 to 6 servings   Vickie Wilkinson

Shrimp And Green Noodles

1	(6 ounce) package spinach noodles	½	teaspoon Dijon mustard
2	pounds shrimp, peeled	1	tablespoon chopped chives
½	cup butter	4	tablespoons dry sherry
1	(10¾ ounce) can cream of mushroom soup	1	cup sour cream
1	cup mayonnaise	¾	cup grated sharp Cheddar cheese

Cook noodles according to package directions. Line 3-quart casserole dish with noodles, forming nest. In a large frying pan, sauté shrimp in butter until pink, approximately 5 minutes. Place shrimp in center of dish. Combine remaining ingredients, except cheese and pour over shrimp and noodles. Sprinkle cheese on top. Bake at 350 degrees for 30 minutes.

Yield: 6 to 8 servings   Joyce Paine

 ## Shrimp Delight

1½	to 2 pounds boiled shrimp	1	cup mayonnaise
2	(10¾ ounce) cans cream of mushroom soup	2	(2 ounce) jars chopped pimentos
6	slices buttered toast, crumbled	1	cup chopped onion
	salt and pepper to taste	1	tablespoon Worcestershire sauce
3	hard boiled eggs	½	cup slivered almonds

Mix all ingredients except ⅓ of breadcrumbs. Place into buttered 13x9x2-inch casserole dish. Top with remaining breadcrumbs. Bake, uncovered, at 350 degrees for 20 to 30 minutes.

Yield: 6 to 8 servings   Jane Willis

Shrimp Mold

1½	teaspoons gelatin	¾	cup chopped celery
1	(10¾ ounce) can tomato soup	¾	cup chopped green onions
1	(8 ounce) package cream cheese	½	teaspoon salt
1	cup mayonnaise	1	(4½ ounce) can small shrimp

Dissolve gelatin in ¼ cup cold water. Heat soup to boiling, and dissolve cream cheese in soup. Add gelatin and let cool. Add mayonnaise. (If needed, use the blender for a smooth blend.) Add celery, onions and salt. Stir together. Mash shrimp with fork and add to mixture. Pour into mold or ring. Refrigerate for 3 to 4 hours until congealed.

Yield: 8 to 10 servings   Sue Ellen Clyatt

 ## Lobster and Chicken Cantonese Dinner

1	clove garlic, minced	1	teaspoon prepared brown gravy sauce
¼	cup butter		
1	(6 ounce) can sliced water chestnuts, drained	3	cups chicken broth
		1½	teaspoons salt
1	(5 ounce) can bamboo shoots, drained	1	(6½ ounce) can lobster or 1 package frozen lobster tails, cooked
¼	pound sliced fresh mushrooms		
		2	chicken breast halves, skinned, boiled and sliced
1	(10 ounce) package frozen peas, slightly thawed		
		1	(3 ounce) can chow mein noodles
¼	cup cold water		
¼	cup cornstarch	2	eggs, hard-cooked and chopped
1	tablespoon soy sauce		

Cook garlic in butter for 1 minute. Add water chestnuts, bamboo shoots, mushrooms and peas. Cook 3 minutes. Combine water, cornstarch, soy sauce, brown gravy, chicken broth and salt. Add to vegetable mixture. Cook over moderate heat until thickened, stirring constantly. Fold in lobster and chicken. Heat thoroughly. Serve over chow mein noodles. Garnish with chopped eggs. Serve with Chinese fried rice and Sweet 'n Sour Sauce.

Chinese Fried Rice:

2	tablespoons vegetable oil	½	teaspoon salt
2	cups chopped onion	1	tablespoon soy sauce
2	cups cooked rice		green pepper, cooked
2	eggs		shrimp or ham, optional

Fry onions in oil. Sauté rice 2 minutes. Beat eggs, salt and soy sauce together and add to rice and onions. Fry until brown on high heat, turning with a spoon. Green pepper, cooked shrimp or ham may be added.

Sweet 'n Sour Sauce:

¾	cup sugar	½	cup vinegar
¼	cup soy sauce	1	(8 ounce) can crushed pineapple, undrained
2	tablespoons cornstarch		

Cook all ingredients until thickened.

Yield: 6 to 8 servings

Bobbie Ann Mitchell

To complete the Cantonese dinner, serve with a hot mustard sauce, fresh or frozen egg rolls, orange sherbet for dessert and hot tea.

 ## *Savannah Seafood Casserole*

1 pint heavy cream	1½ pounds shrimp, cooked and peeled
2 tablespoons butter	
2 tablespoons all-purpose flour	1 teaspoon Worcestershire sauce
1 (14 ounce) can artichoke hearts, drained	1 teaspoon paprika
	1 tablespoon lemon juice
1 pound crabmeat	2 tablespoons ketchup
	sherry to taste

Make cream sauce of cream, butter and flour. Mix with remaining ingredients and place in a 13x9x2-inch casserole. Bake, uncovered, at 350 degrees until heated well and bubbly.

Yield: 8 to 12 servings   Mary Dasher

Grilled Fresh Tuna

¼ cup orange juice	1 clove garlic, minced
¼ cup soy sauce	½ teaspoon oregano
2 tablespoons ketchup	white pepper to taste
2 tablespoons parsley	4 tuna steaks
1 tablespoon lemon juice	

Combine orange juice, soy sauce, ketchup, parsley, lemon juice, garlic, oregano and pepper. Marinate tuna for 1 hour in refrigerator. Grill six minutes on each side basting with marinade over medium low heat. Fish is done when flaky.

Yield: 4 servings   Pat Chitty

Seafood Casserole

8 tablespoons butter or margarine	4 tablespoons chopped parsley
9 tablespoons all-purpose flour	¼ cup sherry
1 cup evaporated milk	1 tablespoon Worcestershire sauce
1½ cups milk	1 tablespoon horseradish
1 cup consommé soup	1 teaspoon prepared mustard
2 tablespoons cornstarch, mixed with a little milk	1 teaspoon soy sauce
1 tablespoon lemon juice	¼ teaspoon cayenne pepper
4 tablespoons ketchup	5 pounds seafood; crabmeat, cooked shrimp, scallops, boneless fish, etc.
1 clove garlic, pressed	5 hard cooked eggs, sliced
½ teaspoon salt	2 cups grated Cheddar cheese
2 teaspoons monosodium glutamate	1 cup buttered breadcrumbs

Melt butter or margarine and blend in flour. Heat together evaporated milk, milk and consommé soup. Add to butter and flour and stir until thick. Add cornstarch, which has been mixed with a little milk, and remaining seasonings. Blend well. Add seafood and eggs, stirring gently. Place in greased 3-quart casserole dish. Top with cheese and buttered breadcrumbs. Bake, uncovered, at 350 degrees for 30 minutes.

Yield: 8 to 10 servings   Myra Jane Bird

Tuna Cheese Muffins

1 (6½ ounce) can tuna, drained	¼ teaspoon Worcestershire sauce
1 cup grated Swiss cheese	⅛ teaspoon hot pepper sauce
½ cup mayonnaise	3 English muffins
1 tablespoon lemon juice	

Mix tuna, cheese, mayonnaise, lemon juice, Worcestershire sauce and hot pepper sauce. Split English muffins in half. Spread tuna mixture on each muffin. Broil for 3 to 4 minutes.

Yield: 6 open-faced sandwiches   Marcia Felts

Jerry's Bluefish With Mustard Sauce

2	pounds bluefish fillets or other fish fillets, fresh or frozen
3	cups water
¾	cup lemon juice
6	tablespoons margarine or butter, melted
3	tablespoons lemon juice
4	teaspoons prepared mustard
¾	teaspoon salt
½	teaspoon paprika
	chopped fresh parsley

Thaw fish, if frozen. Cut fillets into serving size portions. Place fillets in a single layer in a well greased 13x9x2-inch baking dish. Mix water with ¾ cup lemon juice and pour over fish. Marinate in refrigerator for 20 minutes. Combine margarine, 3 tablespoons lemon juice, mustard, salt and paprika. Mix well. Place fish on well greased broiler pan, approximately 15x10x1-inch. Brush generously with mustard mixture. Broil 4 inches from source of heat for 4 to 6 minutes. Turn carefully. Brush generously with sauce and broil for 4 to 6 minutes longer or until fish flakes easily when tested with fork. Sprinkle fish with parsley. Warm remaining sauce and serve with fish.

Yield: 6 servings   Jane Rainey

Grilled Salmon Steaks

4	salmon steaks, 1-inch thick
⅓	cup unsalted butter, softened
2	tablespoons chopped green onion
1	teaspoon dried dill weed or 1 tablespoon fresh dill
1	teaspoon salt
¼	teaspoon freshly ground pepper
1	clove garlic, minced
4	lemon wedges

Dry steaks with paper towel. Combine remaining ingredients and spread generously on one side of steaks. Grill over medium heat, buttered side down, for 5 to 6 minutes. Butter top side, turn and grill for 5 to 6 minutes or until firm. Serve any remaining butter mixture on top. Garnish with lemon wedges.

Yield: 4 servings   Claire Buescher

Crispy Baked Fillets

1   **pound fish fillets, fresh or frozen and thawed in refrigerator**

      freshly ground black pepper to taste
2   **tablespoons oil**
⅓   **cup crushed corn flakes**

Wash and dry fillets and cut into serving pieces. Pepper fillets, dip in oil, and coat with crushed corn flakes. Arrange in a lightly greased 8x8x2-inch baking dish. Bake, uncovered, at 500 degrees for 10 minutes without turning or basting.

Yield: 4 servings   Suzanne Sullivan

Each fillet has only 260 calories.

Baked Fish

2   **pounds fresh fish fillets, flounder or grouper**
1   **cup mayonnaise**

⅔   **cup freshly grated Parmesan cheese**
⅔   **cup dry Italian breadcrumbs**

Preheat oven to 400 degrees. Place fish fillets in lightly greased 8x8x2-inch baking dish. Mix mayonnaise, cheese and Italian breadcrumbs in bowl. Spoon on top of each fillet. Bake, uncovered, at 400 degrees for 15 to 30 minutes, depending on thickness of fish.

Yield: 4 to 6 servings   Pam Mackey

Game, Lamb & Veal

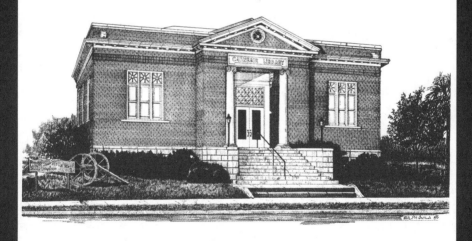

Lowndes County Historical Society
Carnegie Library
Built 1913

Antelope Ragout

1½	pounds antelope, cut in one-inch cubes	½	teaspoon thyme
1	small clove garlic, chopped	1½	cups chicken broth
1	onion, chopped	1	small package dry instant onion soup mix
½	pound sliced fresh mushrooms	2	cups sliced carrots
2	tablespoons margarine	½	cup frozen peas
3	tablespoons brandy	1	tablespoon cornstarch
	salt and pepper to taste	2	tablespoons water

Brown the antelope, garlic, onion and mushrooms in margarine for 3 minutes. Add the brandy and flame. Add salt, pepper, thyme, chicken broth and onion soup. Cover and simmer 1½ hours. Add carrots and peas for last half hour. Thicken with cornstarch, which has been added to 2 tablespoons water. Serve over rice or noodles.

Yield: 6 to 8 servings   Chris Roan

What! NO Antelope?! Try veal instead.

Delicious Baked Dove

18	dove		juice and grated rind of ½ lemon
2	tablespoons butter		
2	tablespoons cooking oil	2	teaspoons liquid smoke
	salt and pepper	1	tablespoon Worcestershire sauce
9	strips bacon, halved		
⅛	teaspoon garlic salt	¼	cup sherry wine
		¼	cup water

Brown dove in mixture of butter and oil. Salt and pepper liberally while browning. Remove dove from skillet. Wrap each dove in bacon and place in 13x9x2-inch baking dish. Sprinkle with garlic salt, lemon juice and rind, liquid smoke, Worcestershire sauce and more salt and pepper. Deglaze the skillet, in which the dove were browned, with the sherry and water. Pour over dove. Bake, covered, at 325 degrees for 1½ hours.

Yield: 6 servings   Claire Buescher

Dove Breast Stroganoff

12	to 18 dove breasts	½	cup sauterne
	salt and pepper to taste	½	teaspoon oregano
1	medium onion, chopped	½	teaspoon rosemary
2	tablespoons butter	1	teaspoon bottled brown
1	(10¾ ounce) can cream of		bouquet sauce
	celery soup	1	cup sour cream

Arrange birds in a 13x9x2-inch baking dish. Do not crowd. Salt and pepper dove. Sauté onion in butter. Add celery soup, sauterne, oregano, rosemary and bouquet sauce. Pour over meat. Bake, covered, at 325 degrees for 1¼ hours, turning birds occasionally. Stir in sour cream. Bake, uncovered, an additional 30 minutes.

Yield: 4 to 8 servings   Martha Grow

Marinated Wild Game

1½	cups vegetable oil	½	cup wine vinegar
¾	cup soy sauce	1½	teaspoons parsley flakes
¼	cup Worcestershire sauce	1	clove garlic, crushed
2	tablespoons dry mustard	25	to 30 cleaned dove
2¼	teaspoons salt	15	bacon slices, cut in half
⅓	cup lemon juice		

Mix oil, soy sauce, Worcestershire sauce, dry mustard, salt, lemon juice, vinegar, parsley and garlic until well blended. Place marinade and 25 to 30 cleaned dove in sealable plastic bags for 6 to 8 hours, turning occasionally. Remove dove from marinade and wrap ½ piece of bacon around each. Place on grill over medium heat and cook for 25 to 30 minutes or until bacon is done, turning halfway through.

Yield: 6 to 8 servings   Vickie Wilkinson

Other wild game can be substituted for dove.

Bacon Dove Bake

6	dove breasts		garlic powder to taste
	salt and pepper to taste	6	slices of bacon

Sprinkle each dove breast with salt, pepper and garlic powder. Wrap each dove with one slice of bacon. Wrap dove in aluminum foil. Bake at 250 degrees for 2 hours.

Yield: 2 servings   Pam Mackey

Dove can also be grilled. Secure bacon with toothpick. Place directly on grill and cook approximately 15 minutes, turning occasionally.

Wild Duck In Grand Marnier Sauce

6	ducks	½	cup sugar
	lemon juice as needed	1	tablespoon wine vinegar
18	celery leaves	2	oranges, reserve rind
1	onion, sliced	½	cup Grand Marnier
1½	cups dry white wine	1	cup water
1	tablespoon honey		salt and pepper to taste

Trim the wings and tips and cut off the necks of ducks. Wash thoroughly inside and out with cold water; dry. Rub cavities with lemon juice and in each put a few celery leaves and onion slices. Place ducks, breast up, on rack in 13x9x2-inch baking pan. Bake, uncovered, at 325 degrees for ½ hour. Drain fat from pan and add wine. Baste ducks and continue cooking 1½ hours, basting with pan juices every 20 minutes. If a very crisp skin is desired, brush ducks with honey 15 minutes before removing from oven and do not baste again. Transfer ducks to hot serving dish. Skim excess fat from juices in basting pan. In heavy saucepan, combine sugar and wine vinegar. Cook mixture over medium heat until sugar melts and begins to caramelize. Add juice of 2 oranges, Grand Marnier and grated rind of 1 orange. Stir well and cook 5 minutes. Combine this mixture with juices in roasting pan. In a small saucepan, cook ¼ cup orange peel, cut into thin strips, in 1 cup of water for 5 minutes, then drain. Add cooked orange strips to other mixture. Season with salt and pepper to taste and pour sauce over ducks or serve separately.

Yield: 4 servings   Phyllis Drury

Mary Caroline's Duck Recipe

4 ducks	1½ cups butter
1 celery rib, quartered	½ cup bourbon
½ to 1 apple, sliced and divided	⅔ cup sherry, pale and dry
2 (10½ ounce) cans consommé	1 (5 ounce) jar currant jelly
1 can water	4 tablespoons Worcestershire sauce
	cornstarch or arrowroot

Stuff 4 ducks with celery and sliced apples. Place ducks in a roaster. Pour consommé and water over ducks. Cover and bake at 350 degrees for 3 hours. Remove meat from bones and place in 3-quart rectangular greased casserole dish. In medium saucepan, melt butter. Add bourbon, sherry, jelly and Worcestershire sauce. Heat mixture and pour over ducks. May need to be thickened with cornstarch or arrowroot.

Yield: 6 to 8 servings   Marilyn Kemper

Delicious served over wild rice.

Buttermilk Pheasant

1 pheasant	self-rising flour as needed
1 quart buttermilk	oil as needed
freshly ground pepper to taste	

Cut up pheasant for frying (same as chicken). Marinate in buttermilk and pepper overnight. Drain excess buttermilk, then flour. Cook in deep frying pan with hot oil until golden brown.

Yield: 4 servings   Pat Chitty

Pheasant cooks faster than chicken.

 ## White Oak Hunting Lodge Quail

24	quail	1	cup sherry
2	cups butter	½	cup currant jelly

Place quail in 13x9x2-inch casserole dish, breast side up. Melt butter and add sherry and jelly. Pour over quail and bake, uncovered, at 250 degrees for approximately 3 hours. Baste while cooking.

Yield: 12 to 14 servings   Suzanne Sullivan

Smothered Quail

	salt and pepper to taste	½	cup butter
	all-purpose flour as needed		garlic powder to taste
12	quail	½	to 1 cup white
	vegetable oil		Chardonnay wine

Salt, pepper and flour quail, then fry in oil. Drain excess oil from pan after removing the quail and placing them in a Dutch oven. Make a thin flour and water gravy in frying pan. Add butter, garlic powder and wine. Pour over quail. Bake, covered, at 350 degrees for 1 hour.

Yield: 4 to 6 servings   Denise Retterbush

Quail Casserole

2	cups cooked quail, boned	1	(10¾ ounce) can cream of
¼	cup onion, chopped fine		chicken soup
1	cup cooked rice	1	section round buttery
⅔	cup chopped celery		crackers, crushed
½	cup mayonnaise	½	cup margarine, melted
3	hard boiled eggs, chopped		

Mix quail, onion, rice, celery, mayonnaise, eggs and soup. Place in 2-quart casserole dish. Combine crackers and margarine. Spread over top of casserole. Bake, uncovered, at 350 degrees for 30 to 40 minutes. Serve hot.

Yield: 8 servings   Vickie Wilkinson

Chicken or turkey could be substituted for quail.

Mama's Quail

salt and pepper	margarine
all-purpose flour	cream sherry
quail	water

Salt, pepper and flour the quail. Melt margarine in an iron frying pan. Brown the quail. Place the quail in a Dutch oven. Pour the margarine from the skillet over the birds. Mix equal parts sherry and water. Pour over quail. Bake, uncovered, at 250 degrees for 3 hours. Baste with the liquid while cooking. If the quail starts to dry out, add more sherry and water. This recipe can be adjusted for a small or large crowd.

Yield: determined by number of quail   Vickie Wilkinson

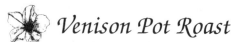 # Venison Pot Roast

1	(6 to 8 pound) venison roast	1	tablespoon salt
3	to 6 slices bacon	10	whole black peppercorns
2	cups Burgundy wine	2	bay leaves
½	cup cider vinegar	1	clove garlic, crushed
2	celery tops	1	cup water
1	medium onion, sliced	¼	cup flour
4	slices lemon	2	tablespoons salad oil
1	large carrot, pared and sliced		

Wipe roast with damp paper towels. Arrange bacon slices over surface of meat. Combine wine, cider vinegar, celery tops, onion, lemon slices, carrot slices, salt, peppercorns, bay leaves, garlic and water. Pour over roast. Cover and refrigerate for 24 hours, turning occasionally. Remove roast from marinade. Coat with flour and place in Dutch oven. Reserve 2 cups of the marinade. Brown roast on all sides in hot oil. Add 1 cup of the marinade and bring to boil. Reduce heat and simmer, covered, for 4 hours or until roast is very tender. Baste occasionally during cooking with pan liquid. Add remaining 1 cup of marinade as needed.

Yield: 6 to 8 servings   Suzanne Sullivan

Venison Steak

2 to 3 pounds venison steak	1 cup flour
½ cup vinegar	pepper to taste
1 cup water	garlic salt to taste
salt, approximately 4 tablespoons	shortening as needed

Pound steak until tender. Soak in vinegar, water and salt for 1 hour. Remove from liquid and dry. Dip in flour, pepper and garlic salt. Fry in shortening over medium heat until done.

Yield: 6 to 8 servings
Suzanne Sullivan

Grilled Lamb With Rosemary

1 fresh leg of lamb, boned and butterflied

Spread meat out in one large piece. Some areas will be thicker than the rest. Cut off as much of outside fat as possible. Shave off the fill (membrane) and cartilage bone. Clean up as much as possible without letting meat become detached. Lay meat, bone side up; will form two large lobes. Slash lobes 1 to 2 inches deep, depending on thickness, to allow even cooking. Use long skewers to keep shape.

Marinade:

4 tablespoons olive oil	juice and grated rind of
2 tablespoons soy sauce	½ lemon
1 or 2 cloves garlic, pressed	1 teaspoon rosemary, crumbled

Mix all ingredients. Rub meat with marinade and place in a marinade container. Reserve half of marinade and pour remainder over meat. Refrigerate for several hours before grilling or marinate overnight, turning meat often. Remove from refrigerator 30 minutes before grilling. Use gas grill on medium to low heat. Turn every 5 minutes and brush with reserved marinade for up to 45 minutes, depending on thickness and how rare desired.

Yield: 6 to 8 servings
Pat Chitty

This is better cooked medium rare instead of well-done.

233

Veal Roll Ups

2 (4 each) packages veal scallopini	1 (16 ounce) can tomatoes, crushed
8 slices bacon	1 teaspoon parsley
1 small onion, diced	pinch of basil
1 clove garlic, pressed	pinch of oregano
oil as needed	1 chicken bouillon cube
	¼ cup red wine

Cut veal in half lengthwise. Place bacon on top of veal and roll up with bacon inside and secure with toothpick. Sauté onion and garlic in small amount of oil in an electric frying pan. Add tomatoes, parsley, basil, oregano, bouillon and wine. Bring to boil at 250 degrees, then turn down to simmer for approximately 20 minutes. Water may need to be added. Add roll-ups and bring to boil on 250 degree heat for 2 minutes. Then turn over for a few more minutes. Reduce heat and simmer for 5 minutes. Serve with rice.

Yield: 6 servings   Pat Chitty

Veal Scallopini

½ pound veal cutlets, ¼ inch thick	vegetable cooking spray
1½ tablespoons all-purpose flour	2 teaspoons vegetable oil
¼ teaspoon salt	⅓ cup Chablis
¼ teaspoon freshly ground pepper	2 tablespoons lemon juice
	lemon slice, optional

Trim fat from veal. Place on sheet of waxed paper. Flatten to ⅛ inch thick. Cut into 2-inch pieces. Combine flour, salt and pepper. Dredge veal in flour mixture. Coat large skillet with cooking spray. Add oil and place over medium to high heat until hot. Add veal and cook 1 minute on each side or until lightly browned. Remove veal from skillet and set aside. Pour wine and lemon juice into skillet; bring to boil. Return veal to skillet, turning to coat with sauce. Reduce heat to simmer 1 to 2 minutes until sauce is slightly thickened. Garnish with lemon twist.

Yield: 2 servings   Pat Chitty

Serve with new potatoes and carrots or pasta.

Sweet Treasures

Valdosta City Hall
Built 1910

Alice's Apple Cake

1½ cups vegetable oil	½ teaspoon salt
2 cups sugar	2 teaspoons vanilla
3 eggs	3 cups peeled and chopped
3 cups all-purpose flour	apples
1 teaspoon baking soda	1 cup chopped pecans

Preheat oven to 325 degrees. Mix oil and sugar. Add eggs, flour, soda, salt and vanilla. Beat until well blended. Stir in apples and nuts. Place in greased and floured 10-inch tube pan. Bake at 325 degrees for 1½ hours. While cake is baking, prepare the following topping.

Topping:

1 cup brown sugar	½ cup margarine
½ cup milk	

Mix brown sugar, milk and margarine in small saucepan. Heat and stir until blended. Boil 2 minutes. Have topping ready as cake is removed from oven. Pour over hot cake in pan and allow it to soak in. Let cake cool completely before removing from pan.

Yield: 1 cake   Denise Retterbush

Miss Morris' Old-Fashioned Applesauce Cake

2 cups all-purpose flour	1 cup sugar
½ teaspoon salt	2 eggs
1 teaspoon baking soda	1 cup cold applesauce
1 teaspoon cinnamon	¾ cup raisins
½ teaspoon cloves	½ cup chopped walnuts or
½ teaspoon nutmeg	pecans
½ cup vegetable shortening	

Sift together flour, salt, soda, cinnamon, cloves and nutmeg and set aside. In large mixing bowl, cream shortening and sugar. Add eggs; beat 1½ minutes. Add cold applesauce, raisins and nuts. Add sifted ingredients to mixture and mix well. Pour in greased and floured 10-inch tube pan. Bake at 350 degrees for 50 to 55 minutes.

Yield: 1 cake   Sue Clary

May be frosted with cream cheese frosting.

Fresh Apple Spice Cake

1½ cups vegetable oil
2 cups sugar
3 eggs
3 cups sifted all-purpose flour
1½ teaspoons cinnamon
1 teaspoon salt
1 teaspoon baking soda
2 teaspoons vanilla
3 cups peeled and chopped apples
1 cup chopped pecans

Combine oil, sugar and eggs; beat 3 minutes with electric mixer. Sift flour, cinnamon, salt and soda together; add to oil mixture. Add vanilla, apples and nuts. Pour into greased and floured 10-inch tube pan. Bake at 350 degrees for 1 hour and 20 minutes. May be made as a 13x9x2-inch sheet cake and baked for approximately 45 minutes to 1 hour, depending on oven.

A good snack cake without the icing or ice with the following recipe.

Icing:

1 (8 ounce) package cream cheese, softened
1 teaspoon vanilla
¼ cup margarine or butter, softened
¾ (16 ounce) box confectioners' sugar

Combine cream cheese, vanilla, margarine and sugar. Spread on cooled cake.

Yield: 1 cake

Sally Kurrie

Dodie's Applesauce Cake

2 cups sugar	1¾ teaspoons baking soda
1 cup vegetable oil	3 teaspoons cinnamon
4 eggs, beaten	1 teaspoon nutmeg
2 cups sifted all-purpose flour	pinch of salt
	2 cups applesauce

Mix sugar and oil; add eggs. Beat well. Add flour, soda, cinnamon, nutmeg and salt. Beat well. Add applesauce. Mix well. Place in 3 greased and floured 9-inch cake pans. Bake at 350 degrees for 25 to 30 minutes.

Cream Cheese Frosting:

1 (8 ounce) package cream cheese, softened	2 teaspoons vanilla
½ cup margarine, softened	1 cup chopped pecans for garnish, optional
1 (16 ounce) box 4X confectioners' sugar	

Beat cream cheese and margarine together until creamy. Gradually add confectioners' sugar. Add vanilla; mix. Frost cake and garnish with approximately 1 cup pecans.

Yield: 1 three-layer cake   Nancy Parris

Blueberry Cake

1 butter recipe yellow cake mix	1 cup sour cream
1 (8 ounce) container frozen non-dairy whipped topping, thawed	1 cup confectioners' sugar
	1 teaspoon vanilla
	1 (21 ounce) can blueberry pie filling

Prepare cake according to directions and bake in three greased and floured 9-inch cake pans. To make icing, mix non-dairy whipped topping, sour cream, confectioners' sugar and vanilla. Spread between the layers then cover with ½ cup blueberry filling. Ice sides and top of cake. Place remaining filling in center of top layer and let drip over sides. The longer it stands, the more moist the cake will be. Cover and refrigerate.

Yield: 1 three-layer cake   Mary Corbett

May use coconut instead of blueberries.

239

Carrot Cake

2	cups all-purpose flour	3	cups finely grated raw
2	teaspoons baking soda		carrots
1	teaspoon salt	2	cups sugar
1½	cups vegetable oil	2	teaspoons cinnamon
4	eggs, beaten		

Sift together flour, soda and salt. Add oil, eggs and carrots; mix well, for 2 to 3 minutes on medium-high speed of electric mixer. Add sugar and cinnamon; beat well, 1 to 2 minutes. Grease and flour three 8-inch cake pans, pour in batter. Bake at 350 degrees for 40 minutes or until center is firm. Also makes 60 cupcakes that require 20 minutes at 350 degrees. Cool and frost with the following icing.

Icing:

1	(16 ounce) box	2	teaspoons vanilla
	confectioners' sugar	1	cup chopped pecans
½	cup margarine, softened	1	(3½ ounce) can shredded
1	(8 ounce) package cream		coconut, optional
	cheese, softened		

Cream margarine and sugar. Add cream cheese, vanilla and pecans. Mix and add coconut. Spread evenly between layers and on outside of cake.

Yield: 1 three-layer cake or 60 cupcakes   Pam Woodward

Vanilla Wafer Cake

1	cup margarine, softened	½	cup milk
2	cups sugar	1	(7 ounce) package flaked
6	eggs		coconut
1	(12 ounce) box vanilla	1	cup chopped pecans
	wafers, crushed		

Cream butter; add sugar and beat until smooth. Add eggs one at a time, beating well after each. Add vanilla wafers, alternating with milk. Add coconut and pecans. Pour batter into greased and floured tube pan; may use 13x9x2-inch pan. Bake at 275 degrees for 1½ hours.

Yield: 1 cake   Debbie Davis

Good as a coffee cake, too.

240

Glazed Almond Amaretto Cheesecake

Topping:

½ cup sugar
¼ cup water
1 cup sliced almonds

1 teaspoon Amaretto, or other almond flavored liqueur

In small saucepan, combine sugar and water. Bring to a boil and boil for 2 minutes. Remove from heat; stir in sliced almonds and 1 teaspoon Amaretto. Remove almonds to waxed paper with slotted spoon and separate. Let almonds cool.

Crust:

2 cups graham cracker crumbs

¼ cup finely chopped almonds
⅓ cup butter, melted

Preheat oven to 350 degrees. In medium bowl, combine graham cracker crumbs, chopped almonds and butter. Press in bottom and 1½-inches up the sides of 10-inch springform pan.

Filling:

2 (8 ounce) packages cream cheese, softened
1 cup sugar
3 eggs
1 cup sour cream

½ cup whipping cream
¼ cup Amaretto, or other almond flavored liqueur
½ teaspoon almond extract

In large bowl, combine cream cheese and sugar. Beat until light and fluffy. Add eggs one at a time, beating well after each addition. Add sour cream, whipping cream, ¼ cup Amaretto and almond extract; blend well. Pour into prepared crust. Bake at 350 degrees for 60 to 75 minutes or until center is set. To minimize cracking: place shallow pan half-full of hot water on lower rack during baking. Arrange prepared almonds in 2-inch wide circle around outer edge of cheesecake for last 15 minutes of baking. Carefully remove sides of pan; cool. Refrigerate several hours or overnight before serving.

Yield: 1 cake
Tonya Smith

Cuisine D'or Oreo Cheesecake

Crust:

1¼ cups graham cracker crumbs

¼ cup firmly packed light brown sugar

⅓ cup unsalted butter, melted

1 teaspoon cinnamon

Blend graham cracker crumbs, butter, brown sugar and cinnamon. Press onto bottom and sides of 9 or 10-inch springform pan. Refrigerate until firm, approximately 30 minutes.

Cookie Filling:

4 (8 ounce) packages cream cheese, softened

1½ cups sugar, separated

2 tablespoons all-purpose flour

4 extra large eggs

2 large egg yolks

⅓ cup whipping cream

2 teaspoons vanilla, separated

2 cups sour cream

1½ cups coarsely chopped chocolate sandwich cookies

Preheat oven to 425 degrees. Beat cream cheese in large bowl on lowest speed until smooth. Beat in 1¼ cups sugar and flour until well blended. Beat in eggs and egg yolks until smooth. Stir in whipping cream and 1 teaspoon vanilla. Pour half of batter into prepared crust. Sprinkle with chopped cookies. Pour remaining batter over, smoothing with spatula. Bake at 425 degrees for 15 minutes. Reduce oven temperature to 225 degrees. Bake at 225 degrees for 50 minutes, covering top loosely with foil, if browning too quickly. Raise oven temperature to 350 degrees. Blend sour cream, remaining sugar and remaining vanilla in small bowl. Spread over cake. Bake 7 additional minutes. Remove from oven and refrigerate immediately. Cover with plastic wrap and chill overnight.

Swiss Fudge Glaze:

1 cup whipping cream

8 ounces semi-sweet chocolate, chopped

1 teaspoon vanilla

5 chocolate sandwich cookies, halved crosswise

1 maraschino cherry, halved

(Cuisine D'or Oreo Cheesecake, continued on next page)

(Cuisine D'or Oreo Cheesecake, continued)

Scald cream in heavy medium saucepan over high heat. Add chocolate and vanilla, stir 1 minute. Remove from heat; stir until chocolate is melted. Refrigerate glaze for 10 minutes. Set cake on platter and remove springform. Pour glaze over top of cake. Using pastry brush, smooth top and sides. Arrange cookie halves cut side down around outer edge of cake. Place cherry halves in center. Refrigerate cake until ready to serve.

Yield: 10 servings   Mary Corbett

This cake should be prepared one day ahead and glazed shortly before serving.

Everyone's Favorite Chocolate Cheesecake

2	cups all-purpose flour	1	teaspoon baking soda
2	cups sugar	½	cup buttermilk
1	teaspoon salt	2	eggs
1	cup margarine	1	tablespoon vanilla
4	tablespoons cocoa	1	tablespoon cinnamon
14	tablespoons water		

Stir flour, sugar and salt together. Bring to boil margarine, cocoa and water and pour over flour mixture. Mix in soda, buttermilk, eggs, vanilla and cinnamon and mix well. Pour into greased and floured 16x11x2-inch pan. Bake 20 minutes at 400 degrees. Five minutes before cake is done, prepare following frosting.

Frosting:

½	cup margarine	1	(16 ounce) box
4	tablespoons cocoa		confectioners' sugar
6	tablespoons milk	1	teaspoon vanilla
		1	cup chopped pecans

Bring to a boil margarine, cocoa and milk. Remove from heat; add confectioners' sugar, vanilla and chopped nuts. Mix and pour over cake immediately upon taking from oven.

Yield: one 16x11x2-inch sheet cake   Suzanne Sullivan

Nutty Pumpkin Cheesecake

Crust:

1 (6 ounce) package
   Zwieback toast, crumbled

¼ cup light brown sugar
6 tablespoons butter, melted

Toss together toast crumbs, brown sugar and melted butter. Press firmly and evenly into the bottom of a 9-inch springform pan and chill.

Filling:

3 (8 ounce) packages cream cheese, softened
½ cup sugar
1 cup light brown sugar
4 large eggs

1 (16 ounce) can pumpkin
1 teaspoon cinnamon
½ teaspoon ginger
¼ teaspoon cloves
1 cup heavy cream

Beat cream cheese until very smooth. Gradually add sugar and brown sugar, beating until mixed. Beat in eggs, one at a time. Beat in pumpkin, cinnamon, ginger, cloves and cream. Pour into prepared pan. Bake at 325 degrees for 1 hour and 40 minutes.

Topping:

6 tablespoons butter
1 cup light brown sugar
1 cup coarsely chopped pecans

whipped cream or whipped topping for garnish

Combine butter and sugar; mix until crumbly. Stir in nuts. At the end of baking time, sprinkle evenly over cheesecake. Bake an additional 10 minutes at 325 degrees. Cool cake. Refrigerate at least several hours or overnight. Garnish with whipped cream or whipped topping.

Yield: 1 cake

Cathy Alday

Pumpkin Marble Cheesecake

Crust:

1½ cups gingersnap crumbs	⅓ cup margarine, melted
½ cup finely chopped pecans	

Combine crumbs, pecans and margarine; press into bottom and ½-inch up sides of a 9-inch springform pan. Bake at 350 degrees for 10 minutes.

Filling:

2 (8 ounce) packages cream cheese, softened	3 eggs
	1 cup canned pumpkin
¾ cup sugar, separated	¾ teaspoon cinnamon
1 teaspoon vanilla	¼ teaspoon ground nutmeg

Combine cream cheese, ½ cup sugar, and vanilla, mixing at medium speed until well blended. Add eggs one at a time mixing well after each addition. Reserve 1 cup batter. Add remaining sugar, pumpkin, cinnamon and nutmeg to remaining batter; mix well. Alternately layer pumpkin and cream cheese batters over crust. Cut through batters with a knife several times for marbled effect. Bake at 350 degrees for 55 minutes. Loosen cake from rim of pan; cool before removing rim of pan. Chill.

Yield: 10 to 12 servings   Charlotte Thomas

Company's Coming Chess Cake

1 box yellow cake mix	3 eggs
½ cup margarine, melted	1 (16 ounce) box 4X confectioners' sugar
1 (8 ounce) package cream cheese, softened	

Mix together cake mix, margarine and 1 egg; press into bottom of greased 13x9x2-inch cake pan. Mix together cream cheese, 2 eggs and confectioners' sugar; pour on top of first layer. Bake at 350 degrees for 45 minutes. Do not overcook. After cake has cooled, cut into small squares to serve.

Yield: 24 to 28 squares   Donna Clary

Miss Morris' Best German Chocolate Cake

1	(8 ounce) package German chocolate	2½	cups sifted cake flour
½	cup boiling water	½	teaspoon salt
1	cup butter	1	teaspoon baking soda
2	cups sugar	1	cup buttermilk
4	eggs, separated	1	teaspoon vanilla

Melt chocolate in boiling water; cool. Cream butter and sugar until fluffy. Add egg yolks, one at a time, beating well after each. Add melted chocolate; mix well. Sift flour, salt and soda. Add flour alternately with buttermilk to chocolate mixture; beat until smooth. Beat egg whites until stiff. Fold in stiffly beaten egg whites and vanilla. Pour into three well greased and floured 9-inch layer pans. Bake at 350 degrees for 30 to 40 minutes. Cool and frost.

Frosting:

2	cups evaporated milk	2	teaspoons vanilla
2	cups sugar	2	cups chopped pecans
1	cup butter or margarine	2	cups shredded coconut
6	egg yolks		

Combine milk, sugar, butter or margarine and egg yolks. Cook until mixture comes to a boil. Reduce heat to low and stir constantly until thickened, approximately 25 minutes. Remove from heat and add vanilla; mix well. Stir in pecans and coconut. Cool before frosting the cake.

Yield: 1 three-layer cake   Sue Clary

 ## *Dottie's Chocolate Layer Cake*

½	cup butter, softened (no margarine, please)	½	cup milk
		1¾	cups cake flour
1	cup sugar	2½	teaspoons baking powder
2	eggs	1	teaspoon vanilla

Grease and flour six to eight (or up to twenty) 9-inch round cake pans. The more layers the better the cake! Cream butter and sugar. Add eggs, one at a time. Add milk and flour (with baking powder added), alternately. Add vanilla and mix well. Pour in prepared pans. Bake at 375 degrees for approximately 30 minutes. Frost with following recipe.

Icing:

2	cups sugar	½	cup butter
½	cup cocoa	1	teaspoon vanilla
⅔	cup milk		

Depending on the number of layers this recipe may need to be doubled. Sift sugar and cocoa together. Add milk. Cook over medium heat until it comes to a boil. Cook 4 minutes or until forms soft ball when dropped in cold water. Add butter and vanilla. Beat until spreading consistency.

Yield: 1 multi-layer cake   Dottie Keller

Popcorn Cake

¼	cup vegetable oil	4	quarts popped popcorn, microwave or regular
½	cup margarine		
1	(16 ounce) package marshmallows	1	pound salted peanuts
		1	pound plain M&Ms

Combine oil, margarine and marshmallows in saucepan; cook over medium heat until marshmallows and butter melt, stirring often. Cool 1 minute. Combine popcorn, peanuts and M&Ms in large bowl. Add marshmallow mixture, stirring until well blended. Press approximately half of popcorn mixture into greased 10-inch tube pan, packing well. Press remaining popcorn mixture into pan. Let set approximately 2 hours. Invert popcorn cake from pan onto cake plate. You may have to set the pan in a little warm water before inverting.

Yield: 1 cake   Denise Rountree

Kids love this recipe! Enjoy!

Unforgettable Coconut Cake

2½	cups sifted cake flour	1½	cups sugar
2½	teaspoons baking powder	½	cup shortening
½	teaspoon salt	¼	cup butter, softened
1	cup milk		Lemon-Apricot Filling,
¼	cup water		recipe follows
1½	teaspoons vanilla		Fluffy White Frosting,
4	egg whites, room		recipe follows
	temperature	3	to 4 cups shredded coconut

Combine flour, baking powder and salt; set aside. Combine milk, water and vanilla; set aside. Beat egg whites until foamy; gradually add ¼ cup sugar, 1 tablespoon at a time, beating until soft peaks form; set aside. Cream shortening, butter and 1¼ cups sugar in large mixing bowl; beat at medium speed of electric mixer for 3 minutes. Add flour mixture alternately with milk mixture, beginning and ending with flour. Mix after each addition. Fold in beaten egg whites. Pour batter into three greased and floured 9-inch round cake pans. Bake at 350 degrees for 15 to 20 minutes or until toothpick inserted in center comes out clean. Cool in pans 10 minutes; remove from pans and let cool completely. Spread Lemon-Apricot Filling between layers and Fluffy White Frosting on top and sides of cake. Sprinkle with coconut.

Lemon-Apricot Filling:

2	cups dried apricots, diced	⅓	cup lemon juice
⅔	cup sugar	1	tablespoon butter
1	tablespoon cornstarch	2	egg yolks, beaten
⅛	teaspoon salt	1	tablespoon grated lemon
¾	cup water		rind

Combine apricots, sugar, cornstarch, salt, water, lemon juice and butter in medium saucepan; stir well. Bring to a boil over medium heat, stirring constantly, and boil 3 to 4 minutes or until thickened. Reduce heat; cook 1 minute, stirring constantly. Gradually stir one-fourth of hot mixture into egg yolks. Add back to remaining hot mixture, stirring constantly. Remove from heat; stir in lemon rind. Let cool; cover and chill 1 hour.

(Unforgettable Coconut Cake, continued on next page)

(Unforgettable Coconut Cake, continued)

Fluffy White Frosting:

1 cup sugar	⅛ teaspoon cream of tartar
¼ cup cold water	⅛ teaspoon salt
2 egg whites	1½ teaspoons vanilla

Combine sugar, water, egg whites, cream of tartar and salt in top of double boiler. Beat at low speed for 30 seconds or just until blended. Place over boiling water; beat constantly on high speed for 7 minutes or until stiff peaks form. Remove from heat. Add vanilla; beat 2 minutes or until frosting is thick enough to spread.

Yield: 1 three-layer cake   Mary Corbett

Dirt Cake

1 (20 ounce) package chocolate sandwich cookies	3⅓ cups milk
¼ cup butter, softened	2 (3⅓ ounce) packages vanilla instant pudding
1 cup confectioners' sugar	1 (8 ounce) package frozen whipped topping, thawed
1 (8 ounce) package cream cheese, softened	

Crush cookies in food processor. Cream together butter, sugar and cream cheese. In another bowl, blend well the milk, instant pudding and whipped topping. Combine with butter, sugar and cream cheese mixture. In a 10 to 12 cup container, make thin alternate layers of cookie crumbs and cream cheese pudding mixture, starting and ending with cookies. Freeze or chill.

Yield: servings for 10 to 12 hungry adults   Chris Roan

This is a great cake for a child's party. Freeze it in a child's clean plastic bucket and serve with a clean sand shovel.

Variation: For "Sand" cake, use vanilla sandwich cookies instead of chocolate sandwich cookies.

 *Fruit Cake*

1	pound chopped candied cherries	1	cup butter, softened
1	pound chopped candied pineapple	1	cup sugar
		5	eggs
1	pound chopped white raisins	2	teaspoons vanilla
		1	teaspoon nutmeg
4	cups chopped pecans or walnuts	1	teaspoon cinnamon
		1	orange rind, grated
2	cups all-purpose flour	1	lemon rind, grated

Chop fruit and nuts; dredge with part of flour. Mix ingredients in order: butter, sugar, eggs, flour, cherries, pineapple, raisins, nuts, vanilla, nutmeg, cinnamon, orange rind, lemon rind. Pour in greased and floured 10-inch tube cake pan or three 8½x4½x2½-inch loaf pans. Bake at 300 degrees for 2 hours or longer.

Yield: 1 tube cake or 3 loaf cakes   Jan Carter

Pistachio Cake

1	box white cake mix	1	(3 ounce) package pistachio instant pudding
¾	cup vegetable oil		
¾	cup water	¼	cup chopped pecans
4	eggs		

Combine cake mix, oil, water, eggs and pudding. Beat 4 minutes at medium speed. Place nuts in bottom of greased and floured Bundt cake pan. Pour in batter. Bake at 350 degrees for 35 to 40 minutes. Cool 10 minutes. Remove from pan and ice immediately with following recipe.

Icing:

½	cup water	2	cups confectioners' sugar
1	tablespoon butter, melted	½	teaspoon vanilla

Beat together water, melted butter, sugar and vanilla with a fork. While cake is hot, punch holes over top of cake with fork. Spoon icing over cake, allowing it to run down into holes. Pry holes open with fork if necessary.

Yield: 1 Bundt cake   Vallye Blanton

Pear Cake With Caramel Drizzle

3	eggs, beaten	1	teaspoon baking soda
1¾	cups sugar	2	teaspoons baking powder
1	cup vegetable oil	1	teaspoon salt
1	tablespoon vanilla	3	cups peeled, chopped pears
1	teaspoon allspice		or apples
1½	cups all-purpose flour	1	cup chopped pecans
1	cup whole wheat flour		

Combine eggs, sugar and oil. Mix on medium speed of mixer. Add vanilla, allspice, flour, whole wheat flour, baking soda, baking powder and salt. Stir in pears and pecans. Pour into greased and floured Bundt pan. Bake at 375 degrees for 50 minutes or until toothpick inserted in center comes out clean. Cool 10 minutes. Remove from pan and cool completely. Glaze with the following caramel drizzle.

Caramel Drizzle:

¼	cup butter	1	cup sifted confectioners'
¼	cup brown sugar		sugar
2	tablespoons milk	½	teaspoon vanilla
		½	teaspoon salt

Melt butter until light brown; add brown sugar. Melt and remove from heat. Stir in milk, stirring constantly. Add sugar, vanilla and salt; beat with mixer on medium speed until it reaches a glaze consistency. Pour on cooled cake.

Yield: 1 cake
Lisa Harris

Delicious as a breakfast cake.

Analease's Poppy Seed Cake

1	box white cake mix	½	cup sweetened pineapple juice
1	(5 ounce) package vanilla instant pudding	1	tablespoon almond flavoring
5	eggs	1	tablespoon poppy seeds
½	cup oil		sugar for topping
½	cup water		

Prepare tube pan by cutting out, greasing and flouring a paper liner for bottom of pan. Grease and flour rest of pan. Mix cake mix, pudding, eggs, oil, water, juice, flavoring and poppy seeds for 5 minutes. Pour into prepared pan. Bake at 300 degrees for 50 minutes. Check for doneness. Take from oven and sprinkle sugar on top while warm. Cool 10 minutes then remove from pan.

Yield: 1 cake

Carol Giles

Mother's Pound Cake

1	cup butter, softened	1	teaspoon almond extract
3	cups sugar	½	teaspoon baking powder
½	cup vegetable shortening	¼	teaspoon salt
5	eggs	3	cups cake flour
1	teaspoon vanilla extract	1	cup milk

Cream butter, sugar and shortening 100 strokes. Add eggs one at a time, beating well after each addition. Sift baking powder and salt with flour. Add to creamed mixture alternating with milk, mixing well after each addition. Stir in vanilla and almond extract. Bake in a greased and floured 10-inch tube pan at 325 degrees for 1 hour and 15 minutes or until tester comes out clean.

Yield: 1 cake

Cheryl Arnold

Buttered Rum Pound Cake

1	cup butter, softened	1	(8 ounce) carton sour
3	cups sugar, divided		cream
6	eggs, separated	1	teaspoon vanilla extract
3	cups all-purpose flour	1	teaspoon lemon extract
¼	teaspoon baking soda		

Cream butter; gradually beat in 2½ cups of sugar. Add egg yolks one at a time, beating well after each. Combine flour and baking soda; add to creamed mixture alternately with sour cream, beginning and ending with flour mixture. Stir in flavorings. Beat egg whites at room temperature until foamy; gradually add ½ cup sugar, one tablespoon at a time, beating until stiff peaks form. Fold into batter. Pour into a greased and floured 10-inch tube pan. Bake at 325 degrees for 1 to 1½ hours or until wooden pick comes out clean. Cool in pan 10 to 15 minutes. Remove from pan and place on serving plate. While warm, prick cake surface with wooden pick or meat fork. Pour warm buttered rum glaze over cake. Allow cake to stand several hours or overnight before serving.

Buttered Rum Glaze:

6	tablespoons butter	3	tablespoons water
3	tablespoons rum	½	cup chopped walnuts
¾	cup sugar		

Combine butter, rum, sugar and water in a small saucepan. Bring to a boil. Boil for 3 minutes, stirring constantly. Remove from heat and stir in walnuts. Pour warm glaze over cake.

Yield: 1 cake   Cheryl Arnold

Glazed Chocolate Pound Cake

3 cups cake flour	3 cups sugar
1 teaspoon baking powder	1 teaspoon vanilla
½ cup cocoa	5 eggs
1 cup butter, softened	1¼ cups milk
½ cup vegetable shortening	

Preheat oven to 300 degrees. Sift cake flour, baking powder and cocoa together. Cream butter, shortening and sugar. Add eggs one at a time, beating well after each. Add vanilla. Add dry ingredients alternately with milk. Lightly grease and flour a 9-inch tube pan; pour in batter. Bake at 300 degrees for 1 hour and 22 minutes. Cool 5 to 10 minutes in pan. Remove from pan and cool on wire rack. Glaze.

Glaze:

½ cup vegetable shortening	¼ cup cocoa
2 cups sugar	1 tablespoon vanilla
⅔ cup milk	½ cup chopped pecans

Melt shortening in pan, add sugar, milk and cocoa. Boil hard for 2 minutes, stirring constantly. Remove from heat; add vanilla. Cool 5 minutes. Beat until creamy then add pecans or you may sprinkle pecans on top of iced cake. Cool glaze. Spread glaze over cooled pound cake.

Yield: 1 cake

Pat Chitty

Lemon Pound Cake

2 cups butter, softened	9 eggs, room temperature
3 cups sugar	1 (1 ounce) bottle pure lemon
3 cups cake flour	extract

Grease and flour a 10-inch tube pan. Cream butter and sugar until mixture turns a white color. Add cake flour, 1 cup at a time, alternating with 3 eggs at a time. Add lemon extract. Place in cold oven. Bake at 325 degrees for 1 hour and 20 minutes.

Yield: 1 cake

Scarlett Cooper

Crunchy Top Pound Cake

½ cup butter, softened
1 cup margarine, softened
1 (8 ounce) package cream
   cheese, softened

3 cups sugar
6 eggs
3 cups all-purpose flour
2 teaspoons vanilla

Cream butter, margarine and cream cheese together. Add sugar, eggs and flour alternately. Add vanilla to mixture; pour into greased and floured 10-inch tube pan. Set in cool oven. Bake at 300 degrees for 1½ hours.

Yield: 1 cake   Jani Martin

Excellent plain, or delicious iced with cream cheese icing recipe provided with Red Velvet Cake.

 ## Sour Cream Pound Cake

1 cup butter, softened
3 cups sugar
6 eggs
1 tablespoon almond
   flavoring

3 cups cake flour
¼ teaspoon soda
¼ teaspoon salt
1 cup sour cream

Beat butter slightly. Add part of sugar and mix until smooth. Add remaining sugar and beat until very smooth and fluffy. Add eggs, one at a time, beating well after each. Stir in flavoring. Add dry ingredients alternately with sour cream. Pour in greased and floured Bundt or tube pan. Bake at 325 degrees for 30 minutes. Reduce heat to 300 degrees and bake for 45 to 50 minutes or until cake is done. Cool cake 5 minutes before taking from pan.

Yield: 1 cake   Martha Barham

Red Velvet Cake

2½ cups all-purpose flour	2 eggs
1 teaspoon baking soda	1 teaspoon vanilla
1½ cups sugar	1 teaspoon vinegar
1 teaspoon salt	1 cup buttermilk
2 teaspoons cocoa	1 ounce red food coloring
2 cups vegetable oil	

Sift together flour, soda, sugar and salt. Add cocoa. Mix vegetable oil, eggs, vanilla, vinegar, buttermilk and food coloring. Add flour mixture to liquid mixture and blend well. Pour into 3 greased and floured 9-inch round cake pans. Bake at 350 degrees for 25 minutes. Cool completely before icing with cream cheese icing.

Cream Cheese Icing:

1 (8 ounce) package cream cheese, softened	1 (16 ounce) box confectioners' sugar
½ cup butter or margarine, softened	1 teaspoon vanilla
	1 cup chopped pecans, optional

Blend cream cheese and butter or margarine. Add sugar, vanilla and nuts; blend until smooth.

Yield: 1 three-layer cake   Jani Martin

Cream Cheese Icing is delicious when used to ice Cream Cheese Pound Cake, cupcakes or Red Velvet Cake.

Chocolate Sin Cake

	butter for pan	1	cup unsalted butter, room
8	ounces semi-sweet		temperature
	chocolate	1¼	cups sugar
		6	large eggs

Liberally butter a 9x1½-inch round cake pan. Line bottom with waxed paper; butter the paper. Preheat oven to 350 degrees. In top of double boiler, melt chocolate over hot water. Add butter and stir until butter has melted and mixture is smooth. Whisk sugar gradually into chocolate mixture until mixture is thick and smooth. Remove from heat. In separate bowl, beat eggs until foamy. Stir eggs into chocolate mixture until well incorporated. Pour mixture into prepared pan; place pan in 14x11-inch baking pan. Add enough boiling water to come halfway up the side of baking pan. Bake at 350 degrees in the center of oven 1½ hours. Remove cake pan and let set 5 minutes. Invert onto plate. Serve with coffee whipped cream.

Coffee Whipped Cream:

1	cup heavy cream	1	tablespoon strong coffee
2	tablespoons confectioners'		
	sugar		

Beat cream until it just begins to hold shape. Sift confectioners' sugar over top and beat until cream holds soft peaks. Stir in coffee. Spoon onto cake per serving.

Yield: 8 to 10 servings

Sharon Swindle

Caramel Frosting

3 cups sugar, divided	1 cup milk
1 tablespoon all-purpose flour	¾ cup butter or margarine
	1⅛ teaspoons vanilla extract

Sprinkle ½ cup sugar in a shallow, heavy 3½-quart Dutch oven. Place over medium heat. Cook, stirring constantly, until sugar melts (sugar will clump) and syrup is light golden brown. Remove from heat. Combine remaining 2½ cups sugar and flour in a large saucepan, stirring well; add milk, and bring to a boil, stirring constantly. Gradually pour one-fourth of hot mixture into caramelized sugar, stirring constantly. Add remaining hot mixture (mixture will lump, but continue stirring until smooth). Return to heat. Cover and cook over low heat 2 minutes. Uncover and cook, without stirring, over medium heat until candy thermometer registers 238 degrees. Add butter, stirring to blend. Remove from heat, and cool, without stirring, until temperature drops to 110 degrees (about 1 hour). Add vanilla, and beat mixture with a wooden spoon or at medium speed of an electric mixer, until frosting reaches spreading consistency.

Yield: frosting for 1 two-layer cake   Janice Worn

Fluffy White Frosting

1 egg white	¼ teaspoon cream of tartar
½ cup water	¼ teaspoon salt
1 tablespoon light corn syrup	1 teaspoon vanilla extract
1 cup sugar	

Place egg white in small mixing bowl. Beat until foamy. Place water, corn syrup, sugar, cream of tartar and salt in a small saucepan and stir well. Cook until mixture comes to a boil or until sugar is melted. Pour slowly into egg white and add vanilla. Beat with an electric mixer on high speed for 6 minutes or longer until firm peaks form.

Yield: frosting for 1 two-layer cake   Janice Worn

Double for a three-layer cake.

Cream Cheese Frosting

1 (8 ounce) package cream cheese, softened
½ cup margarine, softened
1 (16 ounce) box 4X confectioners' sugar

2 teaspoons vanilla
1 cup chopped pecans for garnish, optional

Beat cream cheese and margarine together until creamy. Gradually add confectioners' sugar. Add vanilla; mix. Frost cake and garnish with approximately 1 cup pecans.

Yield: frosting for 1 three-layer cake   Nancy Parris

Chocolate Frosting

2 cups white sugar
½ cup light brown sugar
2 squares unsweetened chocolate

1 tablespoon white corn syrup
1 scant cup sweet milk
6 tablespoons butter

Cook the two sugars, chocolate, corn syrup and milk until soft ball stage. Remove from heat and add butter. Cool. Whip until creamy. Add a small amount of milk if icing hardens.

Yield: frosting for 1 two-layer cake   Suzanne Sullivan

Sea Foam Frosting

¾ cup sugar
¼ cup water
¼ cup light corn syrup

3 egg whites
1 teaspoon vanilla extract

Combine sugar, water and corn syrup in small saucepan. Cook over medium heat until sugar dissolves and mixture begins to boil. Boil without stirring until mixture reaches 242 degrees. Just before syrup reaches temperature, beat egg whites until stiff but not dry. Pour syrup in thin streams over egg whites while beating at high speed on electric mixer. Beat until mixture is stiff and glossy and holds shape nicely. Beat in vanilla extract.

Yield: frosting for 1 two-layer cake   Janice Worn

This is a good frosting on banana cake.

Aunt Mildred's Ice Box Cookies

1	cup butter, softened	1	teaspoon baking soda
2	cups brown sugar	3½	cups all-purpose flour
2	eggs	1	cup finely chopped pecans
½	teaspoon salt		

Cream butter and sugar. Add eggs and mix well. Sift salt and baking soda with flour. Add to first mixture. Add nuts and mix well. Shape into a long roll, wrap and refrigerate overnight. To bake, slice very thinly. Bake at 350 degrees approximately 8 minutes or until crisp.

Yield: 4 to 6 dozen cookies   Susan Golden

Colossal Chocolate Chip Cookies

½	cup butter, softened	1½	cups all-purpose flour
¾	cup brown sugar	½	teaspoon salt
3	tablespoons sugar	¾	teaspoon baking soda
1	large egg	1¼	cups semi-sweet chocolate
1½	teaspoons vanilla		chips, separated

Cream butter, sugar and brown sugar. Add egg and vanilla. Add flour, salt and baking soda. Add 1 cup chocolate chips. Grease a 12-inch pizza pan, or foil pan, if using as a gift. Pour and press dough to within ½-inch of edge of pan. Sprinkle remaining ¼ cup chocolate chips on top and press down. Place foil pan on regular cookie sheet to bake. Bake at 350 degrees for 20 to 30 minutes. Let cool.

Yield: one 12-inch cookie   Marcia Felts

This recipe is a quick and neat gift. It can be used for a new neighbor, a child who made honor roll, a birthday, or any occasion. Cover gift cookie with plastic wrap and add a bow.

Mom's Chewy Chocolate Cookies

1   box fudge cake mix
1   (8 ounce) container
    whipped topping, thawed

1   egg, lightly beaten
¾   cup confectioners' sugar

Combine cake mix, whipped topping and egg. Stir until well mixed. Do not use mixer. Drop by teaspoon into confectioners' sugar; roll to coat. Place 1½-inches apart on a greased cookie sheet. Bake at 350 degrees for 10 to 12 minutes.

Yield: approximately 4 dozen cookies   Libby George

Great for children's project!!

"Cut Out" Sugar Cookies

½   cup butter, softened
1   cup sugar
1   egg, beaten
½   teaspoon vanilla

2   to 2¼ cups all-purpose
    flour
2   teaspoons baking powder
½   teaspoon salt

Cream butter and sugar. Add egg and vanilla. Sift together flour, baking powder and salt; add to creamed mixture. Divide dough into 2 parts. Chill 1 hour. Roll dough, one part at a time, to ¼ to ½-inch thickness and cut with cookie cutters. Keep other part of dough chilled until ready to use. Bake cookies on ungreased cookie sheets at 375 degrees for 8 to 10 minutes. Frost with Confectioners' Sugar Glaze.

Confectioners' Sugar Glaze:
5   to 6 teaspoons water
1   cup confectioners' sugar

food coloring

Blend water and sugar until smooth. Add food coloring for desired color. Brush glaze over cookies and let dry before moving or eating. Add less water to make thick glaze, add more to make thin glaze.

Yield: 2 dozen cookies   Jana Yates

This is a great recipe for all holiday "cut out" cookies. It doubles easily for a perfect classroom treat. Cookies may be frozen until ready to glaze.

261

Elsie's Ginger Snaps

1½ cups shortening
2 cups sugar
2 eggs
½ cup molasses
4 cups all-purpose flour
2 teaspoons ground cinnamon
2 teaspoons ground ginger
1 teaspoon ground cloves
4 teaspoons baking soda
¼ teaspoon salt
granulated sugar for rolling

Cream together shortening, sugar, eggs and molasses. Add flour, cinnamon, ginger, cloves, baking soda and salt. Mix well. Shape into 1-inch balls and roll in granulated sugar. Place 2-inches apart on ungreased cookie sheet. Bake at 350 degrees for 10 minutes for soft cookies, longer for hard cookies.

Yield: approximately 12 dozen cookies   Carol Giles

The $250 Cookie Recipe

2 cups butter, softened
2 cups sugar
2 cups brown sugar
4 eggs
2 teaspoons vanilla
4 cups all-purpose flour
5 cups oatmeal, blended *
1 teaspoon salt
2 teaspoons baking powder
2 teaspoons baking soda
5 cups semi-sweet chocolate chips
1 (8 ounce) milk chocolate candy bar, grated
3 cups chopped pecans

* For blended oatmeal, measure and blend in a blender to a fine powder.

Cream butter, sugar and brown sugar. Add eggs and vanilla. Mix together with flour, oatmeal, salt, baking powder and baking soda. Add chocolate chips, grated candy bar and nuts. Roll into balls and place 2-inches apart on an ungreased cookie sheet. Bake 6 to 10 minutes at 375 degrees.

Yield: 9 to 10 dozen cookies   Vickie Wilkinson

Recipe can be halved—these are wonderful!

Grandmother's Forgotten Cookies

2   egg whites
⅛   teaspoon salt
¾   cup sugar
1   teaspoon vanilla

1   cup chopped pecans
1   (6 ounce) package semi-
     sweet chocolate chips

Preheat oven to 350 degrees. Beat egg whites until soft peaks form. Gradually beat in salt, sugar and vanilla until very stiff. Fold in nuts and chocolate. Spoon small teaspoonfuls onto greased cookie sheet. Place cookies in oven and turn it off. They are done the next morning.

Yield: approximately 5 dozen cookies   Melissa Carter

May line cookie sheets with aluminum foil for easy clean-up.

Peaches and Cream Cookies

¾   cup butter or margarine,
     softened
1   (3 ounce) package cream
     cheese, softened
¾   cup sugar

1   tablespoon grated lemon
     peel
2   cups all-purpose flour
¼   teaspoon salt
¼   cup peach preserves

In large bowl with electric mixer at medium speed, beat butter, cream cheese, sugar and lemon peel until light and fluffy. With mixer at low speed, beat in flour and salt to blend well. Flatten dough to disk shape; wrap in plastic; refrigerate 30 minutes. After chilling, roll dough into small balls then press center with finger. Fill each with peach preserves. Bake at 350 degrees for 10 to 12 minutes.

Yield: approximately 36 cookies   Mary Corbett

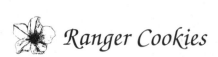 *Ranger Cookies*

½ cup vegetable shortening
½ cup margarine, softened
1 cup sugar
1 cup dark brown sugar
2 eggs
2 cups all-purpose flour

½ teaspoon salt
1 teaspoon baking soda
1 tablespoon vanilla
1 cup shredded coconut
1 cup quick oatmeal
1 cup crispy rice cereal

Mix together all ingredients to make stiff batter. Drop by half teaspoonfuls onto ungreased cookie sheet. Bake at 350 degrees until light brown, 7 to 8 minutes.

Yield: 10 to 12 dozen cookies

Jan Carter

Toffee Cookies

½ cup margarine
½ cup butter
½ cup brown sugar

½ cup chopped pecans
24 cinnamon graham cracker halves

Mix margarine, butter, brown sugar in saucepan and boil 2 minutes, no longer. Add nuts. Completely line bottom of jelly roll pan with graham cracker halves. Pour mixture over crackers. Bake at 325 degrees for 12 to 15 minutes. Remove to waxed paper immediately and cut in half before cool. Put in airtight tins when cooled.

Yield: 48 cookies

Jan Girardin

Almond Creme Pie

1 cup plus 2 teaspoons sugar	3 tablespoons butter
½ cup all-purpose flour	1 teaspoon vanilla extract
¼ teaspoon salt	1½ teaspoons almond extract
3 cups milk	¼ cup slivered almonds
4 eggs, separated	1 (9-inch) baked pie shell

In double boiler, combine 1 cup sugar, flour and salt. Gradually stir in milk. Cook and stir over medium heat until thick and bubbly. Reduce heat to low; cook and stir 2 minutes more. Remove from heat. In medium bowl beat egg yolks lightly and stir hot mixture into egg yolks, one cup at a time. Return to double boiler. Bring to a gentle boil; cook and stir 2 minutes or until thick. Remove from heat. Stir in butter, vanilla extract, almond extract and almonds. Pour into baked pie shell. Beat egg whites in medium bowl with 2 teaspoons sugar until stiff peaks form. Spread meringue evenly over pie. Bake in 350 degree oven for 12 to 15 minutes or until meringue is lightly browned. Chill until firm.

Yield: 8 servings   Mary Beth Meyers

Sour Cream Apple Pie

1 cup sour cream	1 egg
¾ cup sugar	3 cups tart, peeled and diced
1 teaspoon vanilla	apples
2 tablespoons all-purpose flour	1 (9-inch) unbaked deep dish pie shell
½ teaspoon salt	

Beat sour cream, sugar, vanilla, flour, salt and egg. Stir in apples. Mix well and pour into unbaked pie shell. Bake at 400 degrees for 25 minutes. While baking, prepare the following topping.

Topping:

½ cup brown sugar	¼ cup butter
⅓ cup all-purpose flour	

Combine brown sugar, flour and butter. Sprinkle on top of pie and bake for an additional 20 minutes at 400 degrees.

Yield: 8 servings   Mary Corbett

265

Blueberry Pie

1 cup sugar	2½ cups blueberries, fresh or
¼ cup cornstarch	frozen, rinsed with running
1 (3 ounce) package	water
blackberry gelatin	1 (9-inch) baked pie shell
1½ cups cold water	frozen non-dairy whipped
dash of salt	topping or whipped cream
	for garnish

Combine sugar, cornstarch, gelatin, water and salt in pan; cook over medium heat until clear. Cool. Add blueberries; pour into 9-inch pie shell; refrigerate until set. Serve with frozen non-dairy whipped topping or whipped cream.

Yield: 8 servings

Vickie Wilkinson

Chocolate Velvet Pie

1 (11½ ounce) package milk	1 cup heavy whipping cream,
chocolate morsels	whipped
1 (8 ounce) package cream	1 (9-inch) prepared chocolate
cheese, softened	crumb pie crust
1 teaspoon vanilla extract	extra whipped cream for
	garnish

In a double boiler over hot, not boiling, water, melt chocolate morsels. Stir until smooth. In large bowl, mix cream cheese, melted chocolate and vanilla extract. Beat until fluffy and light. Fold in whipped cream. Pour into crust. Refrigerate 3 hours or until firm. Garnish with whipped cream.

Yield: 6 to 8 servings

Cathy Sheats

This is a rich dessert, like a chocolate cheesecake. It is good for a dinner party served in small slices with the whipped cream.

Easy Chocolate Pies

1	cup margarine	4	eggs, beaten
1	cup semi-sweet chocolate chips	1	cup shredded coconut
		1	cup chopped pecans
2	cups sugar	2	unbaked (9-inch) pie shells

Melt margarine and chocolate chips over low heat. Add sugar, eggs, coconut and pecans. Mix well. Pour into pie shells. Bake at 350 degrees for 45 minutes.

Yield: 2 pies, 6 to 8 servings each   Kathy Turner

German Chocolate Pies

3	cups sugar	4	eggs, beaten
	dash of salt	½	cup butter or margarine, melted
7	tablespoons powdered cocoa	2	cups shredded coconut
1	(12 ounce) can evaporated milk	1	cup chopped pecans
1	teaspoon vanilla extract	2	(9-inch) unbaked pie shells

Combine sugar, salt and cocoa in bowl. Stir in evaporated milk, vanilla, eggs and melted butter. Blend well. Stir in coconut and pecans. Pour batter into pie shells. Bake at 350 degrees for 40 minutes or until set around edges of pies.

Yield: 2 pies, 6 to 8 servings each   Mary Corbett

Coconut Pie

1   (16 ounce) package
    shredded coconut
2   unbaked (9-inch) pie shells
6   eggs

2½ cups sugar
½   cup buttermilk
½   cup butter, melted

Divide coconut into the 2 pie shells. Mix eggs, sugar, buttermilk and butter; beat until thoroughly mixed. Pour over coconut in shells. Bake at 300 degrees for 45 to 55 minutes.

Yield: 2 pies, 6 to 8 servings each   Becky Stewart

Miss Morris' Coconut Pie

1   (9-inch) baked pie shell
2½ cups milk, reserve ½ cup
    for egg mixture
⅓   cup cornstarch
1   cup sugar
½   teaspoon salt

3   egg yolks
1   cup shredded fresh or
    packaged coconut
2   teaspoons butter
1   tablespoon orange flavoring

Bake pie shell according to package directions and let cool. Scald 2 cups milk. Slowly mix cornstarch, sugar, salt and egg yolks with ½ cup milk. Stir egg yolk mixture and coconut into scalded milk. Cook over medium heat stirring constantly in heavy saucepan or double boiler until thick. Remove from heat. Add butter and flavoring. Pour into pie shell.

Flavors blend if prepared ahead and allowed to stand in refrigerator. May be covered with whipped cream or with egg white meringue if preferred:

Egg White Meringue:
3   egg whites
¼   teaspoon cream of tartar
¼   cup sugar

2   tablespoons shredded
    coconut

In small bowl, with mixer at high speed, beat egg whites until foamy. Gradually beat in sugar and cream of tartar. Beat until stiff peaks form; spread on coconut pie. Sprinkle coconut on top of meringue. Bake in 350 degree oven for 15 to 20 minutes or until lightly browned.

Yield: 8 servings   Sue Clary

No-Bake Coconut Lovers' Cream Pie

2	envelopes unflavored gelatin	3	eggs
¼	cup cold water	1	(9-inch) graham cracker pie crust
1	(15 ounce) can cream of coconut	2	cups whipped topping
1	cup light cream or half-and-half	2	tablespoons shredded coconut, toasted

In a small saucepan, sprinkle gelatin over cold water; let stand 1 minute. Stir over low heat until completely dissolved, approximately 3 minutes. In blender or food processor, process cream of coconut, light cream and eggs until blended. While processing, gradually add gelatin mixture and process until blended. Chill mixture in blender or processor container approximately 15 minutes. Turn into prepared pie shell. Chill until firm, approximately 3 hours. Top with whipped topping and toasted coconut.

Yield: 8 servings   Karen Eager

Cranberry Ice Cream Pie

1	pound chocolate sandwich cookies, about 42	1	tablespoon Grand Marnier or other orange liqueur
1	quart vanilla ice cream, softened	1½	cups whole cranberry sauce

Grind cookies and reserve ½ cup crumbs for garnish. Pat remaining crumbs firmly into generously buttered, deep 9-inch baking dish. Beat 1 cup vanilla ice cream until soft. Add liqueur and cranberry sauce; beat until combined. Spread over crust. Freeze about 45 minutes, then spread remaining ice cream over first layer. Sprinkle top with reserved crushed cookies. Cover and freeze approximately 6 hours. Slice pie with serrated knife and serve frozen.

Yield: 8 servings   Cathy Sheats

Must be prepared in advance.

Sunny Cream Cheese Pie

Crust:

1	cup graham cracker crumbs	½	cup margarine, melted
		1	tablespoon sugar

Combine crumbs, margarine and sugar. Press into bottom and sides of 9-inch pie plate. Bake at 350 degrees for 15 minutes.

Filling:

1	(8 ounce) package cream cheese, softened	2	eggs
1	(14 ounce) can sweetened condensed milk	¼	cup fresh lemon juice
		1	tablespoon vanilla

Combine cream cheese, milk, eggs, lemon juice and vanilla. Mix thoroughly and pour into pie crust. Bake at 325 degrees for 10 to 12 minutes.

Yield: 8 servings   Claire Hiers

Good served with cherry or blueberry pie filling on top or any fresh fruit desired.

Toffee Bar Pie

1¼	cups chocolate wafer crumbs	1	(12 ounce) package semi-sweet chocolate chips
¾	cup margarine, divided	2	cups confectioners' sugar
12	(¾ ounce) toffee bars, frozen	1	(13 ounce) can evaporated milk
½	gallon vanilla ice cream, softened	1	teaspoon vanilla

Crush chocolate wafers. Melt and add ¼ cup margarine. Press into 13x9x2-inch pan; refrigerate. Crush toffee bars and mix with ice cream. Pour into crust and freeze, overnight is best. Heat ½ cup margarine and chocolate chips until melted. Mix in sugar and evaporated milk. Let cool approximately 10 minutes while stirring. Add vanilla. Pour over ice cream mixture and serve.

Yield: 20 servings   Vallye Blanton

Great for large gatherings, young and old.

Gail's Fudge Sundae Pie

Fudge Sauce:

1 (6 ounce) package semi-sweet chocolate chips

½ cup margarine

2 cups confectioners' sugar

1⅓ cups evaporated milk

1 teaspoon vanilla

Melt chocolate chips and butter over low heat, stirring until melted. Add sugar and evaporated milk. Bring to a boil over medium heat while stirring. Boil 5 minutes. Add vanilla. Double if doubling pie recipe. Any unused sauce can be used later over ice cream.

Filling:

¼ cup corn syrup

2 tablespoons firmly packed light brown sugar

3 tablespoons margarine

2½ cups crispy rice cereal

¼ cup peanut butter

¼ cup fudge sauce

3 tablespoons corn syrup

1 quart vanilla ice milk

In a saucepan, combine ¼ cup corn syrup, brown sugar and margarine. Cook over low heat until boiling. Remove from heat. Add rice cereal. Press into 9-inch pie plate or, if doubling recipe, 13x9x2-inch pan. Stir peanut butter, fudge sauce and 3 tablespoons corn syrup together. Spread over crust mixture. Freeze. Soften ice milk. Spread over top of frozen pie. Return to freezer until solid. Remove from freezer 10 to 15 minutes before serving. Cut into portions. Top each portion with remaining fudge sauce.

Yield: one 9-inch pie or, if doubled, 13x9x2-inch pan   Carol Giles

Kelly's Chocolate Sin Pie

1	(9-inch) prepared chocolate cookie crumb pie crust
7	(1.45 ounce) milk chocolate bars with almonds, reserve 1 for topping
1	(12 ounce) container frozen whipped topping, thawed
½	cup chopped almonds, optional

Chop 6 chocolate bars in blender, food processor or by hand; melt in microwave until completely melted, approximately 2 minutes, stirring after each minute. Pour melted bars in large bowl and mix with whipped topping. May add optional ½ cup almonds at this point. Pour into pie crust. Break remaining chocolate bar into pieces and scatter over top of pie. Refrigerate at least 1 hour before serving.

Yield: 8 servings
Sharon Coleman

Also tastes great frozen.

Mint Ice Cream Pie

Sauce:

1	cup miniature marshmallows
1	cup evaporated milk
1	cup semi-sweet chocolate chips

Heat marshmallows, evaporated milk and chocolate chips over medium heat until well blended and chips and marshmallows are melted. Stir gently. Cool. Makes enough for 2 pies.

Filling:

1	(9-inch) chocolate crumb pie crust
1	quart mint ice cream, softened

Spoon softened ice cream into pie crust. Pour cooled sauce over ice cream. Freeze.

Yield: 8 servings
Ellen Clary

This is quick and easy!! Mint ice cream can be substituted with favorite flavor ice cream.

Ice Cream Pie Spectacular

2 egg whites	1 pint coffee ice cream, softened
¼ teaspoon salt	1 pint vanilla ice cream, softened
½ cup sugar	
1½ cups chopped pecans, almonds or walnuts	

Generously butter a 9-inch pie plate. Beat egg whites with salt until frothy. Add sugar gradually, beating well after each addition. Continue beating until stiff peaks form and egg white does not slide when bowl is tilted. Fold in nuts. Turn into pie pan. Spread evenly with spoon over bottom and sides of pan. Prick bottom and sides with fork. Bake at 400 degrees for 10 to 12 minutes or until lightly browned. Allow to cool then chill. Spoon coffee ice cream into chilled pie shell. Top evenly with vanilla ice cream. Set in freezer until ready to serve. Serve with Raisin-Caramel Sauce.

Raisin-Caramel Sauce:

3 tablespoons butter	½ cup golden raisins
1 cup firmly packed light brown sugar	1 teaspoon vanilla extract pinch of salt
½ cup cream or evaporated milk	

Heat butter in small saucepan. Add brown sugar and heat over slow heat, stirring constantly until smooth, approximately 10 minutes. Remove from heat. Add cream very slowly, stirring until blended after each addition. Heat 1 minute longer. Stir in raisins and vanilla extract. Add pinch of salt. Serve warm or cold.

Yield: 8 servings   In Memory of Beverly Williams

Pie can be made in prepared chocolate crumb crust for quick preparation.

Simply Delicious Lemon Pie

1 cup sugar	2¾ to 4 tablespoons butter or
3 egg yolks	margarine
1 egg	juice and rind of 1 lemon or
3 level tablespoons	3 to 4 tablespoons bottled
cornstarch	lemon juice
1½ cups boiling water	1 (9-inch) pie shell, baked

In saucepan, mix sugar, egg yolks, whole egg and cornstarch thoroughly. Gradually add boiling water. Boil until clear, stirring constantly so it will not become lumpy. Add butter, lemon juice and rind. Cook slowly until egg is done or until thick. Pour into baked pie shell and spread with meringue.

Meringue:

1 tablespoon cornstarch	3 egg whites
8 tablespoons sugar, divided	dash of salt
½ cup water	

Mix cornstarch and 2 tablespoons sugar with water. Cook until clear; set aside. Beat egg whites and salt until foamy and forms stiff peaks. Add cornstarch mixture and continue beating until creamy. Gradually add remaining 6 tablespoons sugar, one at a time and beat until glossy. Spread on pie, making sure edges are sealed. Bake at 350 degrees for 30 minutes or until golden brown.

Yield: 8 servings

Pam Edwards

Mocha Meringue Pie

3	egg whites	1	cup whipped cream
½	teaspoon baking powder	½	cup confectioners' sugar
¾	cup sugar	1	quart coffee ice cream,
	pinch of salt		softened
1	cup chocolate wafer crumbs		chocolate candy bar curls
½	cup chopped pecans		for garnish
1	teaspoon vanilla		Kahlúa, optional

Beat egg whites, baking powder, sugar and salt until stiff and glossy. Fold in chocolate crumbs, pecans and vanilla. Place in a 10-inch greased pie pan. Bake at 350 degrees for 30 minutes. Cool. Whip together whipped cream and confectioners' sugar. Fill cooled pie shell with ice cream and freeze. Before serving, spread whipped cream and confectioners' sugar mixture over ice cream. Top with chocolate candy bar curls. Drizzle with Kahlúa before serving, if desired.

Yield: 10 servings   Beth Sullivan

Can substitute vanilla ice cream and it is still a yummy dessert.

Peanut Parfait Ice Cream Pie

1¾	cups graham cracker crumbs	½	gallon vanilla ice cream, softened
⅓	cup margarine, melted	1	(10 ounce) jar hot fudge sauce
¼	cup sugar		
1	cup dark corn syrup	1	(10 ounce) jar dry-roasted peanuts
4	tablespoons chunky peanut butter		whipped cream, optional
			cherries, optional

Mix cracker crumbs, margarine and sugar to form crust. Press into bottom of 9-inch springform pan. Mix corn syrup and peanut butter to form caramel sauce. Layer pie as follows: ice cream, fudge sauce, caramel sauce and peanuts on top. Freeze several hours before serving. Decorate with whipped cream and cherries, if desired. Slice into small servings as this is very rich!

Yield: 12 to 16 servings   Marcia Felts

Pumpkin Pie With Praline Topping

½ cup sugar
1 tablespoon all-purpose
   flour
½ teaspoon salt
1 teaspoon ground ginger
1 teaspoon ground cinnamon
¼ teaspoon ground nutmeg
⅛ teaspoon ground cloves

¼ cup margarine, softened
1½ cups canned pumpkin
½ cup unsulphured molasses
3 eggs
1 cup evaporated milk
2 (9-inch) pie shells, unbaked
   and chilled

Mix sugar, flour, salt, ginger, cinnamon, nutmeg and cloves. Blend in margarine, pumpkin and molasses. Beat in eggs, one at a time. Stir in milk. Pour into pie shells. Bake at 350 degrees for 1 hour or until tip of knife inserted in center comes out clean. Cool.

Topping:
2 tablespoons margarine
¼ cup firmly packed brown
   sugar

½ cup chopped pecans
½ pint whipping cream,
   whipped

Stir margarine and sugar in small skillet over medium heat until bubbly. Add pecans and cook 2 minutes, stirring constantly. Remove from heat and pour onto aluminum foil. Cool. Crumble into small pieces. Spoon whipped cream over cooled pie. Sprinkle praline crumbs over whipped cream. Serve cold.

Yield: two 9-inch pies

Claire Buescher

Spectacular Pecan Pies

1 cup all-purpose flour
2 (16 ounce) packages light
   brown sugar
1 cup milk
6 eggs, beaten
½ cup margarine, melted

1 teaspoon vanilla
1 cup chopped pecans, more
   if desired
   unbaked (9-inch) pie shells,
   2 deep or 3 shallow

Mix flour and sugar. Add milk and beaten eggs; mix well. Add margarine, vanilla and pecans; stir well. Pour into unbaked pie shells. Bake at 350 degrees for 45 to 55 minutes.

Yield: 2 deep or 3 shallow pies

Nancy Parris

Freezes well!!

276

Almond Cake Squares

2 eggs	1 cup butter, melted
1 cup sugar	½ teaspoon almond extract
1 cup all-purpose flour	

Combine eggs and sugar. Beat with electric mixer until thick and lemon colored. Stir in flour and butter. Pour batter into a greased and floured 13x9x2-inch pan. Bake at 350 degrees for 30 minutes. Remove from oven and spread topping over cake.

Almond Topping:

½ cup butter	1 tablespoon all-purpose
½ cup sugar	flour
½ cup slivered almonds	1 tablespoon milk

Combine all topping ingredients in a saucepan. Cook over low heat, stirring constantly until sugar is completely dissolved and mixture thickens. It will be light yellow. Spread over warm cake. Return to oven on center rack. Turn broiler on and watch until top is golden brown and bubbly. Cool and cut into squares.

Yield: 28 squares   Marcia Felts

Try this one at breakfast!

Blonde Brownies

¾ cup margarine, melted	½ teaspoon salt
1 (16 ounce) box brown sugar	1 (12 ounce) package semi-
3 eggs, beaten	sweet chocolate chips
2¾ cups all-purpose flour	1 teaspoon vanilla extract
2½ teaspoons baking powder	

Preheat oven to 350 degrees. In large bowl, pour margarine over sugar; mix well. Add eggs and stir. Sift together flour, baking powder and salt. Add dry ingredients to sugar mixture and stir to combine. Stir in chocolate chips and vanilla. Pour into greased 13x9x2-inch baking pan. Bake for 30 minutes. Cool completely in pan and cut into bars.

Yield: 2 dozen bars   Sally Gaskins

Would be good with nuts added, if desired.

Black Forest Brownies

1	(16 ounce) jar maraschino cherries	1¼	cups all-purpose flour
⅔	cup margarine	¾	cup quick or old fashioned oatmeal, uncooked
1	(6 ounce) package semi-sweet chocolate chips, divided	1	teaspoon baking powder
		¼	teaspoon salt
1	cup sugar	½	cup chopped nuts, optional
1	teaspoon vanilla	2	teaspoons vegetable shortening
2	eggs, beaten		

Preheat oven to 350 degrees. Drain cherries, slice 12 in half and set aside. Chop remaining cherries. In large saucepan, melt margarine and ½ cup chocolate chips over low heat; stir until melted. Remove from heat; cool slightly. Add sugar, vanilla and eggs and mix well. Stir in flour, oatmeal, baking powder and salt. Add chopped cherries and nuts. Spread in greased 13x9x2-inch baking pan. Bake for 25 minutes or until brownies pull away from sides of pan. Cool completely. In heavy saucepan over low heat melt remaining ½ cup chocolate chips and shortening; stir until mixture is melted and smooth. To microwave, place chocolate and shortening in glass container. Microwave on high 1 minute. Stir until smooth. If needed, microwave an additional 30 seconds. Drizzle chocolate over brownies. Cut into 2½-inch squares. Place cherry half on each square.

Yield: 2 dozen bars   Elaine Bridges

Company Brownies

½	cup plus 2 tablespoons margarine or butter, softened	1	teaspoon vanilla
		2	eggs
1	cup sugar	6	tablespoons cocoa
		½	cup all-purpose flour

Preheat oven to 325 degrees. Cream butter, sugar and vanilla. Beat in eggs. Blend in cocoa, then flour. Bake in greased 8x8x2-inch pan for 25 to 30 minutes. Cool. Cut into squares.

Yield: 16 squares   Terry Thomson

Moist and delicious. Makes an easy dessert when served warm with whipped topping. Yummy!

Butter Pecan Turtle Bars

Crust:

½ cup margarine, softened
1 cup firmly packed brown
  sugar

2 cups all-purpose flour
1 cup pecans, chopped

Cream margarine with brown sugar, beating at medium speed of electric mixer. Gradually add flour, mixing well. Press mixture into an ungreased 13x9x2-inch pan. Sprinkle with pecans; set aside.

Filling:

⅔ cup margarine, melted
½ cup firmly packed brown
  sugar

1 cup milk chocolate morsels

Combine margarine and brown sugar in a small saucepan. Bring to a boil over medium heat, stirring constantly. Boil 30 seconds, continue to stir. Remove from heat and pour hot mixture over crust. Bake at 350 degrees for 18 minutes or until bubbly. Remove from oven; immediately sprinkle with chocolate morsels. Let stand 2 to 3 minutes, cut through chocolate with a knife to create a marbled effect. Cool. Cut into squares.

Yield: 4 dozen bars   Kim Strickland

Bowen's Butterscotch Bars

4 eggs
1 (16 ounce) package brown
  sugar
2 cups biscuit baking mix

2 cups chopped pecans or
  walnuts
1 (6 ounce) package
  butterscotch morsels
1 teaspoon vanilla

Beat eggs on medium speed until frothy. Add sugar, beat until thick. Add remaining ingredients and mix well. Pour into a greased and floured 13x9x2-inch pan. Bake at 325 degrees for 45 minutes. Cool. Cut into bars.

Yield: 28 bars   Barbara Hendrix

Easy bar cookie to take and to store.

Chewies

½ cup margarine, softened	2 cups self-rising flour
1 (16 ounce) package light brown sugar	1 teaspoon vanilla
3 eggs	1 cup chopped nuts

Cream together margarine and sugar. Add eggs and beat well. Add flour, vanilla and nuts. Pour into 13x9x2-inch greased baking dish and bake at 300 degrees for 45 minutes. Will fall after baking.

Yield: 24 to 28 squares   Kathy Turner

Chocolate Cheesecake Squares

1 box chocolate cake mix with pudding	1 (16 ounce) box confectioners' sugar
3 eggs	1 (8 ounce) package cream cheese, softened
½ cup margarine, melted	
1 cup chopped pecans, divided	

Mix cake mix, 1 egg, margarine and ½ cup pecans; press into 16x11x2-inch greased pan. Mix sugar, 2 eggs and cream cheese with spoon or blender. Add pecans. Spread on top of first layer. Bake at 300 degrees for 60 to 65 minutes, until brown. Cool before cutting into squares.

Yield: 4 dozen squares   Kim Strickland

Patti's Chocolate Fondue

3 (3 ounce) Toblerone milk chocolate bars	½ cup light cream
	2 tablespoons rum

Combine all ingredients in small saucepan. Heat on low, stirring constantly until chocolate is melted and smooth. Pour into fondue pot. Ready to serve with bananas, strawberries or pound cake squares.

Yield: serves 4 to 6 people for dessert,   Susan Golden
approximately 1 cup

Chocolate Cups

2	cups semi-sweet chocolate chips	12	(2¾-inch) paper cupcake liners
2	teaspoons shortening		ice cream, mousse, fruit or other fillings

Melt chocolate chips with shortening; let cool slightly. Place twelve 2¾-inch paper cupcake liners in muffin tins. With narrow, soft pastry brush, thickly and evenly coat inside of each cup with melted chocolate. Chill cups 10 minutes or until firm; apply another coating of melted chocolate to any thin spots. Cover with plastic wrap and chill until very firm, approximately 1 hour. Carefully pull paper away. Cover and chill another hour. Fill with ice cream, mousse, fruit or other filling.

Yield: 12 cups   Honey Hendrick

Miniature paper cupcake liners (1¾-inch) can also be used. Makes an elegant dessert.

Chocolate Delight

1	cup all-purpose flour	1	(8 ounce) package cream cheese, softened
½	cup margarine, softened		
1½	cups chopped pecans, divided	3	cups milk
1	(9 or 10-ounce) container frozen whipped topping	1	(3 ounce) package instant vanilla pudding
1	cup sifted confectioners' sugar	1	(3 ounce) package instant chocolate pudding

Mix flour, margarine and 1 cup pecans; press into lightly greased 13x9x2-inch dish. Bake at 350 degrees for 20 minutes. Cool one hour. Mix 1 cup frozen whipped topping, sugar and cream cheese; spread over crust. Mix both puddings with 3 cups milk. Beat until slightly thickened. Spread over cream cheese mixture. Chill until set. Cover with remaining frozen whipped topping. Sprinkle with remaining ½ cup pecans. Refrigerate until ready to serve.

Yield: 12 to 15 servings   Pam Mackey

Chocolate Refrigerator Cupcakes

Cakes:

½ cup butter
1½ ounces (1½ squares)
   unsweetened chocolate
1 cup sugar
⅔ cup unsifted all-purpose
   flour

1 teaspoon vanilla
1 cup coarsely chopped
   pecans
   miniature cupcake liners

Melt butter and chocolate in double boiler. Blend in sugar, flour and vanilla. Stir in pecans. Place baking cups in miniature muffin tin and fill half-full with batter. Bake 12 minutes at 350 degrees; these will not look done. Prepare icing recipe below during baking time. Ice cakes while they are hot and fill to top of muffin cups. Place in refrigerator.

Icing:

2 tablespoons butter
1½ ounces unsweetened
   chocolate (1½ squares,
   usually)

¾ (16 ounce) package
   confectioners' sugar
1 tablespoon cold coffee

Melt butter and chocolate. Add confectioners' sugar slowly. Add coffee to make smooth.

Yield: 24 cupcakes   Vickie Wilkinson

These freeze very well.

Dutch Sand Tarts

1 cup butter, softened
1 teaspoon vanilla extract
½ teaspoon almond extract
   dash of salt
1½ cups sugar

1 egg
2 cups all-purpose flour
1 cup semi-sweet chocolate
   chips

Cream butter, vanilla, almond extract and salt. Add sugar gradually; cream well. Beat in egg. Stir in flour and chocolate chips. Roll into small balls and place on baking sheet. Flatten slightly. Bake at 350 degrees for 10 to 15 minutes.

Yield: 3 to 4 dozen cookies   Susan Golden

282

Chocolate Éclair Dessert

1 (16 ounce) box graham crackers	1 (9 ounce) container frozen whipped topping, thawed
2 (3 ounce) packages instant French vanilla pudding	additional whipped topping, pecans and/or cherries for garnish, optional
3 cups milk	

Line bottom of 11x7x2-inch baking dish with whole graham crackers. Mix pudding with milk and beat with electric mixer 2 minutes; fold in whipped topping. Spread half pudding mixture over crackers. Top with another layer of crackers. Add remaining pudding mixture and top with final layer of crackers. Refrigerate while preparing glaze.

Glaze:

6 tablespoons cocoa	3 tablespoons milk
4 tablespoons margarine	1 teaspoon vanilla
2 tablespoons corn syrup	1½ cups confectioners' sugar

Melt cocoa and margarine. Blend in corn syrup, milk and vanilla. Mix in sugar. Pour and spread over top layer. Refrigerate 6 hours before serving. Cut into squares and top each with spoonful of whipped topping, pecans or cherries, if desired.

Yield: 12 servings   Marcia Felts

No bake! Easy and excellent for busy cooks.

Crème Celeste

1 cup heavy cream	1 cup sour cream
½ cup sugar	2 tablespoons cognac
1½ teaspoons gelatin	whipped cream or fruit for garnish
3 tablespoons cold water	

Combine heavy cream and sugar in saucepan. Cook and stir over low heat until sugar is dissolved. Soften gelatin in water and add to cream/sugar mixture and stir until gelatin is dissolved. Remove from heat. With fork, stir in sour cream and cognac. Pour mixture into greased 3 to 4 cup mold and chill until serving time. Unmold onto chilled platter; garnish with whipped cream or fruit such as strawberries or peaches.

Yield: 6 servings   Marilyn Kemper

Libby's Famous Chocolate Peanut Butter Bars

1½ cups graham cracker
crumbs
1 (16 ounce) box
confectioners' sugar

1½ cups peanut butter
1¼ cups margarine, divided
1 (12 ounce) package semi-
sweet chocolate chips

In large bowl, mix graham cracker crumbs and confectioners' sugar. Melt peanut butter and ¾ cup margarine together; pour over cracker crumbs and sugar and mix thoroughly. Press into bottom of 13x9x2-inch pan. Melt chocolate chips and ½ cup of margarine together; spread over peanut butter layer. Cool to room temperature before cutting into small bars; refrigerate.

Yield: 7 to 8 dozen bars

Libby George

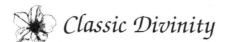 *Classic Divinity*

2 cups sugar
½ cup white corn syrup
pinch of salt
½ cup water

2 egg whites, beaten
1 teaspoon vanilla
1 cup chopped pecans

Combine sugar, syrup, salt and water in a heavy saucepan and bring to a boil. Boil to 240 degrees on a candy thermometer. While syrup boils, beat egg whites until stiff peaks form. Pour ⅓ syrup mixture slowly into egg whites, beating constantly. Cook remaining syrup mixture to 265 degrees. Pour slowly into egg white mixture and beat until it holds its shape. Add vanilla and nuts. Drop by teaspoonfuls onto buttered marble slab or waxed paper. Can be easily doubled.

Yield: 4 dozen candies

Grace Alvarez

Chocolate Surprise Bars

First layer:

4 ounces unsweetened chocolate

1 cup margarine

4 eggs

2 cups sugar

2 teaspoons vanilla

1 cup all-purpose flour

1 cup toasted, chopped nuts

1 teaspoon cinnamon

Preheat oven to 350 degrees. In a small saucepan, melt chocolate and margarine together. Cool slightly. In a medium bowl, beat eggs, sugar and vanilla. Add chocolate mixture and blend well. Sift flour and cinnamon together; blend with chocolate mixture and mix well. Stir in nuts. Pour into well-greased 13x9x2-inch pan. Bake at 350 degrees for 30 minutes. Do not overbake. Cool completely.

Second layer:

2 tablespoons margarine, softened

3 tablespoons sour cream

½ teaspoon cinnamon

½ teaspoon cocoa

½ teaspoon vanilla

2½ cups sifted confectioners' sugar

3 tablespoons toasted, chopped nuts

Blend butter and sour cream well. Add cinnamon, cocoa, vanilla and sugar; mix thoroughly. Stir in nuts. Spread over first layer. Refrigerate until firm.

Third layer:

1½ tablespoons margarine

1½ ounces (1½ squares) unsweetened chocolate

Melt margarine and chocolate together in saucepan over low heat. Dribble over frosted brownies. Refrigerate until firm. Cut into 2x1-inch bars.

Yield: approximately 48 bars

Elaine Bridges

Be sure to toast all nuts in this recipe.

Helen Smith's Fudge

4½ cups sugar
1 (12 ounce) can evaporated milk
1 teaspoon vanilla
1 cup margarine

1 (12 ounce) package semi-sweet chocolate chips
1 (6 ounce) package semi-sweet chocolate chips
1 cup chopped pecans

Mix sugar and evaporated milk in saucepan; bring to a boil over medium heat and cook for 7 minutes. Remove from heat. Add vanilla and margarine. Add chocolate chips. Beat with mixer on low until chocolate loses its gloss. Add nuts and pour into greased 13x9x2-inch pan. Cut when cool.

Yield: 40 pieces of fudge   Jeanne Cowart

Old-Fashioned Fudge

4 tablespoons light corn syrup
4 cups sugar
6 tablespoons cocoa

¾ cup milk
3 tablespoons butter
1 teaspoon vanilla
1 cup chopped pecans

Cook corn syrup, sugar, cocoa and milk over slow heat until sugar dissolves. Continue cooking slowly, stirring only to prevent burning. Remove from heat and, without stirring, add butter. Return to heat. Cook until thick or soft ball stage. Remove from heat. Cool. Add vanilla and nuts. Beat vigorously until thick and loses its gloss. Pour into greased 11x7x2-inch baking dish. Cut when cool.

Yield: 4 dozen squares   Zan Martin

 # Heavenly Hash Candy

1 pound milk chocolate
1 cup chopped nuts

12 large marshmallows, diced, or 1 heaping cup miniature marshmallows

Put milk chocolate in top of double boiler over hot water. Stir until melted. Pour half into 13x9x2-inch pan lined with waxed paper. Cover with chopped nuts and marshmallows. Pour remaining chocolate over nuts and marshmallows. When cool, break into pieces.

Yield: 2 to 3 dozen pieces   Suzanne Sullivan

Kahlúa Soufflé

½ cup sugar, divided	3 eggs, separated
1 envelope unflavored gelatin	½ pint whipping cream,
dash of salt	whipped or 1 (8 ounce)
1 cup cold water	carton frozen non-dairy
½ cup Kahlúa or other coffee-	whipped topping
flavored liqueur	chocolate curls, optional

Combine ¼ cup sugar, gelatin, salt, cold water and Kahlúa in saucepan. Cook over low heat until gelatin dissolves, stirring constantly. Stir a small amount of gelatin mixture into slightly beaten egg yolks. Gradually add yolk mixture to gelatin mixture, stirring constantly. Cook over low heat, stirring constantly, until mixture coats a metal spoon, approximately 3 minutes. Chill until slightly thickened, stirring occasionally. Fold whipped topping into gelatin mixture. Beat egg whites until foamy; gradually add ¼ cup sugar and continue beating until stiff peaks form. Fold egg whites into gelatin mixture. Pour into 1-quart soufflé dish. Chill until firm, approximately 6 hours. Garnish with chocolate curls, if desired.

Yield: 8 servings   Jane Stanaland

Peanut Blossoms

½ cup butter, softened	1¾ cups sifted all-purpose
½ cup peanut butter	flour
½ cup sugar	1 (6 ounce) package milk
½ cup brown sugar	chocolate kisses (36 kisses)
1 egg	granulated sugar for
1 teaspoon vanilla	coating balls

Preheat oven to 375 degrees. Cream butter, peanut butter, sugar and brown sugar. Add unbeaten egg and vanilla. Blend in flour. Shape dough into balls using a rounded teaspoon. Roll in sugar and place on ungreased cookie sheet. Bake for 8 minutes, then remove from oven. Remove silver foil from candies. Place 1 chocolate candy on top of each, pressing down firmly. Return cookies to oven and bake at 375 degrees for 2 to 5 minutes until golden brown.

Yield: 3 dozen cookies   Jana Yates

Kids love these!

Magic Marshmallow Crescent Puffs

¼	cup sugar	16	large marshmallows
1	teaspoon cinnamon	¼	cup butter or margarine,
2	(8 ounce) cans crescent		melted
	dinner rolls	¼	cup chopped nuts

Combine sugar and cinnamon. Separate 2 cans crescent roll dough into 16 triangles. Dip a marshmallow in melted butter then in sugar-cinnamon mixture. Place marshmallow on wide end of triangle. Fold corners over marshmallow and roll toward point, completely covering marshmallow and squeezing edges of dough to seal. Dip point side in butter and place buttered side down in greased deep muffin pans. Repeat with remaining marshmallows. Place pan on cookie sheet during baking. Bake at 375 degrees for 10 to 15 minutes or until golden brown. Immediately remove from pans and drizzle with icing. Sprinkle with nuts. Serve warm.

Icing:

| ½ | cup confectioners' sugar | ½ | teaspoon vanilla |
| 2 | to 3 teaspoons milk | | |

Combine sugar, milk and vanilla. Blend until smooth.

Yield: 16 puffs

Suzanne Sullivan

Try this as a brunch or bridge snack!

Caramel Popcorn Treat

1⅓	cups sugar	½	cup light corn syrup
1	cup butter	2	quarts popped corn
1	teaspoon vanilla		

Mix sugar, butter, vanilla and syrup and cook over medium heat. Stir 10 to 15 minutes or until caramel brown. While hot, pour over popcorn, coating as much as possible. Pour on greased cookie sheet and let cool. Break up.

Yield: 2 quarts

Mary Perry

Nuts also make a good addition.

David's Favorite Bread Pudding

5	eggs, beaten	1	tablespoon vanilla extract
1	cup sugar	¼	cup golden raisins
½	cup butter, softened	12	(1-inch thick) slices French
2	cups heavy cream		bread
¼	teaspoon cinnamon		vanilla ice cream, optional

Preheat oven to 350 degrees. Beat eggs and set aside. In large bowl, cream sugar and butter. Add eggs, cream, cinnamon and vanilla; mix well. Stir in raisins and pour into greased 11x7x1½-inch baking pan. Arrange bread on mixture; let stand 5 minutes. Turn bread over; let stand 5 to 10 minutes. This should soak up most of mixture. Set this pan in larger pan and fill larger pan with water to about a half-inch from top of smaller pan. Cover entirely with foil and bake 45 to 50 minutes. Uncover pudding for last 10 minutes to brown top slightly. This dessert should be moist and soft. Serve warm with a scoop of vanilla ice cream.

Yield: 8 to 10 servings   Denise Retterbush

This recipe is best if you time your baking to be complete just as you complete your meal and serve it straight from the oven.

 # Snickerdoodles

1	cup butter, softened	2	teaspoons cream of tartar
1½	cups sugar	1	teaspoon baking soda
2	eggs	¼	teaspoon salt
2⅔	cups sifted all-purpose	2	tablespoons sugar
	flour	2	teaspoons cinnamon

Cream butter and sugar; add eggs and beat thoroughly. Add sifted flour, cream of tartar, baking soda and salt. Mix well and chill. Form into 1-inch balls. Mix 2 tablespoons sugar and 2 teaspoons cinnamon. Roll dough balls in cinnamon mixture. Place 2 inches apart on ungreased cookie sheet. Bake at 400 degrees for 8 to 10 minutes.

Yield: 4 dozen cookies   Susie Kaiser

Apple-Cheese Cobbler

1   **pound pasteurized process cheese**
1   **cup butter**
1½ **cups all-purpose flour**

1¾ **cups sugar**
3   **(16 ounce) cans sliced apples, drained (not pie filling)**

Melt cheese and butter in microwave. Add flour and sugar; blend well. Arrange apples in bottom of lightly greased 13x9x2-inch baking dish. Pour cheese mixture over apples. Bake at 350 degrees for 20 to 30 minutes.

Yield: 12 to 15 servings   Claire Hiers

Do not use pie filling in place of canned sliced apples. This is also a good side dish, or brunch dish.

Hot Cranberry Apple Dessert

3   **cups peeled, chopped tart apples**
2   **cups raw cranberries**

⅔ **cup brown sugar**
⅔ **cup white sugar**

Combine apples, cranberries and sugars in 3-quart casserole.

Topping:
1½ **cups quick cooking oatmeal, uncooked**
1½ **cups brown sugar**
½ **cup all-purpose flour**

⅔ **cup chopped pecans**
½ **cup butter, melted**
    whipped cream or ice cream, optional

Mix oatmeal, brown sugar, flour, chopped nuts and melted butter. Spoon topping over cranberries and apples. Bake at 350 degrees for 1 hour. Serve with whipped cream or ice cream.

Yield: 12 to 14 servings   Barbara Hornbuckle

Reheats well in microwave.

Orchard Apple Crisp

5	medium size red cooking apples	½	cup all-purpose flour
1	cup quick or old-fashioned oats, uncooked	¼	teaspoon salt
¾	cup firmly packed brown sugar	½	cup butter or margarine, softened
			milk or ice cream, optional

Peel and slice apples. Arrange in ungreased 2-quart baking dish. Combine oats, brown sugar, flour and salt. Cut in butter and crumble mixture over apples. Bake at 350 degrees for 30 to 35 minutes or until brown and bubbly. Apples should be tender. Serve warm with milk or ice cream.

Yield: 6 servings   Floye Luke

Carol's Creamy Banana Pudding

2	(3 ounce) boxes instant vanilla pudding	1	(12 ounce) container non-dairy whipped topping
1	(14 ounce) can sweetened condensed milk	5	to 6 bananas
3	cups whole milk	1	(12 ounce) box vanilla wafers

Mix pudding and whole milk until it begins to thicken. Stir in sweetened condensed milk. Fold in ¼ of the non-dairy whipped topping. In a 2-quart dish, layer vanilla wafers then banana slices then ½ pudding mixture; repeat layers. Cover bananas and wafers completely with pudding. Refrigerate until set, approximately 15 minutes. Remove from refrigerator and cover pudding with remaining non-dairy whipped topping, approximately 9 ounces. Return to refrigerator until ready to serve.

Yield: 12 servings   Carol Giles

Super-Easy Blueberry Crunch

1   (20 ounce) can crushed pineapple, undrained
2   to 3 cups blueberries, fresh or frozen
1   cup sugar, divided
1   box yellow cake mix
1   cup margarine or butter, melted
1   cup chopped pecans

Grease a 13x9x2-inch baking dish and layer as follows: pineapple, blueberries, ¾ cup sugar, dry cake mix, melted margarine, pecans, and ¼ cup sugar. Bake at 325 degrees for 35 to 40 minutes until brown on top. Serve warm or cold.

Yield: 12 to 16 servings   Kathy Lincoln

Delicious topped with whipped cream or ice cream.

Peach Melba Trifle

1   (14 ounce) can sweetened condensed milk
1½ cups water
1   (3¾ ounce) package instant vanilla pudding mix
1   pint whipping cream, whipped
¼   cup plus 1 tablespoon cocktail sherry, orange juice, or peach brandy
1   (10 ounce) prepared angel food cake, torn into small pieces, approximately 8 cups
1½ pounds fresh peaches, pared and sliced, or 1 (29 ounce) can sliced peaches, drained
¼   cup red raspberry preserves
toasted almonds and additional preserves for garnish, optional

In large bowl combine milk and water, mix well. Add pudding mix; beat until well blended. Chill 5 minutes. Fold in whipped cream and 1 tablespoon sherry. Place 4 cups cake pieces in 2-quart glass bowl. Sprinkle with 2 tablespoons sherry. Top with ½ peaches, ¼ cup preserves and ½ pudding mixture. Repeat layer with remaining cake, sherry, peaches and pudding. Chill. Garnish with almonds and additional preserves if desired. Refrigerate leftovers.

Yield: 16 to 20 servings   Sharon Swindle

Holiday Date Roll

1	(8 ounce) package chopped dates	1	teaspoon baking powder
1	cup water	½	teaspoon salt
¾	cup sugar, divided	½	teaspoon ground allspice
⅛	teaspoon salt	¾	cup coarsely chopped pecans
3	eggs	2	tablespoons confectioners' sugar
1	cup all-purpose flour		

Combine dates, water, ¼ cup sugar and ⅛ teaspoon salt. Bring to boil, lower heat. Cook over low heat, stirring constantly until thickened, approximately 5 minutes. Remove from heat and cool. In large bowl, beat eggs at high speed for 5 minutes. Gradually beat in ½ cup sugar. Combine flour, baking powder, ½ teaspoon salt and allspice; gradually add to egg mixture. Add date mixture to egg mixture and beat until blended. Spread in greased, floured 15x10x1-inch jelly roll pan. Sprinkle chopped nuts over top. Bake at 325 degrees for 20 to 25 minutes or until top springs back when pressed with finger. Turn onto towel well covered with powdered sugar. Roll up immediately, rolling cake and towel together. Cool on rack. Unroll and spread with Cream Cheese Filling. Reroll and wrap in plastic wrap to hold roll together. Refrigerate.

Cream Cheese Filling:

1	(8 ounce) package cream cheese, softened	½	teaspoon vanilla
4	tablespoons butter, softened	1	cup confectioners' sugar, sifted

Combine well cream cheese, butter, vanilla and powdered sugar. Spread as directed above.

Yield: 12 servings   Sharon Swindle

Freezes well.

Judy's Fruit Whip

1 (21 ounce) can cherry pie
filling
1 (20 ounce) can crushed
pineapple, drained well
1 (14 ounce) can sweetened
condensed milk

2 cups miniature
marshmallows
1 cup chopped pecans
1 (10 ounce) container non-
dairy whipped topping

Mix pie filling, pineapple, milk, marshmallows, nuts and topping; stir well. Refrigerate overnight.

Yield: 16 to 20 servings   Carol Giles

Sweet enough to be dessert but may be used as a salad.

Pilgrim's Pumpkin Pudding

1 (29 ounce) can pumpkin
1 cup sugar
4 eggs
1 (12 ounce) can evaporated
milk
1½ teaspoons pumpkin spice,
nutmeg or cinnamon
1 teaspoon salt

1 teaspoon vanilla extract
6 tablespoons margarine,
melted
¾ to 1 cup chopped pecans
1 box yellow cake mix
whipped topping or
whipped cream for garnish

Grease 13x9x2-inch dish. Mix pumpkin, sugar, eggs, evaporated milk, pumpkin spice, salt, and vanilla extract. Pour into greased baking dish. Sprinkle dry cake mix over mixture. Garnish with nuts, drizzle margarine over cake. Bake at 325 degrees for 1 hour and 15 minutes. Serve with dollop of whipped cream or non-dairy whipped topping.

Yield: 16 to 20 servings   Floye Luke

Mayhaw Trifle

1 (5.1 ounce) box instant
  vanilla pudding mix
2 cups milk
1 (10¾ ounce) frozen,
  prepared pound cake,
  thinly sliced

1 (11 ounce) jar mayhaw
  wine jelly
1 (12 ounce) container non-
  dairy whipped topping

Prepare pudding according to package directions. Arrange thin slices (half of cake) of pound cake in glass bowl. Spoon 5½ ounces of jelly over cake. Cover with half of pudding. Top with half of whipped topping. Repeat layers once more. Refrigerate until serving time.

Yield: 16 to 20 servings   Floye Luke

A super dessert.

Frozen Strawberry Crumb

¾ cup all-purpose flour
3 tablespoons brown sugar
½ cup chopped pecans
½ cup melted butter
2 egg whites
⅔ cup sugar

1 (10 ounce) package frozen
  strawberries, thawed
2 tablespoons lemon juice
1 cup whipping cream,
  whipped

Combine flour, brown sugar, nuts, and butter in ovenproof bowl. Bake at 350 degrees for 20 minutes, stirring occasionally. Remove from oven. Spread half of mixture in 13x9x2-inch baking dish. Save other half for topping. With electric mixer, beat egg whites until foamy. Add lemon juice, sugar and strawberries and beat at high speed for 8 more minutes. Fold in whipped cream. Pour over crumbs. Top with rest of crumbs. Freeze overnight.

Yield: 16 servings   Beth Sullivan

Super! Try on your supper club. Men like it, too.

Mother's Day Strawberry Torte

2	(3½ ounce) packages instant vanilla pudding	1	(6 ounce) package strawberry gelatin
2	cups milk	2½	cups boiling water
1	(8 ounce) container non-dairy whipped topping	2	(10 ounce) packages frozen strawberries, partially thawed
1	prepared angel food cake, approximately 13 ounces, broken into bite-size pieces	12	fresh whole strawberries additional whipped topping

In medium mixing bowl combine pudding with milk, mixing well. Stir in whipped topping and cake pieces. Spread mixture in 13x9x2-inch pan; chill. In large bowl, combine gelatin with water, stirring to dissolve. Add strawberries. Chill until slightly thickened. Pour gelatin mixture over cake layer and chill until set. Cut into squares and top each square with additional whipped topping and a whole strawberry.

Yield: 12 servings   Mary Beth Meyers

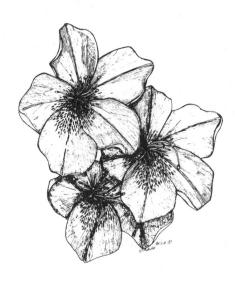

Local Chef's Treasures

The Crescent/Valdosta Garden Center
Built 1898

Ahh David! Flowers and Foods R.S.V.P. - *Ahh David! offers complete floral and catering services. Outstanding in taste and appearance, each selection is prepared with special care. Assists with all entertaining needs.*

Pasta With Vodka

1	(16 ounce) package penne or other tubular pasta	1	(16 ounce) can Italian plum tomatoes; drained, seeded and pierced
5	tablespoons unsalted butter		
⅔	cup vodka, preferably Polish or Russian	¾	cup heavy cream
		½	teaspoon salt
¼	teaspoon hot red pepper flakes	¾	cup freshly grated Parmesan cheese

In large pot of salted boiling water, cook pasta 8 to 10 minutes. Drain well. Melt butter over moderate heat, add vodka and red pepper flakes. Simmer 2 minutes. Add tomatoes and cream, simmer 5 minutes longer. Salt to taste. Add pasta. Reduce heat to low, add cheese and mix thoroughly. Pour into heated bowl and serve immediately.

Yield: 4 servings   David Clyatt

German Hot Potato Salad

10	pounds Irish potatoes, boiled and coarsely mashed	1	cup sugar
		¾	cup apple cider vinegar
1	pound bacon	¾	cup water
3	medium onions, chopped		salt and pepper to taste
3	tablespoons all-purpose flour	¼	cup pimento pepper

Boil whole potatoes and peel, then coarsely mash. Fry bacon until crisp. Drain most of grease from pan and add chopped onions. Sauté until clear. Add flour and stir until roux. Add sugar, vinegar, water, salt and pepper. Combine with potatoes. Pour into 13x9x2-inch baking dish and garnish top with pimento peppers. Bake at 350 degrees for 30 minutes or until well heated.

Yield: 8 servings   David Clyatt

Baked Vidalia Onion Dip

2	cups chopped Vidalia or sweet onions	2	cups slivered almonds
2	cups grated Swiss cheese	½	cup pimento peppers
2	cups mayonnaise	¼	teaspoon cayenne pepper

Mix all ingredients together and place in 13x9x2-inch baking dish. Bake at 325 degrees until completely melted, approximately 20 minutes. Serve with butter crackers.

Yield: 20 servings   David Clyatt

Artichokes, water chestnuts or asparagus tips may be added to this recipe.

Mustard Dip

1	cup hot water	¾	cup apple cider vinegar
1	cup sugar	½	gallon mayonnaise
1	cup prepared mustard		

Mix hot water and sugar. Add mustard and vinegar. Blend well and add mayonnaise. Refrigerate.

Yield: 1 gallon   David Clyatt

Great on meats, poultry and fresh vegetables.

Salad Dressing

1	garlic bud	1	tablespoon fresh lemon
1	teaspoon salt	1	tablespoon Parmesan cheese
6	tablespoons virgin olive oil		
1	tablespoon red wine vinegar	1	tablespoon Worcestershire sauce
1	tablespoon Dijon mustard		

Mash garlic and salt together to puree. Add all remaining ingredients and blend well.

Yield: 1 cup   David Clyatt

May be enjoyed on salads, potatoes or other fresh or steamed vegetables. Great on romaine lettuce.

Marinade for Poultry or Meat

1	cup water	1	(6 ounce) can pineapple
1	cup soy sauce		juice
1	cup sugar	1	tablespoon garlic salt
½	teaspoon five spices	1	teaspoon dried or freshly grated ginger

Blend all ingredients together and pour over poultry or meat. Marinate poultry 3 to 4 hours. Meat may take longer or even overnight.

Yield: marinade for 10 pounds of poultry or meat   David Clyatt

Holiday Egg Nog

12	eggs	1	fifth brandy
8	half-pint cartons whipping cream	3	cups sugar
			freshly grated nutmeg
1	quart half-and-half		

Separate eggs. Beat egg whites until stiff. In separate bowl beat cream. Add half and half while beating stiff cream. Slowly add brandy, then gradually add sugar. While continuing to beat, add egg yolks and then stiffly beaten egg whites. Sprinkle with freshly grated nutmeg.

Yield: 24 servings   David Clyatt

Refreshing Mid-Summer Iced Tea

3	large lemons	1	(46 ounce) can pineapple
2	quarts water		juice
1	pound sugar	1	tablespoon almond extract
2	cups strong tea	1	tablespoon vanilla extract
	pinch of salt		fresh mint sprigs

Grate lemon rinds, add 1 quart water and sugar. Boil 5 minutes to make syrup. Add strong tea, salt, juice of 3 lemons, 1 quart water, pineapple juice and extracts. Mix well and pour over cubes of ice. Add sprigs of mint for refreshing taste.

Yield: 1 gallon   David Clyatt

Bynum's Diner - *Family dining featuring "down-home" cooking. Family owned and operated, Bynum's has served Valdosta, since 1950. Open for breakfast and lunch.*

Chicken and Dumplings

1 (7 to 8 pound) baking hen	2½ cups all-purpose flour
salt and pepper to taste	1 to 1½ cups warm water

Cut hen into quarters, add salt and pepper. Place in Dutch oven and boil until tender. Remove meat from bones and reserve stock water. In bread bowl, sift flour, add warm water and mix with hands to make dough. Roll as thin as possible on floured surface. Cut into small strips and put into boiling stock water, one at a time. Avoid letting them stick. Put meat into pot with dumplings and remove from heat.

Yield: 8 to 10 servings   Jackie Bynum

China Garden, USA - *China Garden offers authentic Chinese and Japanese cuisine. There are two locations in Valdosta. Open noon and evening every day. Banquet facilities and catering.*

China Garden, U.S.A. Egg Roll

1 pound chicken meat	3 pounds green cabbage, shredded
2 tablespoons rice wine	
2½ teaspoons salt	¼ pound fresh mushrooms, sliced
1¼ teaspoons black pepper	
2 egg whites, beaten	1 carrot, peeled and shredded
1 teaspoon cornstarch	2 celery ribs, chopped
¾ teaspoon monosodium glutamate	10 pieces China Garden or commercial egg roll skin
3 tablespoons salad oil	1 egg, beaten
½ pound onion, chopped	6 cups salad oil

Remove skin from chicken and cut meat into paper-thin slices. Marinate chicken for 20 minutes in rice wine, 2 teaspoons salt, 1 teaspoon pepper,

(China Garden, U.S.A. Egg Roll, continued on next page)

(China Garden, U.S.A. Egg Roll, continued)

egg white, cornstarch and ½ teaspoon monosodium glutamate. Heat 3 tablespoons of oil in pan. Stir-fry onions until fragrant, adding chicken, which has been removed from marinade. Continue to stir-fry adding cabbage, mushrooms, carrots, celery and ½ teaspoon salt, ¼ teaspoon pepper and ¼ teaspoon monosodium glutamate. Place handful of cooked meat and vegetables on the corner of egg roll skin. Tightly roll over once, then fold up two sides. Brush beaten egg on top of skin and complete the roll-up. Heat oil for deep frying. Deep-fry egg roll for 8 minutes over medium heat until golden, then remove.

Yield: 10 rolls   Mike and May Gung

Chicken Lo Mein

10	pounds half-cooked Chinese egg noodles	4	ounces cooking oil
1	pound sliced chicken	3	pounds cabbage, sliced
1	tablespoon monosodium glutamate	¼	pound carrots, shredded
		½	pound green onions
3	ounces soy sauce	1	pound salad oil
½	tablespoon pepper	¼	pound bacon
½	tablespoon sesame oil	1	tablespoon salt

Boil noodles in amount of water according to package for approximately three minutes. Cook thoroughly to avoid raw flour in center. Marinate chicken in monosodium glutamate, soy sauce, pepper, sesame oil and cooking oil. Cut green onions into 1-inch sections. Heat salad oil in wok. Brown the bacon, onion, and seasoned chicken slices. Add cabbage, carrots and green onions and cook 1 minute. Add noodles and salt. Mix well and stir-fry for 3 minutes.

Yield: 40 servings   Mike and May Gung

Shrimp Fried Rice

10	pounds uncooked rice	1	(16 ounce) package frozen
6	ounces salad oil		green peas and carrots
½	pound bacon	2	tablespoons salt
1	pound (90 to 110 count)	1	tablespoon monosodium
	shrimp, peeled		glutamate
1	pound onion, chopped	½	tablespoon pepper
6	eggs, beaten	2	ounces soy sauce

Cook rice in 5 quarts water. Heat oil in wok to 350 degrees. Brown bacon and cook shrimp in oil. Add onion, eggs, (avoid over-shoveling) peas and carrots. Cook for 1 minute. Add rice and seasonings: salt, monosodium glutamate, pepper and soy sauce. Continue to cook and stir evenly. Keep temperature above 185 degrees, but avoid scorching.

Yield: 40 servings   Mike and May Gung

Chocolate Expressions - *A love for chocolate and a love for people turned Chocolate Expressions from a hobby into a business. Everything from boxed chocolates to Easter bunny suckers and everything in-between, including sugar-free chocolate. Nationwide shipping.*

Butter Mints

⅓	cup butter	1	(16 ounce) box powdered
⅓	cup corn syrup		sugar
			granulated sugar as needed

Flavorings: **Color:**
3   drops, if oil base or ½   paste or liquid to desired
      teaspoon, if alcohol base   color

Melt butter. Stir in corn syrup until blended. Pour over powdered sugar and work into a dough. Flavor and color as desired or leave plain. Roll in granulated sugar and press into molds. Pop out and let air dry on each side for 12 hours.

Yield: 3 dozen ¼-inch mints   Lyndell Abramczyk

You can also mold these in chocolate. They are good either way.

Cookies and Creme

1	pound white chocolate (almond bark)	3	double-stuffed chocolate sandwich cookies

Melt chocolate in double boiler, microwave or crockpot. Crush all three cookies including cream center. Add cookies to melted chocolate. Spoon into candy mold and refrigerate until set. Alternate method: spread entire mixture onto a 13x9-inch cookie sheet and tap until thin and evenly spread. Refrigerate until set, remove and break up into various size pieces.

Yield: Based on placing ingredients in miniature peanut butter cup mold, nickel width and ½-inch deep, yield will be 5 dozen quarter size candies. Cookie sheet method yield will vary. Lyndell Abramczyk

Covington's - *Covington's is a unique dining experience in downtown Valdosta. Open for breakfast and lunch and private dinner parties. Catering is also available. Features a gallery wall where paintings by local artists are displayed.*

She-Crab Soup

3	tablespoons butter	1	cup lump crabmeat
3	tablespoons all-purpose flour		salt and white pepper to taste
5	cups chicken broth	8	tablespoons sherry
1½	cups heavy cream		

Melt butter in 3-quart saucepan. Stir in flour and cook slowly for 3 minutes, stirring constantly. Add stock and mix well with wire whisk. Cook very slowly, uncovered, for 20 minutes. Add cream, crabmeat, salt and pepper. Top each bowl with 1 tablespoon sherry.

Yield: 8 servings Sue Cox

Covington's Cinnamon Rolls

1 package dry yeast	3 to 3½ cups all-purpose flour
1 cup warm water (110 degrees)	sugar and cinnamon as desired
¾ cup non-fat dry milk	margarine as needed
4 tablespoons sugar	1 cup powdered sugar
3 tablespoons shortening	milk
1 egg, beaten	
½ teaspoon salt	

Dissolve yeast in warm water and dry milk in mixing bowl; let stand 4 to 5 minutes. Add sugar, shortening, beaten egg, salt and half the flour. Beat on low speed of electric mixer using paddle until smooth. Gradually add remaining flour. Beat until dough pulls away from the sides of mixing bowl. Depending on flour and humidity, entire 3½ cups may not be needed. Be sure dough is well-beaten and smooth, almost shiny. Place dough in a greased bowl and turn to grease all sides. Cover with a damp towel and allow to rise in a warm, draft-free place for approximately 1 hour or until doubled in size. If desired, as soon as covered with a damp towel, refrigerate overnight, then allow to return to room temperature before going to the next step. Punch dough down with fists. Pour onto a floured surface and knead a few times. Roll dough into a 10x12-inch rectangle. Brush with melted margarine. Sprinkle lightly with desired amount of sugar and cinnamon. Roll up jellyroll fashion. Cut roll into ¾-inch slices. Place slices in a 13x9x2-inch greased pan. Brush lightly with melted margarine. Allow to rise, free from drafts, for 30 to 40 minutes or until almost doubled in size. Bake at 400 degrees for 5 minutes or until lightly brown, making sure rolls separate without being sticky. Because of difference in ovens, baking times will vary. Brush rolls lightly with melted margarine. Combine powdered sugar with a little milk and mix until smooth; slightly thick. Pour over rolls that have been out of oven for about 5 minutes. Use a French whip or pierced spoon. It is important to ice while rolls are still warm so icing will glaze. However, if iced right out of oven, icing will dissolve. It's best to remove the rolls, brush with margarine, then make the icing and put on rolls.

Yield: 1½ dozen rolls

Sue Cox

The type of flour used is very important. A soft wheat flour is the best.

Mom and Dad's Italian Restaurant - *Authentic Italian restaurant featuring fresh homemade breads, sauces, pasta and wonderful desserts. Family owned and operated. Private party rooms available.*

Zuppa Di Pesce (Fish Soup)

2 pounds clean squid	1 cup dry white wine
2 dozen little neck clams	1 to 1½ cups canned Italian
2 pounds mussels	tomatoes, chopped in own
⅔ cup olive oil	juices
½ cup chopped onions	1 pound shrimp, peeled
1 tablespoon chopped garlic	salt and pepper to taste
3 tablespoons chopped parsley	

Cut squid into ½-inch rings; set aside with tentacles. Soak clams and mussels in cold water and wash. Empty water and replace with clean water continuing until water is clear. Put all clams and mussels into covered pot of boiling water. When clams and mussels open, remove from water. Reserve 6 of each for garnish. Separate meat from shell on remaining clams and mussels. Put olive oil in deep saucepan, add onions, and sauté on medium heat until translucent. Add chopped garlic. When garlic becomes lightly colored, add chopped parsley, stir and add wine. Boil for about 30 seconds. Add tomatoes with juice, and simmer for about 20 minutes. Add clams, mussels, shrimp and squid to sauce. Salt and pepper to taste. Cook until shrimp change to a white color. Top with reserved clams and mussels. Serve immediately with plenty of crusty bread on the side.

Yield: 6 servings   Massimo and Cindy Pistelli

J.P. Mulldoon's - *Mulldoon's offers fine dining in a most relaxing atmosphere. Open for lunch and dinner. Enjoy a superb meal and piano entertainment. Catering also available.*

Chicken Breasts with Zinfandel and Peaches

	salt and pepper to taste	16	slices of fresh or frozen
4	(6 ounce) boned, skinless		peaches
	chicken breasts	8	ounces Zinfandel wine

Salt and pepper chicken breasts. Sauté in heavy skillet until almost done. Pour in peaches with juice and wine. Sauté until chicken is done and peach liquid is thick.

Yield: 4 servings

Stuart Mullis

Spicy Broiled Fresh Grouper

3	to 6 pounds grouper fillets	¼	cup ketchup
½	teaspoon paprika		onion salt to taste
½	cup cooking oil		salt and pepper to taste
½	teaspoon hot pepper sauce		chopped parsley for
	juice of ½ lemon		garnish
1	teaspoon prepared mustard		

Mix all ingredients except grouper and parsley in a bowl. Place grouper, skin side down, into broiler pan and brush heavily with sauce mixture. Broil close to heat until half done. Brush again with mixture and broil an additional 6 minutes. Sprinkle with parsley and serve.

Yield: 10 to 12 servings

Stuart Mullis

Nicky's Restaurant - *A local tradition located in beautiful downtown Valdosta. Open for breakfast and lunch. Nicky's features a buffet of delicious homestyle cooking and also boasts some old Greek family recipes. Catering available.*

Squash Casserole

3	cups sliced yellow squash	¼	cup Parmesan cheese
½	cup cubed fresh bread		salt and pepper to taste
1	cup sweet milk	3	tablespoons butter
2	eggs		

Cook squash until tender. Drain and mash thoroughly. Mix together with cubed bread, milk, eggs, and Parmesan cheese. Season and pour into greased 2-quart casserole dish and dot with butter. Bake at 350 degrees for 30 minutes until set.

Yield: 6 to 8 servings   Katina Balanis

Moussaka

2	medium eggplants	2	tablespoons tomato paste
	olive oil		dash of cinnamon
1½	pounds ground beef	½	cup red wine
2	onions, chopped		grated Parmesan cheese
5	tablespoons butter		

Cream Sauce:

¼	cup all-purpose flour	2	cups milk
3	eggs		

Slice peeled eggplant lengthwise. Brush slices with oil and broil lightly. Sauté beef with onions in 5 tablespoons butter. Add tomato paste, cinnamon and wine. Simmer until liquid is absorbed. Overlap a layer of eggplant in bottom of a greased 2-quart casserole dish and sprinkle lightly with cheese. Cover eggplant with meat mixture and sprinkle again with cheese. Repeat layers until all eggplant and meat is used, ending with a layer of eggplant. Combine flour, eggs and milk to make cream sauce. Pour sauce on top of eggplant, then sprinkle generously with cheese. Bake at 375 degrees for 1 hour or until set.

Yield: 6 to 8 servings   Katina Balanis

Spanakopeta

2	pounds fresh spinach	1	egg, beaten
1	bunch green scallions, chopped	¼	pound feta cheese phyllo pastry sheets
4	tablespoons olive oil		melted butter as needed

Wash spinach and discard stems. Drain and cut in small pieces. Sauté onion in oil until soft, adding spinach for a few minutes. Stir in egg and crumbled feta. Cut sheets of phyllo lengthwise in 3-inch strips and brush with butter. Place one tablespoon of spinach mixture at end of strip and fold over into triangle shape. Continue folding until all is completed. Brush lightly with butter. Bake at 400 degrees for 10 to 15 minutes until golden.

Yield: 40 appetizers   Katina Balanis

Sweet Potato Soufflé

3	well-beaten eggs	1	(8 ounce) can chunk pineapple, undrained
1	cup milk		
3	cups boiled, peeled, mashed sweet potatoes	½	cup chopped pecans
½	cup butter	¼	cup raisins
½	cup sugar		miniature marshmallows

Mix eggs and milk with mashed sweet potatoes. Then add butter, sugar, and pineapple juice. Beat these ingredients together and place in 2-quart casserole dish. On top, place pecans, raisins and chunk pineapple. Bake at 350 degrees for 30 minutes. Just before removing from oven, spread evenly with marshmallows.

Yield: 6 to 8 servings   Katina Balanis

Everyone's Favorite Fried Eggplant

1	fresh eggplant	all-purpose flour	
3	cups water	oil for frying	
½	cup sugar		

Peel and slice eggplant into wedges. Soak eggplant in combined sugar and water for one hour. Drain eggplant and dredge in flour. Fry in heated oil until crispy and golden brown.

Yield: 6 to 8 servings   Katina Balanis

Ocean Pond - *The home of "swamp salad," Ocean Pond is a Lowndes County tradition as old as the tales of the "big one that got away." Rocking on the porch and listening to the frogs makes that famous fried chicken taste even better. Private parties only.*

Overnight Chicken Divan

2	(10 ounce) packages frozen broccoli spears	1	teaspoon paprika
1	(10¾ ounce) can cream of chicken soup	1	teaspoon dry mustard
½	cup mayonnaise	¼	teaspoon curry powder
½	cup sour cream	8	chicken breasts, cooked, boned and chopped
2	tablespoons sherry	⅓	cup grated Parmesan cheese

Cook and drain broccoli and arrange in 13x9x2-inch pan. Mix soup, mayonnaise, sour cream, sherry, paprika, mustard, and curry. Spoon half of mixture over broccoli, add chicken on top then spoon remaining mixture on top. Chill overnight. Let stand at room temperature for 30 minutes. Bake at 350 degrees for 25 minutes. Top with Parmesan cheese and bake an additional 5 minutes.

Yield: 8 servings   Barbara Grondahl

O'Ryley's - *A unique addition to Valdosta's restaurant community, O'Ryley's is a family cafe featuring billiards and a touch of class. Open for lunch and dinner with an intriguing menu and homemade desserts. Catering available.*

Fresh Carrot Puff

2	pounds carrots, peeled, cooked and pureed	1½	tablespoons all-purpose flour
2	teaspoons lemon juice	½	teaspoon salt
2	tablespoons minced scallions	¼	teaspoon cinnamon
¼	pound butter or margarine, softened	1	cup milk
¼	cup sugar	3	eggs
		1	egg white, stiffly beaten

Preheat oven to 350 degrees. Combine all ingredients except egg white. Mix well. Fold in egg white. Pour into well-greased, 2-quart soufflé dish. Bake at 350 degrees for 50 to 60 minutes or until center is firm to touch. Serve immediately.

Yield: 6 to 8 servings   Leslie Beal

Quick-to-Fix Chicken

4	boned, skinless chicken breasts	1	(16 ounce) can Italian style zucchini
½	teaspoon oregano	¼	pound grated mozzarella cheese
½	teaspoon basil		Parmesan cheese as desired
¼	teaspoon rosemary salt and pepper to taste	1	(8 ounce) package linguine, cooked and drained

Wash and pat dry chicken breasts. Season with oregano, basil, rosemary, salt and pepper to taste. Open can of zucchini. Place breasts in oven-proof 9x9x2-inch baking dish and pour zucchini over breasts. Sprinkle with mozzarella cheese and follow with Parmesan. Bake at 375 degrees for 30 to 40 minutes, or until cooked through. Serve over linguine.

Yield: 4 servings   Leslie Beal

Baked Apples

½ cup walnut halves
¼ cup sugar
½ teaspoon ground cinnamon
4 baking apples
1 lemon, halved
¼ cup unsalted butter, melted
2 tablespoons unsalted butter, cut in pieces

¼ cup packed dark brown sugar
¼ cup raisins
4 small cinnamon sticks
apple juice
cream as needed

Preheat oven to 375 degrees. Place walnuts, sugar and cinnamon in a food processor and process until finely ground. Transfer to bowl. Core and peel apples. Sprinkle inside and rub outside well with lemon juice. Brush apples with melted butter. Press walnut mixture evenly onto apples. Transfer to shallow baking dish. Combine brown sugar with butter pieces in a small bowl. Work with a fork to mix. Add raisins and mix with fingers. Fill apples with this mixture. Tuck a cinnamon stick into top of each. Drizzle any remaining melted butter over tops. Pour apple juice ¼-inch deep into dish. Bake at 375 degrees for 1 hour or until apples are tender. Let cool on a rack 15 minutes. Transfer apples to individual shallow bowls. Spoon the juice around the apples and serve while still warm, or at room temperature with cream on the side.

Yield: 4 servings   Leslie Beal

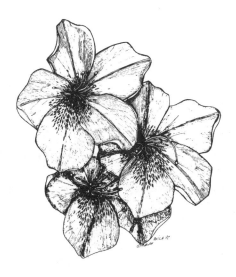

Chocolate Yummies

½	cup butter	1	cup coconut
¼	cup sugar	½	cup chopped pecans
1	teaspoon vanilla	¼	cup margarine
3	tablespoons cocoa	3	tablespoons milk
1	egg	2	tablespoons instant vanilla
2	cups graham cracker		pudding powder
	crumbs	2	cups powdered sugar

Topping:

2	semi-sweet chocolate squares	1	tablespoon butter

In double boiler, cook while stirring the butter, sugar, vanilla, cocoa and egg until it resembles custard. Add crumbs, coconut and pecans to the mixture and pack in 9x9x2-inch square pan. Cream together margarine, milk, and pudding powder. Blend in powdered sugar and spread on base. Let stand 15 minutes. Melt chocolate with butter and spread over pudding mixture. Cool and refrigerate until ready to use. Cut into small squares.

Yield: approximately 3 dozen   Mary K. Moorman

Plaid Peppers Creative Catering - *Creative catering from casseroles to weddings offered by Plaid Peppers. No function too large or too small.*

Fresh Mushrooms with Green Beans

½	pound fresh mushrooms, sliced	¼	cup butter
1	(16 ounce) can green beans, drained	¼	cup soy sauce
		⅛	cup red wine vinegar
1	small onion, diced		salt, pepper and garlic to taste
1	small green pepper, diced		water as needed

Wash mushrooms well. Combine mushrooms with remaining ingredients and simmer for 1½ hours in a skillet over low heat.

Yield: 4 to 6 servings   Pam Vickers

Simply Southern - *Catering available or drop by the shop on Plum Street in historic Remerton. Fresh breads and pastries always available.*

Chicken and Green Noodle Casserole

6	chicken breasts	½	cup margarine, divided and melted
2	(5 ounce) packages green spinach noodles		
1	quart chicken stock	1	(10¾ ounce) can cream of mushroom soup
1	(8 ounce) block Cheddar cheese, cubed	1	(3 ounce) jar pimento stuffed olives, sliced
1	cup chopped green pepper	1	(4½ ounce) jar sliced mushrooms, drained
1	cup chopped onion		
1	cup chopped celery	1	cup cracker crumbs

Boil chicken 30 minutes until tender; save broth. Cut chicken into bite-size pieces. Cook noodles in stock until tender. Drain. Add cheese to noodles and stir until cheese melts. Sauté pepper, onions, and celery in ¼ cup margarine and add to noodles and cheese. Stir in soup, olives and mushrooms, cook until bubbly. Add chicken. Put in 15x10x2-inch casserole dish. Combine ¼ cup margarine and cracker crumbs. Sprinkle over chicken. Bake at 325 degrees for 25 to 30 minutes.

Yield: 6 servings   Donna McLeod

Green Grape Salad

Crust:

½ cup margarine
½ cup slivered almonds

1 cup all-purpose flour
½ cup sugar

Filling:

1 (3 ounce) package lemon
gelatin
½ cup sugar

1 cup boiling water
1 cup sour cream
1 cup halved green grapes

To make crust, melt margarine in skillet. Add almonds, flour and ½ cup sugar. Cook over medium heat until crumbly. Reserve ½ cup crust mixture. Put remaining in bottom of 8x8x2-inch baking dish. To make filling, combine gelatin, ½ cup sugar and boiling water. Stir until dissolved. Beat in sour cream, then fold in grapes. Pour over crust and refrigerate until congealed. Sprinkle the ½ cup cooked crust over top before serving.

Yield: 6 to 8 servings   Donna McLeod

Caution: When cooking crust, do not overcook; will be too hard. A different and delicious salad.

Cream Cheese Pastries

½ cup butter, softened
½ cup margarine, softened
1 (8 ounce) package cream
cheese, softened
¼ cup sugar
2½ cups all-purpose flour

2 teaspoons cinnamon,
divided
½ cup sugar, divided
½ cup finely chopped pecans,
divided

Combine butter, margarine, cream cheese, sugar and flour. Mix well; cover and chill 24 hours. Divide dough into 4 equal portions. Turn each portion out onto a lightly floured surface and roll each into a 12-inch circle. Sprinkle each circle with ½ teaspoon cinnamon, 2 tablespoons sugar and 2 tablespoons pecans. Cut each circle into 12 wedges. Roll up each wedge, beginning at wide end. Place, seam side down, on greased baking sheet. Bake at 325 degrees for 20 minutes.

Yield: 4 dozen   Donna McLeod

The Landmark - *Catering or private dining, luncheons or teas. Menus include many unique and delicious items. Located in historic downtown Valdosta.*

Porc à l'Orange

1	(6 to 7 pound) pork loin	1	tablespoon light brown sugar
1	clove garlic		
1	to 2 teaspoons rosemary	⅔	cup orange juice, divided
½	teaspoon salt	1	to 2 tablespoons Grand Marnier
¼	teaspoon pepper		
2	tablespoons Dijon mustard		orange slices for garnish
2	tablespoons orange marmalade		parsley for garnish

Rub meat with garlic, rosemary, salt and pepper. Brown in pan on all sides, then place in a shallow roasting pan (may place on rack in pan); roast at 325 degrees until temperature of meat is 170 degrees, approximately 30 to 35 minutes per pound. Combine mustard, marmalade, brown sugar and 2 tablespoons orange juice; mix well. About 15 minutes before roast is done, brush with mustard mixture to glaze. Continue roasting 15 minutes. Remove roast to platter, garnish with orange slices and parsley. Skim fat from roasting pan and add remaining orange juice and Grand Marnier to pan drippings. Serve as sauce.

Yield: 12 to 14 servings   Gloria Price

Tarragon and Oregano Butter

2	cups butter	½	cup fresh oregano leaves (if using dried leaves, use 1 scant tablespoon each of tarragon and oregano)
½	cup fresh tarragon leaves		
		1	tablespoon orange juice

Soften butter at room temperature and mix with tarragon, oregano and orange juice. If using dried leaves, first soak them in juice. May pack in bowl or mold or it may be thinly spread on waxed paper, cooled and then cut into shapes for individual servings.

Yield: 2 cups   Gloria Price

Good served with rolls or tea sandwiches for ladies luncheon.

Sweet Potato Apple Casserole

4	to 6 large sweet potatoes, baked	½	cup firmly packed brown sugar
1	teaspoon salt	½	teaspoon ground nutmeg
¼	teaspoon pepper	2	medium cooking apples, cored and thinly sliced
½	cup butter or margarine, divided and melted		

Mash sweet potatoes in a large bowl. Season with salt and pepper and 4 tablespoons melted butter. Combine remaining 4 tablespoons melted butter with brown sugar and nutmeg in bottom of 8x8x2-inch baking dish. Then layer apple slices and top with mashed sweet potatoes. Bake at 350 degrees for 40 to 45 minutes.

Yield: 6 to 8 servings   Gloria Price

The Tavern - *Located at Twin Lakes, The Tavern features steak, seafood, quail, pasta and mouth-watering desserts. Live entertainment on Friday and Saturday nights. Banquet facilities and catering available.*

Chicken Paprikash

2	tablespoons olive oil	1	chicken, cut up
1	cup chopped onion	1	tablespoon all-purpose flour
½	cup Hungarian paprika		
1	cup chicken broth, divided	½	cup sour cream
2	green peppers, thinly sliced		salt and pepper to taste
3	tomatoes, peeled and cut into large pieces		

Sauté onions in olive oil in a Dutch oven over low heat until onions are translucent. Add paprika and half of chicken broth, stir until smooth. Cook 5 minutes more. Stir in green peppers, tomatoes and chicken. Cover and simmer 35 minutes. When chicken is cooked, remove from pot and keep warm. Mix flour with sour cream, add to the cooking liquid. Stir until well blended. Add remaining chicken broth, stir well and cook 5 minutes. Salt and pepper to taste. Spoon sauce over chicken and serve.

Yield: 4 servings   Stan Cox and Bill Thomson

Stuffed Shrimp

16	jumbo shrimp	2	cups breadcrumbs
12	tablespoons butter	½	cup flaked crab
4	tablespoons chopped parsley	½	cup sherry
		½	cup chopped almonds

Preheat oven to 350 degrees. Remove shell of shrimp up to tail. Devein and cut shrimp in butterfly fashion. Place in 13x9x2-inch baking dish. Melt butter. Combine remaining ingredients. Place stuffing in each shrimp cavity. Bake at 350 degrees for 20 minutes or until tails curl up and shrimp meat is bright white.

Yield: 4 servings   Stan Cox and Bill Thomson

Serve with drawn butter and lemon wedge.

Teriyaki Shark Steaks

1	cup teriyaki sauce	4	teaspoons unflavored gelatin
1	cup pineapple juice	4	shark steaks, 1-inch thick

Heat teriyaki sauce and pineapple juice. Add gelatin and simmer 5 minutes. Refrigerate until thickened, about 1½ hours. Broil shark for 4 minutes on each side; while broiling, brush glaze over steaks.

Yield: 4 servings   Stan Cox and Bill Thomson

Shrimp Arnaud

¼	cup peanut oil	¼	clove garlic
¼	cup white vinegar	½	teaspoon salt
1	teaspoon chopped chives	1	pound shrimp; cooked, peeled and cooled
1	teaspoon chili sauce		
½	teaspoon hot mustard	½	teaspoon paprika

Combine oil, white vinegar, chives, chili sauce, hot mustard, garlic and salt. Add cooled shrimp. Toss well. Cover and refrigerate at least 3 hours, tossing occasionally. To serve, drain and sprinkle lightly with paprika.

Yield: 4 appetizers   Stan Cox and Bill Thomson

French Onion Soup

1 (¾ inch) slice French bread	salt and pepper to taste
1½ tablespoons butter	1 teaspoon all-purpose flour
1½ large onions, sliced	¼ cup grated Swiss cheese
1½ cups beef stock	Parmesan cheese, optional
⅛ cup red wine	

Spread French bread with ½ tablespoon of butter. Toast until brown and set aside. In soup pot, melt remaining 1 tablespoon butter. Add onions and slowly cook, covered, until brown. Add stock and wine. Add salt and pepper to taste. Add flour and mix until smooth. Simmer 15 minutes. Pour in ovenproof serving bowl and place toasted bread on top. Place Swiss cheese over bread. If desired, sprinkle with Parmesan cheese and broil until light brown.

Yield: 1 bowl

Stan Cox and Bill Thomson

Valdosta Country Club - *A private club serving Valdostans since 1917. Dining room chefs share new and exciting dishes.*

Bourbon Pecan Pie

6 tablespoons butter	1 cup maple syrup
¾ cup brown sugar	3 tablespoons bourbon
½ teaspoon salt	1 teaspoon vanilla
3 eggs	2½ cups pecan pieces
1 tablespoon all-purpose flour	1 9-inch deep pie crust

Cream together butter, sugar and salt. Add eggs, one at a time. Add flour, syrup, bourbon, vanilla and pecans. Pour into crust. Bake at 350 degrees for 45 minutes.

Yield: 1 pie

Danny Sermons

If preferred, syrup can be ½ cup corn and ½ cup maple.

Veal Medallions

4	(8 ounce) veal medallions, pounded thin	1	carrot, peeled and thinly sliced
1	egg, beaten		salt and pepper to taste
¾	pound ground turkey or chicken	4	scallions

Lay veal flat. Combine egg and ground meat, mixing thoroughly. Spread a layer of ground meat on the veal about ⅛-inch thick leaving the outer edges clean. Then add a layer of carrots. Sprinkle salt and pepper to taste. Lay the scallions in the center (cutting to size to fit the roll). Fold the left and right side in and roll to make a cylinder shape. Bake at 350 degrees for 10 to 15 minutes. Slice in ¼-inch circles and serve.

Yield: 4 servings   Danny Sermons

Champagne Chicken

4	(8 ounce) chicken breasts		garlic powder to taste
	salt and pepper to taste	3	chicken bouillon cubes
	onion powder or flakes to taste	½	cup champagne
		2	cups heavy whipping cream

Grill chicken breasts until done, adding a little of the seasonings for flavor. Bring the champagne to a boil until it has reduced to 10% original volume. Add whipping cream and boil until proper thickness comes about, then add the chicken base and seasonings. Serve over the grilled chicken breasts.

Yield: 4 servings   Danny Sermons

Cocktail Crab Dip

2	pounds imitation or real crabmeat; drained, picked and flaked	2	(8 ounce) packages cream cheese, softened
¼	cup mayonnaise	½	cup cocktail sauce
			salt and pepper to taste

Combine all ingredients in a bowl, either by hand or by a stationary or hand mixer. Serve chilled on toast points or crackers.

Yield: 3 cups   Danny Sermons

Very simple but very delicious.

Index